LOVECRAFTIAN PROCEEDINGS 2

HIPPOCAMPUS PRESS LIBRARY OF CRITICISM

S. T. Joshi, *Primal Sources: Essays on H. P. Lovecraft* (2003)
———, *The Evolution of the Weird Tale* (2004)
———, *Lovecraft and a World in Transition: Collected Essays on H. P. Lovecraft* (2014)
Robert W. Waugh, *The Monster in the Mirror: Looking for H. P. Lovecraft* (2006)
———, *A Monster of Voices: Speaking for H. P. Lovecraft* (2011)
Scott Connors, ed., *The Freedom of Fantastic Things: Selected Criticism on Clark Ashton Smith* (2006)
Ben Szumskyj, ed., *Two-Gun Bob: A Centennial Study of Robert E. Howard* (2006)
S. T. Joshi and Rosemary Pardoe, ed., *Warnings to the Curious: A Sheaf of Criticism on M. R. James* (2007)
Massimo Berruti, *Dim-Remembered Stories: A Critical Study of R. H. Barlow* (2011)
Gary William Crawford, Jim Rockhill, and Brian J. Showers, ed., *Reflections in a Glass Darkly: Essays on J. Sheridan Le Fanu* (2011)
Massimo Berruti, S. T. Joshi, and Sam Gafford, ed., *William Hope Hodgson: Voices from the Borderland: Seven Decades of Criticism on the Master of Cosmic Horror* (2014)
Donald R. Burleson, *Lovecraft: An American Allegory–Selected Essays on H. P. Lovecraft* (2015)
Lovecraft Annual
Dead Reckonings
Lovecraftian Proceedings

Lovecraftian Proceedings 2

Select Papers from the Dr. Henry Armitage
Memorial Scholarship Symposium
NecronomiCon Providence: 2015

Edited by Dennis P. Quinn

Hippocampus Press

New York

Copyright © 2017 by Hippocampus Press. The terms "NecronomiCon Providence" and "Dr. Henry Armitage Memorial Scholarship Symposium" are trademarks of the Lovecraft Arts & Sciences Council, Inc., and used by permission. All works are © 2017 by their respective authors.
Panels from "El Introso" on pages 145–59 are copyright © 2017 by Erik Kriek and reproduced by permission of the artist.
Cover illustration "The Shadow of His Smile" © by Pete Von Sholly.

Published by Hippocampus Press
P.O. Box 641, New York, NY 10156.
http://www.hippocampuspress.com

All rights reserved.
No part of this work may be reproduced in any form or by any means without the written permission of the publisher.

Cover illustration by Pete Von Sholly
Cover design by Barbara Briggs Silbert.
Hippocampus Press logo designed by Anastasia Damianakos.

First Edition
1 3 5 7 9 8 6 4 2

ISBN 978-1-61498-190-9

Contents

Introduction: From Armitage Symposium to *Lovecraftian Proceedings* 7
    DENNIS QUINN

Dreams of Antiquity: H. P. Lovecraft's Great Roman Dream of 1927 13
    BYRON NAKAMURA

The Poet's Nightmare: The Nature of Things according to Lovecraft 31
    SEAN MORELAND

Reordering the Universe: H. P. Lovecraft's Subversion of the Biblical Divine .. 47
    RENÉ J. WEISE

Resisting Cthulhu: Milton and Lovecraft's Errand in the Wilderness 64
    MARCELLO RICCIARDI

"The Discriminating Urban Landscapist": Tradition and Innovation in the Architectural Writings of H. P. Lovecraft 76
    CONNOR PITETTI

Tentacles in the Madhouse: The Role of the Asylum in the Fiction of H. P. Lovecraft 93
    TROY RONDINONE

Unspeakable Languages: Lovecraft Editions in Spanish 109
    JUAN L. PÉREZ-DE-LUQUE

Color out of Mind: Correlating the Cthulhu Mythos Universe to the Autism Disorder Spectrum 119
    LARS G. BACKSTROM

Darwin and the Deep Ones: Anthropological Anxiety in "The Shadow over Innsmouth" and Other Stories 131
    JEFFREY SHANKS

The "Inside" of H. P. Lovecraft's Supernatural Horror in the Visual Arts 145
    NATHANIEL R. WALLACE

H. P. Lovecraft's Optimism 160
    MATTHEW BEACH

Insider, Outsider: From the Commonplace to the Uncanny in H. P. Lovecraft's Narration and Descriptions 176
    DAPHNÉE TASIA BOURDAGES-ATHANASSIOU

H. P. Lovecraft, Georges Bataille, and the Fascination of the Formless: One Crawling Chaos Seen Emerging from Opposite Shores 189
  CHRISTIAN ROY

Ripples from Carcosa: H. P. Lovecraft, *True Detective*, and the Artist-Investigator 208
  HEATHER POIRIER

Lovecraft for the Little Ones: *ParaNorman*, Plushies, and More 225
  FAYE RINGEL AND JENNA RANDALL

Contributors 237

Appendix: Abstracts of Papers Presented at the Dr. Henry Armitage Memorial Scholarship Symposium, NecronomiCon Providence 20–23 August 2015 241

Index 271

Introduction: From Armitage Symposium to *Lovecraftian Proceedings*

Dennis Quinn
Cal Poly Pomona

Interest in Lovecraft and his influence is most certainly on the rise and shows little signs of declining. A cursory search of national and international conferences reveals that Lovecraft has been embraced by academia and is being taken seriously by scholars around the world. Publications too, from books to articles in journals, to journals devoted exclusively to Lovecraft, abound. Lovecraft and his influence have become an industry. The existence of this volume is a testament to that fact. This second volume of *Lovecraftian Proceedings* contains select papers, in revised and peer-reviewed form, from the Dr. Henry Armitage Memorial Scholarship Symposium at NecronomiCon Providence, 21–23 August 2015. The Armitage Symposium set out to foster explorations of Lovecraft's elaborate cosmic mythology, and how this mythology was influenced by, and has come to influence, numerous other authors and artists before and since. But we also looked for submissions that contribute to a greater, critical, and nuanced understanding weird fiction and art (and related science fiction, fantasy, horror, etc.). We indeed found that and more and had an amazing selection of papers.

The Armitage Symposium of 2015 consisted of thirty-seven presentations organized into various topics spanning three days. Topics consisted of such things as space and place, popular culture, language/linguistics, the Cthulhu Mythos, the Lovecraft Circle, the influence of Roman civilization and literature on Lovecraft, as well as philosophical and aesthetic concerns in the Lovecraftian milieu. At its heart, the three days hosted a diverse group of scholars who brought many different perspectives to the works of H. P. Lovecraft and his legacy. This volume consists of fifteen of those papers that have been revised and gone through a double-blind peer review process. One might see from the contributor list a collection of scholars from a variety positions: from undergraduates to tenured professors, from scientists to classicists, from medical researchers to lawyers. This diversity of training and disciplinary expertise certainly influenced how the authors approach and understand the Lovecraftian context. They also come from around the nation and indeed around the world, with an ample selection of international scholars included in these pages. Of the papers included in this volume, one will also note the great diversity of topics and approaches.

Several papers in this volume deal with influences of classic works on Lovecraft. But as the works demonstrate, Lovecraft does not simply reflect tradition; he transforms it and makes it his own. "Dreams of Antiquity: Lovecraft and His Great Roman Dream of 1927," by Byron Nakamura, argues that Lovecraft's dream that was published as "The Very Old Folk" does more than simply use the ancient world as a backdrop to his narrative; it uses it as a framework to project his own attitudes toward race, imperialism, and his own Eurocentric concept of civilization. "*The Poet's Nightmare: The Nature of Things according to Lovecraft*," *by Sean Moreland, argues that the first century BCE Roman poet and atomist Lucretius had a profound influence on how Lovecraft constructed his "gods" in terms of their material composition and how they interact with humans in the world.* "Reordering the Universe: H. P. Lovecraft's Subversion of the Biblical Divine," by Renée J. Weise, examines the biblical and Christian theological influences on Lovecraft's pseudo-pantheon, and how he subverts the message of comfort and salvation for his own brand of cosmic dread and terror.

This volume also contains papers looking at Lovecraft in conjunction with other authors, demonstrating how he can be viewed alongside similar aesthetic and philosophical trends in the Western tradition. "Resisting Cthulhu: Milton and Lovecraft's Errand in the Wilderness," by Marcello Ricciardi, explores how both Lovecraft and Milton reflect a puritanical cosmic consciousness and resonate themes seen in the early Christian desert fathers. "H. P. Lovecraft, Georges Bataille, and the Fascination of the Formless: One Crawling Chaos Seen Emerging from Opposite Shores," by Christian Roy, argues that, being influenced by Nietzsche and others, Lovecraft and Georges Bataille explored their own versions of cosmic dread that also had important common resonances.

Place is extremely important to Lovecraft. This is demonstrated in two papers contained in this volume. In "'The Discriminating Urban Landscapist': Tradition and Innovation in the Architectural Writings of H. P. Lovecraft," Connor Pitetti argues, through examining Lovecraft's attempt to save a group of old Providence warehouses from demolition during the construction of the new Providence County Courthouse in the 1920s, that Lovecraft advocated a particular transformative, modernist art practice as well as a conservative preservationism in order to protect and enrich the cultural tradition of his beloved Providence. "Tentacles in the Madhouse: The Role of the Asylum in the Fiction of H. P. Lovecraft," by Troy Rondinone, shows how Lovecraft uses asylums in some of his narratives to highlight key themes such as how one understands reality, the limits of psychology (and science in general), the fine line between sane and insane, and what Lovecraft saw as the racial degradation of humanity.

Lovecraft's influence on modern popular culture is also examined in these pages. "The 'Inside' of H. P. Lovecraft's Supernatural Horror in the Visual Arts," by Nathaniel R. Wallace, uses Erik Kriek's comic version of "The Outsider," as well as other popular adaptations of Lovecraft's works in video games, films, and graphic novels, to examine the author's original approach to the evocation of supernatural horror in his first-person narratives—often lost in visual representations of his works. "Ripples from Carcosa: H. P. Lovecraft, *True Detective*, and the Artist-Investigator," by Heather Poirier, examines both Robert W. Chambers and Lovecraft through the lens of detective fiction to show how the investigators in the HBO series *True Detective* are a new kind of character derived from atelier fiction, weird fiction, and detective fiction. "Lovecraft for the Little Ones: *ParaNorman*, Plushies, and More," by Faye Ringel and Jenna Randall, explores some of the modern children's adaptations of Lovecraft and then focuses on how the work of Chris Butler, the director of the film *ParaNorman* and several other films in the genre of "KinderGoth," bears close resemblances to many themes seen Lovecraft's more Gothic works.

This collection also contains some other innovative approaches to Lovecraft. "Unspeakable Languages: Lovecraft Editions in Spanish," by Juan L. Pérez-de-Luque, explores the current state of Hispanic Lovecraftian studies with special attention to different stages that the translations of Lovecraft's literary work has undergone in Spanish-speaking countries over the last forty years. "Color out of Mind: Correlating the Cthulhu Mythos Universe to the Autism Disorder Spectrum," by Lars G. Backstrom, argues that Lovecraft's literary world is close to the world lived by those with Asperger's syndrome, particularly as the author characterizes the Cthulhu

Mythos as revealing a world that is a chaotic, unpredictable, and terrifying place. "Darwin and the Deep Ones: Anthropological Anxiety in 'The Shadow over Innsmouth' and Other Stories," by Jeffrey Shanks, shows how the Social Darwinism of the nineteenth and early twentieth centuries informed some of Lovecraft's stories to undergird themes of anthropological anxiety in order to create a sense of existential unease. "H. P. Lovecraft's Optimism," by Matthew Beach, offers a rereading of what has so often been understood as a pervasive and underlying pessimism throughout Lovecraft's fiction to suggest that Lovecraft has something to contribute to the discussions of futurity and optimism currently taking place within literary studies. "Insider, Outsider: From the Commonplace to the Uncanny in Lovecraft's Narration and Descriptions," by Daphnée Tasia Bourdages-Athanassiou, explores how Lovecraft evokes a sense of menacing alterity in a number of his works, using what at first seems to be commonplace as a tool along with a variety of narrative and descriptive techniques in creating a unique Lovecraftian atmosphere.

These essays contained in this volume of *Lovecraftian Proceedings* are not only a representative cross-section of the papers presented at 2015 Armitage Symposium, but they also offer a view into some exciting new directions and trajectories within Lovecraftian studies. Building from previous established works, these essays set out in new ways that will most certainly inspire scholars to build off these works and ask new questions about Lovecraft and his impact on literature, philosophy, religion, popular culture, and many other areas of study. As we look toward more NecronomiCon Providence conventions, and other gatherings like it, and we prepare for what is hoped will be a third volume of *Lovecraftian Proceedings*, and many others, I am excited to see what new discoveries and interpretations will reveal and challenge us about Lovecraft and his legacy.

Before I close the introductory chapter, some heartfelt thanks are in order. I am indebted to the support of many people helping this volume come to fruition (certainly more than I can mention here, as much to do with space as failing memory). First, I must thank Niels-Viggo S. Hobbs and the others at Lovecraft Arts & Sciences Council for their tireless devotion to the promotion of Lovecraft and his influence by, among others, creating a forum for people from around the world to learn about and celebrate the legacy of H. P. Lovecraft in his hometown. It should also be acknowledged that due to Dr. Hobbs and John Sefel's efforts, the first volume of *Lovecraftian Proceedings* came into print and began this important forum to disseminate new works on such things Lovecraftian. Without a volume 1, a volume 2 would be impossible. I must also thank the vision and generosity of Derrick Hussey at Hippocampus Press for believing enough in NecronomiCon Providence and the Armitage Symposium to publish these proceedings, so that these important and innovative works can see the light of day. A special thanks goes to the skill, generosity, wisdom, and nearly divine patience of David E. Schultz, who helped guide me through every part of the editorial process of this volume and most certainly took on parts of the editorial process that I was supposed to do. Of course, any editorial errors that remain are mine alone. I must also give much thanks to S. T. Joshi, who does much more editing and general helping the preparation and publication of this volume than I will ever realize. To him is owed a great debt. I must also give a special thanks to the unnamable: those anonymous though indispensable peer reviewers who agreed to take on one of the most important roles in this publication, knowing full well that they would never be given due credit for their hours of work. But you and I know who you are. Thanks again! Although I know that is of little consolation. Perhaps a couple pints will help. Finally, I must thank the authors of the articles in this volume, whose names are clear for all to see. They were all wonderful to work with, exhibiting much patience and flexibility in the publication process, along with their great knowledge and skill as academics and writers. No doubt, without you and your thought-provoking work, this volume would not exist. I was honored to work with you all.

Abbreviations

AT *The Ancient Track: Complete Poetical Works* (Hippocampus Press, 2013)
CE *Collected Essays* (Hippocampus Press, 2004–06; 5 vols.)
CF *Collected Fiction* (Hippocampus Press, 2015–17; 4 vols.)
IAP S. T. Joshi, *I Am Providence: The Life and Times of H. P. Lovecraft* (2010)
SL *Selected Letters* (Arkham House, 1965–76; 5 vols.)

Dreams of Antiquity: H. P. Lovecraft's Great Roman Dream of 1927

Byron Nakamura
Southern Connecticut State University

> Rome is a subject which has fascinated me uncannily since I first heard of it around the age of six. (SL 4.332)
> —H. P. Lovecraft to Clark Ashton Smith
> 29 November 1933

Introduction

One need not look far to find the imprint of classical antiquity and of the Romans especially on the works of H. P. Lovecraft. Just a brief perusal of his weird fiction, poetry, works of amateur journalism, and epistolary correspondence reveals a plethora of examples bearing the influence of classical civilization.[1] Yet there are few instances in Lovecraft's weird fiction that directly feature the Greco-Roman world. The most well known example is, of course, "The Tree" (1920), one of Lovecraft's Dunsanian-styled short stories, which takes place in Greece during the fourth century BCE.[2] An often overlooked example is, however, Lovecraft's great "Roman Dream" of 1927, first related in a series of letters to Donald Wandrei,

---

1. Joshi, "Lovecraft and Classical Antiquity," provides the first serious attempt to tackle the subject, while Kenneth Hite, "Lost in Lovecraft," is a comprehensive survey for the general reader.

2. See Joshi, "'The Tree' and Ancient History," for commentary on this tale. One could possibly include the author's collaboration with Winifred Virginia Jackson, "The Green Meadow," which is set in classical Greece, but this paper is mainly concerned with work written by HPL himself. See Vaughan, "A Factual Basis for 'The Green Meadow'?"

Bernard Austin Dwyer, Frank Belknap Long, and Clark Ashton Smith.[3] In this dream, Lovecraft assumes the persona of a Roman governmental official of the Late Republic, who along with his fellow Romans (much to their sorrow) encounters an ancient evil from the Spanish hills of Pamplona, which destroys them utterly. A version of this dream tale was later incorporated (with Lovecraft's permission [SL 2.261]) by Frank Belknap Long into his novella, *The Horror from the Hills* (1931), published in *Weird Tales*. Somewhat later another variant of his dream was published after Lovecraft's death as a stand-alone piece in *Scienti-Snaps* (1940) under the title "The Very Old Folk."

Lovecraft's Roman Dream of 1927 provides a window into the author's creative process through a series of letters describing his dream to his literary correspondents. These letters provide insight into the development of this dream into a draft of a short story. Also, his "dream-texts" demonstrate that Lovecraft possessed a detailed and textured understanding of the Roman period. This is not surprising given Lovecraft's well attested fascination with classical antiquity and his ability as a background researcher. Yet Lovecraft's dream does more than use the Roman world as a backdrop to its narrative. It employs the historical canvas to project the author's own attitudes toward race, imperialism, and the decline of Western civilization. Finally, Lovecraft's dream-persona as the Roman official L. Caelius Rufus mirrors the author's social and economic aspirations as a one of a dwindling number of gentrified Anglo-Yankee "equestrians" of early twentieth-century America.

The Great Roman Dream of 1927

On Halloween night 1927, H. P. Lovecraft settled down to his evening's reading, which happened to be James Rhoades's translation of Virgil's *Aeneid*, a work that, according to Lovecraft, was "more faithful to P. Maro than any other versified version I have ever seen—including that of my late uncle Dr. Clark, which did not attain publication" (MTS 177). The next morning the ambiance of All Hallows' Eve combined with Virgil's verses produced "a Roman dream of such supernatural clearness & vividness, &

---

3. MTS 177 (Wandrei); SL 2.188-97 (Dwyer). References to the dream can be found in letters to Long (SL 2.202-8, 2.261, 3.186-87); to Clark Ashton Smith (*Dawnward Spire* 499); and later to C. L. Moore (*Letters to C. L. Moore and Others* 36-37).

such titanic adumbrations of hidden horror, that I verily believe I shall someday employ it in fiction" (MTS 177). This dream was never published as a story by Lovecraft himself, but he described it in detail to a number of his correspondents during the winter of 1927. Consequently, these surviving dream-texts differ from one another, causing some inconsistencies in the secondary literature.[4] Some clarification is therefore needed.

There are two major variants of the dream, which differ structurally and in some important details. The earliest version of the "Roman Dream" derives from a letter to Donald Wandrei dated to Thursday, 3 November 1927 (MTS 177-82). A later letter detailing the dream was sent to Bernard Austin Dwyer on a Friday in November 1927, possibly as early as the day after he wrote to Wandrei (SL 2.188-97). In a letter to Frank Belknap Long in December 1927, Lovecraft refers to an earlier description of the dream sent to Long in November, but that November letter has not been preserved (SL 2.202-8). Fortunately, what must be very close to the original dream text written to Long was later incorporated into Long's *Horror from the Hills*, and it generally follows Dwyer's version.[5] Finally, a reference to the Roman dream appears in a letter to Clark Ashton Smith later in 1933 (SL 4.334). Unfortunately, the original letter containing the specific details is no longer extant, though from the wording of the correspondence it appears that the description written to Smith was perhaps just an abbreviated version. Lovecraft's Roman dream thus survives in two variations, the Wandrei version and the Dwyer version. The Wandrei version was titled "The Very Old Folk" and published in 1940; it has become the main text for subsequent publication in collections and anthologies of Lovecraft's miscellaneous writing.[6] Meanwhile, the Dwyer version with

---

4. The most substantive commentary on HPL's Roman Dream can be found in *IAP* 2.695-97, in which the author remarks that the versions are "surprisingly different in scope and focus," but does not elaborate. Apparently, Joshi, *H. P. Lovecraft: A Comprehensive Bibliography* I-B-v-b32, misdates HPL's letter to Donald Wandrei to 2 November 1927, when in fact it was written on 3 November, and maintains the variants as virtually the same, while Joshi and Schultz make no mention of the existence of any differing versions (*An H. P. Lovecraft Encyclopedia* 286).

5. In a letter to Clark Ashton Smith, HPL mentions that Long had incorporated his Roman dream "without any linguistic change in his 'Chaugnar' story" (*Dawnward Spire* 499); i.e., *The Horror from the Hills*.

6. In *Scienti-Snaps* 3, No. 3 (1940): 4-8, followed by HPL, *Marginalia*, ed. August Der-

some changes was published within Long's *Horror from the Hills* in a two-issue *Weird Tales* serial in 1931 and later published in a single stand-alone volume by Arkham House.[7] Let us now look at the differences in the two variants.

In general both the Wandrei and Dwyer versions of Lovecraft's dream follow the same plot as Lovecraft had summarized it in a letter to Clark Ashton Smith: "You probably recall the one [dream] I had in October, 1927, in which I was a provincial quaestor named L. Caelius Rufus serving in Hispania Citerior and accompanying the proconsul P. Scribonius Libo and a cohort of infantry into the mountains behind Pompelo—where nightmare doom overtook us all" (SL 4.334). Both versions take place in the Late Roman Republic, around 70 or 60 BCE, as Lovecraft vaguely dates it (SL 5.181), and deal with Roman reaction to a group of ancient hill folk whose dark Sabbath rites threaten the Roman colony of Pompelo. In the Wandrei version, the action takes place in Pompelo where the proconsul himself, Scribonius Libo, had summoned the legion commander Gnaeus Balbutius and his adjutant Sextus Asellius (along with a cohort of 300 Roman soldiers), and Lovecraft as Caelius Rufus, a minor Roman official and resident "occult expert," well versed in the forbidden black arts. A debate ensues regarding the proper course of action. Rufus maintains to the proconsul that they should stamp out the old folk from the hills in order to maintain peace and stability and to protect the Roman citizens and Romanized provincials living in Pompelo. Balbutius and Asellius disagree and argue for inaction for fear of antagonizing the local non-Roman Vascones tribe. Rufus wins the debate and convinces Libo to take military action. In the evening all involved accompany the cohort into the Pyrenees mountains, where they are drawn in and obliterated by the shadows

---

leth (Arkham House, 1944); HPL, *Uncollected Prose and Poetry*, eds. S. T. Joshi and Marc A. Michaud (Necronomicon Press, 1978), and HPL, *Miscellaneous Writings*, ed. S. T. Joshi (Arkham House, 1995), pp. 46-51. Recent omnibus editions and collections of HPL's weird fiction have also seen fit to include "The Very Old Folk." See *H. P. Lovecraft: The Complete Fiction* (Barnes & Noble, 2011), pp. 623-28, and the Knickerbocker Classics edition, *The Complete Fiction of H. P. Lovecraft* (Race Point Publishing, 2014), while the definitive text is contained in CF 3.494-500.

7. *Weird Tales* (January 1931): 32-54, and (February-March 1931): 245-72. For the Arkham House edition, see Long, *The Horror from the Hills* 65-75.

of nameless beasts and by the icy mountain wind summoned by the very old folk.

The narrative in the Dwyer version appears to be more cumbersome than the account in Wandrei, yet is more evocative and detailed in parts. Here the story slowly unfolds with Caelius Rufus in the library (reading a copy of Lucretius' *De Rerum Natura*) of his friend Balbutius, in the Spanish city of Calagurris. The two friends debate what to do about the looming threat of the *Miri Nigri* (strange dark folk) and their deity, now specified as the *Magnum Innominandum* (the great unnamed).[8] Rufus had arrived in Calagurris to argue on behalf of Pompelo's local official (aedile) Tib. Annaeus Mela (the aedile appears as Tib. Annaeus Stilpo in the Wandrei version), whose request for military support against the *Miri Nigri* had been rebuffed by the legionary commander Balbutius. Rufus' pleas for the suppression of the *Miri Nigri*'s loathsome rites fall upon deaf ears. Even bringing up the precedent of the Bacchanalian incident of 186 BCE and evidence from the terrible Pergamine scroll, the *Hieron Aigypton* (not found in Wandrei), fails to convince. Frustrated, Rufus goes over Balbutius' head and writes to the proconsul himself, Scribonius Libo, who apparently knows a thing or two about the *Miri Nigri*. The proconsul sympathizes with the quaestor's point of view and orders a cohort of soldiers under Balbutius' command to be dispatched immediately to Pompelo with Rufus in tow.

At Pompelo, Rufus, Balbutius, and his lieutenant Sextus Asellius convene with the proconsul, Libo, and at sunset march into the hills above the town. In the Dwyer version, the cohort's eventual fate is markedly more detailed than in Wandrei. Incessant eldritch drumming greet the doomed men, while the surrounding peaks blaze with flame and demonic laughter bursts through the mountains. In both versions, as the night sky becomes obliterated with shadow, most of the characters are eventually driven mad or trampled by the panicking soldiers, while only the old proconsul Scribo maintains his composure with his last words, "*Malita vetus—*

---

8. Or, "He who must not be named." The *Magnum Innominandum* as the "Not to be named One" makes an appearance in HPL's ghostwritten tale "The Mound" in 1929-30 and was cited in "The Whisperer in Darkness" (1930). Later the deity makes an appearance in an invocation from the *De Vermis Mysteriis* in Robert Bloch's "The Shambler from the Stars" (1935).

malitia vetus est—venit—tandem venit . . ."[9] One other major difference in Dwyer's version is that Rufus' mother is the Roman matron Helvia, the sister of Lucius Helvius Cinna, while in the Wandrei version she is the mother of the aedile Annaeus Stilpo and daughter of Marcus Helvius Cinna. This important connection shall be addressed later in this article.[10]

The dream sequence contained in Belknap Long's *Horror from the Hills*, featuring the elephantine god Chaugnar Faugn, closely follows the structure contained in the Dwyer letter but is evidently rewritten to fit Long's style and seems to be less ornate than Lovecraft's own prose. By in large, the names of the characters have been preserved from the Dwyer version, but certain details are omitted, such as the mention of Lucretius' work, while the *Hieron Aigypton* is referred to as "a hideous manuscript in Greek." Curiously, there is a classical reference to Athens' sacrificial victims sent to King Minos' Minotaur, which appears neither in Dwyer nor in Wandrei. Rufus' or Stilpo's familial connection with the lady Helvia has been dropped, as well as reference to the *Miri Nigri*'s ancient deity, the *Magnum Innominandum*. This is certainly to be expected, since it is Long's Chaugnar Faugn who is behind the cohort's destruction and falls beyond the original context of Lovecraft's dream.[11]

What we have, therefore, are two drafts of Lovecraft's Roman dream, each preserving the basic core of the narrative but differing in some specific details. In addition, we have Lovecraft's later comments reacting to his correspondents' responses and his further ideas of how he thought he

---

9. "The ancient evil—it's the ancient evil—it comes—at last it comes . . ."

10. There are other minor differences between the two versions of HPL's dream, such as the name of the Roman guide (Vercellius in Wandrei, Marcus Accius in Dwyer); Caelius Rufus in the Wandrei version is granted a field commission of the rank, *primus pilus* (first spear), while in the Dwyer version the *primipilus* is Publius Vibulanus; A certain D. Vibulanus appears in Wandrei, but is described as a *subcenturio*. Q. Minncius Laena, a secretary of the proconsul, appears in the Dwyer version but is omitted in Wandrei.

11. Other minor differences in Long's version include Rufus' reading of Cato's *De Re Rustica* (this is an error in fact in Long, since Cato wrote the *De Agri Cultura*, while a later Roman, Columella, composed the agricultural treatise *De Re Rustica*) rather than Balbutius in the Dwyer version; Libo's secretary appears as Q. Trebellius Pollio rather than Q. Minnicius Laena, while a certain Aebutius encounters Rufus in Calagurris, which is not found in Dwyer or Wandrei.

would develop his Roman dream into a viable story. In reaction to Donald Wandrei's amazement at the vividness and unusual power of the Roman dream, Lovecraft admits that "very few [of his dreams] have provided sufficient substance as literary material" (MTS 187). But Lovecraft goes on to say that he credits his close sense of personal identity with the Romans and their phenomenal sway over his imagination to dreams he had about them at an early age. He remarks, "Psychologically I am either a Roman or an Englishman, with no possibility of imaginative expansion" (MTS 188).

In response to Dwyer's comments, however, Lovecraft wrote less about his romance with the Romans than about possible revisions he needed to make in order to turn the dream into a story. Thorny problems involving coordinating the Sabbaths of the *Miri Nigri* with the pre-Julian Roman calendar needed to be solved. It plagued Lovecraft to the point where he considered moving the story ahead to the age of the Roman Empire, when the calendar could easily be synchronized with the Witch-Sabbaths (SL 2.218). Lovecraft also provided additional information about how the language of the *Miri Nigri* was radically different from the Indo-European-based linguistic group of the Celt-Iberians or the anomalous tongue of the Basques of northern Spain. The author further wrote that he ought to have emphasized that the steep wooded slopes would have slowly engulfed the Roman cohort and buried it in an altered landscape. Further additions would have included the discovery of a lost and buried Hispano-Roman town (other than Pompelo) overtaken by the doom summoned by the *Miri Nigri*. The story would begin with the modern-day discovery by a traveler of a rusty Roman *signum* from the doomed cohort, which leads to the excavation of the buried town in question by Spanish archaeologists. The traveler, overtaken with a vision of a terrible stone altar within a circle of monoliths, falls ill and is hospitalized, where he has the Roman dream. He awakens the next morning to shocking news that the excavations of the newly discovered town, as well as the archaeological team, had been destroyed by a terrible avalanche. The *Magnum Innominandum* strikes again. Lovecraft included most of these same observations and musings in his response to Frank Belknap Long, prefacing his comments with an emphatic assertion that his Roman dream was experienced with most of its detail intact, leading one to suspect that Long thought otherwise (SL 2.202–3).

What Lovecraft's letters demonstrate is that he wrote about his Roman dream in a series of drafts farmed out to his correspondents and had given serious thought to developing it into a working story at least by the beginning of 1928. However, nearly a year later, in February 1929, Lovecraft wrote to Long, who was trolling for some ideas for short pieces or a novel: "Another thing you could use is that Hispano-Roman dream I described a year ago October. I probably shan't ever get around to writing it up, so if you can find the letter containing it, you're welcome to the thing" (SL 2.261). What imposed so much on Lovecraft's time previous to this juncture? A good deal of the intervening year was filled with literary revision work for two of his clients, Adolphe de Castro and Zealia Bishop. We also know that Lovecraft was summoned by his wife, Sonia Greene, to New York in the spring of 1928 and that this was followed by extended trips throughout New England. In early August 1928, Lovecraft was preoccupied with the writing of "The Dunwich Horror." And, finally, Sonia Greene began divorce proceedings against Lovecraft at the end of 1928. It is not surprising, therefore, that Lovecraft had a good deal on his plate and was not able to compose his Roman Dream into a proper short story.[12] Indeed, by early 1929 Long had incorporated Lovecraft's Roman dream into his *Horror from the Hills*.

Finally, a very significant reason that might explain Lovecraft's delay in transforming his dream into a publishable story is his utter devotion to historical detail and accuracy, aptly demonstrated by his concern that the *Miri Nigri* Sabbath dates must correspond to the Roman calendar.[13] This slavish attention to detail not only shows the depth of Lovecraft's research but also his commitment to faithfully recreating the world of ancient Rome, a vanished civilization for which he had a profound affinity. It is for this reason that his Roman Dream of 1927 can be read as a reflection of his fears about what he perceived to be major threats to his own civilization.

---

12. For HPL's activities during this time see chapters 18 and 19 of *IAP*.

13. Curiously, HPL commits a historical error by stating that the Roman Legion involved in the dream stationed in Spain was the 12th Legion stationed at Calagurris (*MTS* 178 and *SL* 2.190), when in fact the 12th was raised by Caesar later in 58 BCE. See Keppie 82.

Lovecraft's Roman Nightmare: The *Miri Nigri*, the Yellow Peril, and the Decline of Western Civilization

The setting of Lovecraft's dream during the Late Roman Republic in the province of Hispania Citerior is significant. From a number of examples in his letters, Lovecraft idealized Rome, particularly the Roman Republic, and saw direct parallels between his own age and that of ancient Rome. Of particular concern to Lovecraft was the decline of the modern West due to "mongrelisation" from race-mixing. The Roman dream portrays noble, civilized Romans being overwhelmed and destroyed by a barbaric, foreign people and their god. This mirrors the author's own fears that Western civilization was profoundly threatened by immigration, especially from the "east." The "Yellow Peril" scare of the late nineteenth and early twentieth centuries was one reflection of this fear and was generally grounded in the "nativist" anxieties of middle-class Anglo-Saxon Protestants to which at least culturally Lovecraft belonged (Higham 52–53). The proposed course of action against the strange dark folk proposed by Lovecraft's dream persona, Caelius Rufus, echoes the author's own preferred course of action against the "eastern threat" of his own day: a swift armed response and eradication of the menace at hand.

Lovecraft's Roman Dream took place during the age of Cicero and Caesar, the period of Roman history and culture that the author most admired and had the most affinity toward. Lovecraft's childhood dreams of Rome always took place in the age of the glorious *res publica*, often as a Roman officer, a *tributus militum* (military tribune), riding with Caesar against the savage Gallic tribes (MTS 178). Lovecraft also considered the time period of 106–43 BCE as a veritable literary golden age, which "opens the period of highest perfection in Roman literature" ("The Literature of Rome" [1918]). Cicero, according to Lovecraft, was "synonymous with the height of Attic wit, forensic art, and prose composition"(CE 2.26). It is natural that Lovecraft found connection with a Rome governed by the Senate, a ruling class of aristocrats. Lovecraft in his treatise on political philosophy, "Nietzscheism and Realism" (1921), states that oligarchic rule was the best form of government, preferable to monarchy, despotism, and certainly more preferable to democratic rule (CE 5.69). Lovecraft believed that the cultural and political achievements of the Republic were directly attributable to its aristocratic government: "Aristocracy alone is capable of creating thoughts and objects of value" (CE 5.70).

Therefore, Lovecraft's regard for the Roman Republic went beyond mere admiration on an intellectual level. More than a few selections from his letters indicate that this twentieth-century American Yankee had a profound, even visceral, identification with the ruling elites of ancient Rome. In a letter to Clark Ashton Smith he writes, "The idea of the republic of the consuls and empire of the Caesars being other than my country is simply impossible for me to entertain." And he maintains that "pictures of Roman scenes prompt a kindred feeling mixed with certain unexplainable objections as if to *anachronisms* I cannot consciously place. It is utterly impossible, too, for me to regard Rome in a *detached* way" (SL 4.332). For Lovecraft, the Roman Republic was the ideal civilization.

Consequently, Lovecraft despaired at Rome's decline and the perceived decline of his own civilization, both of which he linked to the arrival and integration of foreign immigrants. Lovecraft bemoaned the twilight of Rome and drew a distinct parallel with his own contemporary society when he wrote, "Those loathsome days after Septimius Severus, when the mixed blood & fading art of the dying empire began to foreshadow the end openly & visibly, have a curious & melancholy parallelism with the present stage of history" (MTS 177).[14] For Lovecraft, a major factor in the decline of Rome, particularly the Roman empire, was "mongrelisation" or race-mixing. In his treatise "The Literature of Rome," he writes that eastern influences had corrupted Roman values, while its people had physically been "reduced to mongrel degeneracy through unrestrained immigration and foreign admixture"(CE 2.30). In some of his letters he reveals similar fears about the decline of America, calling the admission of "alien" and "degenerate" immigrant hordes "the supreme calamity of the western world" (SL 2.305). It is little wonder that a good deal of Lovecraft's anti-immigrant rants can be found in his writings from his New York period and after. The author's fear of aliens and miscegenation also shows up prominently in his weird fiction. "The Lurking Fear," "The Shadow over Innsmouth," and of course, "Horror at Red Hook" are prime examples.

Lovecraft's horror of immigrants and race-mixing strongly resonates in

---

14. A sentiment, unfortunately, reflected in some of the academic literature of the age as HPL might have been influenced by Tenney Frank's prominent article, "Race Mixture in the Roman Empire," written in 1911.

the location of his Roman dream, the Spanish town of Pompelo, which is modern Pamplona. Lovecraft was well aware that Pompelo was a border town along the frontier of Roman civilization in the Pyrenees mountains. Pompelo's inhabitants were Roman citizens, Romanized (acculturated) provincials, and non-Roman Celt-Iberian Vascones. His description of Pompelo's inhabitants as a mixture of "broad-browed Roman colonists & coarse-haired Romanised natives, together with obvious hybrids of the two strains, alike clad in cheap woolen togas & sprinklings of helmeted legionaries & coarse-mantled, black-bearded tribesmen of the circumambient Vascones—all thronged the few paved streets & forum" (MTS 177–78) can easily be seen as drawing on his experiences of New York, another city of mixed population.

The *Miri Nigri*, however, are completely foreign and alien to the ethnic communities in Pompelo, who are either Roman, of mixed Roman, or of fully Celt-Iberian stock. Lovecraft describes the very old folk in starkly racist terms as little, yellow, squint-eyed, sub-humans resembling the central Asian Scythians of antiquity. The language the *Miri Nigri* spoke, which was choppy and unintelligible, was akin to an Asiatic language group referred to later by Lovecraft as "mongoloid" and separate from the language of the Basques of the Pyrenees. It is the abhorrent behavior of the strange dark folk that truly separates them from the cultural milieu of Roman civilization. Their twice-yearly abductions of local townsfolk for their Sabbath rituals had become a common and feared part of life in Pompelo. Yet the catalyst of the story was not the death of townspeople but "certain gloating and inhuman cruelties perpetrated upon a dog," leading to a riot and the subsequent deaths of two of the strange dark folk. The choice of a dog as victim in Lovecraft's dream is surprising, since atrocities against a cat would have been personally more abhorrent to him. Whatever the circumstances, the behavior of the *Miri Nigri* mark them as morally, culturally, and religiously deviant, beyond the sphere of "civilized" folk.

Lovecraft's strange dark folk undoubtedly reflect his ideas regarding the anthropological origins of "elfin fairyfolk" and "dwarves" in Northern Europe, as being derived from Aryan encounters with the "squat, Mongoloid stocks of northern Europe—Lapps and Finns" ("Some Backgrounds of Fairyland" [CE 5.323]). And there is the unmistakable influence of Arthur Machen's "Little People" stories featured in his "The White People" and *The Three Impostors*, among others. Yet Lovecraft's portrayal of the "mongoloid" *Miri Nigri* is clearly linked to the central Asiatic Scythians and can be seen as analogous to the view of Asians as part of the "yellow peril" scare of the late nineteenth and early twentieth centuries.[15] We know that Lovecraft's view of Western civilization's decline was influenced by Oswald Spengler's *Decline of the West*, which argued that Anglo-European western civilization had run its course.[16] For him, the root causes of this decline in America in particular lay in mass democracy, the mechanization of culture, and the unfettered influx of immigrants (*IAP* 774-75). His description of the *Miri Nigri* as a racial threat to Rome echoes the fears of a Chinese or Japanese hegemony over the Western powers as presented in such influential contemporary works as G. G. Rupert's *The Yellow Peril; or, The Orient vs. the Occident* (1911) and Lothrop Stoddard's *The Rising Tide of Color against White World-Supremacy* (1920).

Clearly there are close parallels between the perceived Asiatic threat to Europe and America and the threat of the *Miri Nigri* to Roman Pompelo. For example, Lovecraft's Roman persona, Caelius Rufus, vociferously argues that the *Miri Nigri* "were capable of visiting almost any nameless doom upon the town, which after all was a Roman settlement & contained a great number of our citizens"; and, "Checked in time, before the progress of the rites might evoke anything with which the iron of a Roman *pilum* might not be able to deal, the Sabbath would not be too much for the for the powers of a single cohort." The *Miri Nigri* posed a "horror of such import not only to the wards of the Roman people, but to the peace of mankind as a whole." His call for military action is justified by the premise that the key to good Roman governance was in the defense of its citizens and more importantly of the provincial elites through whom Roman power was extended and maintained. Lovecraft's hawkish attitudes projected onto the past are also reflected in his own personal politics, particularly in the realm of foreign affairs and such conflicts as the Spanish-American War. Lovecraft's jingoism becomes fully apparent in his opinion on American neutrality during the early years of the First World War, culminating in his biting criticism of Woodrow Wilson's "craven pacifism" in his essay "The Renaissance of Manhood" (*CE* 5.15; see *IAP* 486). Furthermore, Lovecraft's militaristic stance (through the mouth of Caelius

---

15. For this imagery, see Tchen, *Yellow Peril!* 39-44, Madison, *Anti-Foreign Imagery* 41-87, and Wu, *The Yellow Peril: Chinese Americans in American Fiction* 183-206.
16. For HPL's use of Spengler, see Joshi, *H. P. Lovecraft: The Decline of the West* 133-45.

Rufus) against the *Miri Nigri* parallels his concern about the growing threat of Russia and Japan, who would both, ironically, be allies with Britain and the United States against the Germans during World War I. In his essay "The Crime of the Century," written in 1915, Lovecraft pleads for reconciliation between the two "Teutonic" powers of Britain and Germany and bids them to "crush successively the rising power of Slav and Mongolian, preserving for Europe and America the glorious culture that has evolved" (*CE* 5.14). Here Lovecraft's fear of eastern threats to Europe and America are played out years later in his Roman Dream as the forces of Roman civilization are overwhelmed by an alien people.

Lovecraft's Roman Face: A Yankee Equestrian in Republican Rome

Thus far we have seen Lovecraft's Roman Dream as a reflection of fears about his own society played out in the historical stage of ancient Rome. Yet what does this dream, indeed this nightmare, tell us about Lovecraft's own personal aspirations? His dream persona, the Roman Lucius Caelius Rufus, is a provincial government official (a quaestor) from Rome's equestrian class, ranking below the old Roman aristocracy but still a member of the Republic's ruling elite. Rufus is a well-educated man with a comfortable private income, for as we shall see his position as a quaestor was not salaried. In Rufus, we have the ideal "gentleman" that Lovecraft longed to be.

Fans of Lovecraft will be well aware of his use of literary characters as his own personal analogues. Randolph Carter, Charles Dexter Ward, and other Lovecraftian heroes exemplify this aspect of Lovecraft's weird fiction (Price 32–36). But his Roman persona deserves special consideration. All his life Lovecraft dreamed or fantasized about being a soldier under Caesar. Two examples, one taken from his youth and other from adulthood, illustrate this. In both his correspondence (*SL* 3.313) and in his brief autobiographical essay "A Confession of Unfaith," Lovecraft relates that while in grade school he had adopted the Roman pseudonym of Lucius Valerius Messala and fantasized about torturing imaginary Christians (*CE* 5.146).[17] This deeply rooted sense of personal *Romanitas* would continue

---

17. Given HPL's sensibilities, it may be possible that the name Lucius Valerius Messala might have been a conflation of Valerius Gratus, the Roman procurator of Judea, and Messala, the anti-Christian antagonist, who were both characters from Lew Wal-

into adulthood. In 1933 Lovecraft wrote: "my sense of personal connexion with my own blood-ancestors of the north utterly vanishes—giving place to a natural and unshakable feeling of *being a Roman*" (SL 4.332).[18] Let us now probe a little deeper into Lucius Caelius Rufus and what he represented to Lovecraft.

A stalwart Roman civil servant with academic knowledge of the occult, Lucius Caelius Rufus functions as the special advisor dealing with the *Miri Nigri* problem for the high-ranking patrician Scribonius Libo. His toga bearing the two narrow stripes (*angusti clavi*), as Lovecraft was keenly aware, places Rufus in the equestrian social class, a step below Libo's status. We know that by the late Republic, aspirants to equestrian status would need to be worth at least 400,000 sesterces. Rufus would thus have enjoyed a very comfortable income.[19] His elected position as a provincial quaestor of Roman Spain meant that he would have exercised regional control over judicial and financial matters and served at the pleasure of the province's proconsul or governor.[20] We can also surmise that Rufus must have had a certain degree of financial independence, because his lower-ranking political office as a quaestor was not salaried. Caelius Rufus is, then, a financially secure, mid-level bureaucrat attached to the serving proconsul of Roman Hispania, Scribonius Libo. If we now investigate Rufus' family background and engage in some prosopography, a number of interesting relationships emerge.

Although none of the featured characters in the Roman Dream are actual historical figures, Lovecraft knew that the family names (*gens*) he gave to his literary characters connected them to actual Roman families. Hence, many of the fictional characters in the dream are firmly grounded within the historical context of the period.[21] Rufus' *gens*, the Caelii, was a promi-

---

lace's *Ben-Hur* (1880), a national bestseller during the author's time until 1936.

18. For additional examples of this sentiment, see SL 4.335–36, 5.181–82, 265–66.

19. Pliny, *Ep.* 1.19. Earlier, during Rome's archaic period, this social designation required members to be able to field a horse in military levies, an expensive proposition. See Hill 84–85 and, for the formation of equestrian culture, Mayer.

20. According to William Smith, *A Dictionary of Greek and Roman Antiquities*, s.v. "Quaestor," a reference book HPL had used and had in library.

21. Yet Quinn, "Endless Bacchanal" 210, cogently observes that some Roman Dream characters, particularly, P. Scribonius Libo and Balbutius, were based on figures

nent, politically active equestrian family, whose most famous member *Marcus* Caelius Rufus (c. 88–48 BCE) was a Roman magistrate and protégé of Cicero and Marcus Crassus.[22] It is unclear whether Lucius Caelius Rufus was based on the historical figure Marcus Caelius, but it is clear that they are intended to be related and are contemporaries. It is most probable that Lovecraft's dream persona is intended to be a member of a well-regarded equestrian family, allied at the time with the great Cicero, and staunch supporters of the Roman Republic.

Another family connection of Lucius Caelius Rufus is to the Helvii family. In the Dwyer version, Caelius Rufus is related to that famous family by his mother, Helvia, and by a certain uncle, Lucius Helvius Cinna. Both are unattested in the historical record, but if they had existed they would be connected to the very real and renowned poet and man of letters Gaius Helvius Cinna (85–44 BCE).[23] It is worth noting, however, that in the Wandrei version Helvia is the mother of a minor character, the provincial aedile Tiberius Annaeus Stilpo. It is uncertain why Lovecraft chose to switch this family relation from Rufus to Stilpo. Perhaps the relationship proved too cumbersome, as it not known whether the Helvii were clearly equestrian. In any case, it is evident that Lovecraft intended to have his Roman persona come from a financially secure and well-respected background.

Finally, we know from internal evidence from both versions of Lovecraft's dream that Lucius Caelius Rufus is an educated man. In the Dwyer version, Rufus is familiar with the Roman philosopher Lucretius and his work, the *De Rerum Natura* (particularly the sections on astronomy), and familiar also with the prose of Cato the Elder. Furthermore, his academic knowledge of "forbidden lore" and his close understanding of erudite, arcane literature such as the hideous *Heiron Aigypton* solidify Lovecraft's dream persona's place among Rome's intellectual if not social elites (Harris 219).

Lovecraft clearly saw himself, in most respects, as a twentieth-century

---

found in the works of Dezső Kosztolányi and William Stearns Davis.

22. Featured prominent in Cicero's defense oration, the *Pro Caelio*, which details the alleged scandal involving Marcus Caelius with Clodia, the mistress of the famous Roman poet Catullus.

23. For Cinna's background, see Wiseman 144–58.

equivalent of the Roman equestrian Rufus. In his eyes, Rufus' status as a full-blooded Roman equestrian is similar to his own Anglo-Yankee background and, as he like to put it, "ancestry of unmixed English gentry" (*SL* 1.296; see also *IAP* 13). Gentry is an important descriptive term meaning well placed socially but not of the aristocracy, which equates to Rome's equestrian order and also reflects the Lovecraft family's social status. His family, especially his maternal grandfather, stemmed from the emerging urban-based, white-collar mercantile middle class in New England (Blumin 250-97). Both Rufus and Lovecraft are highly literate intellectuals with a Lucretian philosophical bent and a shared interest in astronomy. But in other respects, there are significant differences between Lovecraft and Rufus, differences of which Lovecraft would have been painfully aware.

Both the Caelii and Helvii families produced men of letters, while Lovecraft's family (aside from himself) did not—a fact that Lovecraft himself bemoaned and regretted. Even more significantly, Caelius Rufus was financially well off and could afford to serve as an unsalaried minor Roman magistrate, while Lovecraft lived in poverty and lacked a steady source of income for most of his life. Rufus' position as a mid-level Roman official might mirror Lovecraft's wish for steady employment in the civil service, certainly well within his grasp intellectually but difficult to attain due to his lack of advanced formal education. The Roman Dream may also reflect other disappointments for Lovecraft. In Dwyer's version, Lovecraft's dream persona is given a field commission as a *primipilus*, a high-ranking non-commissioned officer in the Roman legion. Lovecraft deeply regretted not being able to enlist in the Rhode Island National Guard during the First World War (*SL* 1.148; cf. *IAP* 224). In the Roman Dream, however, he can march alongside the aristocratic great man Scribonius Libo to face the horrors of the *Magnum Innominandum* and defend the values of Roman and, by extension, of Western civilization.

Conclusion

The value of Lovecraft's Great Roman Dream of 1927 lies in what it reveals about Lovecraft himself, his personal disappointments, and his anxieties about the future of his society. Lovecraft loved the Romans, and Rome remained for him the ideal civilization. Onto the Roman landscape he projected not unknown or unnamable terrors but terrors very real to the author: the terrors of change in the form of foreign immigrants, eastern invaders, and the perceived decline of the west. Lovecraft feared that his world, like that of the Romans, would eventually fall. And on a deeply personal level, his Roman persona Caelius Rufus embodied how he saw himself as, like Rufus, a member of a threatened elite striving to defend the values of Western civilization; but that persona was also a reflection of the author's own failed ambitions and lost opportunities.

Works Cited

Blumin, Stuart M. *The Emergence of the Middle Classes: Social Experiences in the American City, 1760–1900.* Cambridge: Cambridge University Press, 1989.

Frank, Tenney. "Race Mixture in the Roman Empire." *American Historical Review* 21, No. 4 (1916): 689–708.

Harris, William V. *Ancient Literacy.* Cambridge, MA: Harvard University Press, 1989.

Higham, John. *Strangers in the Land: Patterns of American Nativism, 1860–1925.* 3rd ed. New York: Atheneum, 1965.

Hill, H. *The Roman Middle Class in the Republican Period.* Oxford: Oxford University Press, 1952.

Hite, Kenneth. "Lost in Lovecraft: A Guided Tour of the Dark Master's World: To Hear Antiquity's Call." *Weird Tales* 64, No. 2 (2009): 72–75.

Joshi, S. T. *H. P. Lovecraft: The Decline of the West.* Mercer Island, WA: Starmont House, 1990.

———. *H. P. Lovecraft: A Comprehensive Bibliography.* Tampa, FL: University of Tampa Press, 2009.

———. "Lovecraft and Classical Antiquity." *Cynick,* 2, No. 2 (1981): 13–24.

———. *Primal Sources: Essays on H. P. Lovecraft.* New York: Hippocampus Press, 2003.

———. "'The Tree' and Ancient History." *Nyctalops* 4 (1991): 68–71.

Joshi, S. T., and David E. Schultz. *An H. P. Lovecraft Encyclopedia.* Westport, CT: Greenwood Press, 2001; rpt. New York: Hippocampus Press, 2004.

Keppie, Lawrence. *The Making of the Roman Army.* Norman: University of Oklahoma, 1984.

Long, Frank Belknap. *The Horror from the Hills.* Sauk City, WI: Arkham House, 1963.

Lovecraft, H. P. *Letters to C. L. Moore and Others*. Ed. David E. Schultz and S. T. Joshi. New York: Hippocampus Press, 2017.

Lovecraft, H. P., and Clark Ashton Smith. *Dawnward Spire, Lonely Hill: The Letters of H. P. Lovecraft and Clark Ashton Smith*. Ed. David E. Schultz and S. T. Joshi. New York: Hippocampus Press, 2017.

Madison, Nathan Vernon. *Anti-Foreign Imagery in American Pulps and Comic Books, 1920–1960*. Jefferson, NC: McFarland, 2013.

Mayer, Emanuel. *The Ancient Middle Classes: Urban Life and Aesthetics in the Roman Empire, 100 BCE–250 CE*. Cambridge, MA: Harvard University Press, 2012.

Price, Robert M. "Lovecraft as a Character in Lovecraftian Fiction." *Crypt of Cthulhu* No. 52 (Yuletide 1999): 32–36.

Quinn, Dennis. "Endless Bacchanal: Rome, Livy, and Lovecraft's Cthulhu Cult." *Lovecraft Annual* No. 5 (2011): 188–215.

Rupert, G. G. *The Yellow Peril; or, The Orient vs. the Occident*. 3rd ed. Britton, OK: Union Publishing, 1911.

Smith, William. *A Dictionary of Greek and Roman Antiquities*. London: John Murray, 1875.

Stoddard, Lothrop. *The Rising Tide of Color against White World-Supremacy*. New York: Scribner's, 1920.

Tchen, John Kuo Wei. *The Yellow Peril! An Archive of Anti-Asian Fear*. Brooklyn, NY: Verso, 2014.

Vaughan, Ralph E. "A Factual Basis for 'The Green Meadow'?" *Crypt of Cthulhu* No. 11 (Candlemas 1983): 26–27.

Wiseman, T. P. *Cinna the Poet and Other Roman Essays*. Leicester, UK: Leicester University Press, 1974.

Wallace, Lew. *Ben-Hur: A Tale of the Christ*. 1880. New York: Harper & Brothers, 1908.

Wu, William F. *The Yellow Peril: Chinese Americans in American Fiction*. Hamden, CT: Archon, 1982.

The Poet's Nightmare:
The Nature of Things according to Lovecraft

Sean Moreland
University of Ottawa

It has long been commonplace to describe Lovecraft's personality and views as paradoxical. This appears to have been as true for his contemporaries as it is for ours, for Lovecraft often justified his seemingly contradictory views in his letters. Perhaps his most salient explanation of his intellectual and aesthetic habitus comes in an early letter:

> I should describe my own nature as tripartite, my interests consisting of three parallel and dissociated groups—(a) Love of the strange and fantastic. (b) Love of abstract truth and scientific logic. (c) Love of the ancient and the permanent. Sundry combinations of these three strains will probably account for all my odd tastes and eccentricities. (SL 1.110; see also SM 13.)

Lovecraft's longstanding admiration for and fascination with *De Rerum Natura* (hereafter *DRN*), the epic didactic poem by first-century BCE Roman poet Lucretius, was shaped by its unique intersection with all these "parallel and dissociated" domains. Rife with wild imagery, sublime rhetorical effects, and fantastic speculation but nonetheless grounded in materialist metaphysics, *DRN*'s six books of Latin dactylic hexameter verse deploy these features in arguing for the truth and necessity of Epicurean philosophy. Written during a period in Roman history that had particular appeal for Lovecraft, the poem's philosophical perspective is a materialistic monism, in which absolutely everything that exists is composed of two elements: concatenations of atoms (a Greek word Lucretius notably never uses, preferring a succession of more common Latin terms instead) that are constantly combining and collapsing, and the inane, the infinite void, through which they fall and in which they incessantly come apart and recombine. In Lucretius' Epicurean reality, it is only these elements that are permanent; the poem is concerned with, and describes (often in vivid detail), the impermanence of every configuration that arises, has arisen, or will ever arise from them.

It is certainly no secret that Lovecraft read, studied, and deeply admired *DRN*, and yet so far only passing critical attention has been paid to this fact, and this has focused solely on the second of Lovecraft's three parallel domains, that of "abstract truth" and philosophy. For example, S. T. Joshi notes that "the Epicurean philosophy embodied in Lucretius was a central influence in [Lovecraft's] early thought" (61–62). Lovecraft's early embrace of both Epicurean ethics and epistemology is clear from a 1920 letter to Alfred Galpin, to whom he recommends them wholeheartedly:

> As to any especial "creed of speculative scepticism", as Gahal-Bah describes his present need, I would advise Epicureanism as a base. That old geezer had the right idea, and drew from the right sources, largely my old friend Democritus. Read Lucretius' "De Rerum Natura" for the best possible exposition of this unsurpassed philosophy. There are many reasons why moderns can never surpass Epicurus, among them racial inferiority. We are certainly as far below the Greeks as, for example, the Mongolians are below us. (89)

This passage echoes Lucretius' claims for the philosophical supremacy of his Greek master, linking this to Lovecraft's own belief in a racial hierarchy and his anxieties about racial difference and degeneration. Lovecraft continues to play the role of Epicurean evangelist in many of his later letters, describing how the poem shaped both his metaphysical views and his personal ethics. The latter, in particular, remained remarkably consistent throughout the course of his life, as he suggests in a letter to Natalie H. Wooley:

> Now since man means nothing in the cosmos, it is plain that his only logical goal (a goal whose sole reference is to himself) is simply the achievement of a reasonable equilibrium which shall enhance his likelihood of experiencing the sort of reactions he wishes, & which shall help along his natural impulse to increase his differentiation from unorganised force and matter. This goal can be reached only through teaching individual men how best to keep out of each other's way, & how best to reconcile the various conflicting instincts which a haphazard cosmic drift has placed within the breast of the same person. Here, then, is a practical & imperative system of ethics, resting on the firmest possible foundation & being essentially that taught by Epicurus & Lucretius. (*Letters to Robert Bloch* 209–210)

"Ancient and Permanent": *DRN* as Historical Fetish

However, Lucretius' influence on Lovecraft was not as confined to the domains of logos and ethos as these sorts of statements suggest. *DRN* also appealed powerfully to Lovecraft through a pathos strengthened by his curiously intense self-identification with classical Rome, and particularly the period in Roman history that gave rise to Lucretius, Virgil, and Horace. In a 1927 letter to Bernard Austin Dwyer, Lovecraft confesses that Rome "has always exercised the most peculiarly potent effect upon my imagination—forming a second father-land to which all my sense of loyalty, perspective, affection, pride, and personal identity reverts whenever I think myself back into the ancient world" (*SL* 2.188).

The intensity of Lovecraft's imaginative identification with first century BCE Rome is given its most powerful expression in a dream he had in 1927, and which he wrote of in many of his letters, providing his most detailed account in the letter to Dwyer quoted from above. *DRN* figures centrally in the dream, as Lovecraft recalls his dream-self was reading

> It my own library, and there lay on the table the copy of *Lucretius De Rerum Natura* that I had been reading, rolled about three-quarters toward the end to the astronomical part in Book V which I had reached when Cnaeus Balbutius had been announced. I can still see the line where I left off—
>
> LUNAQUE.SIVE.NOTHO.FERTUR.LOCA. LUMINE.LUSTRANS. (*SL* 2.190)

Lovecraft's philosophical reception of *DRN*, and his emotional identification of it with an ideal of Rome that was as much a product of fantasized nostalgia as historical reality, produced a uniquely creative tension. Lovecraft was aware of this tension, as a 1936 letter to Fritz Leiber suggests:

> the purely philosophic side of me—plus a large amount of the aesthetic side—certainly *is* classical. I am a complete materialist in belief—of the line of the Ionians, Leucippus, Democritus, Epicurus, & Lucretius, & such moderns (Hobbes, Condillac, Comte, Dewey, Bertrand Russell, Santayana) as derive from this source. [. . .] All this is joined to a *curious sense of identification* with classic *Rome* . . . . a psychological twist which a superstitious person would attribute to metempsychosis or something of the sort. This feeling—which runs parallel to my still stranger sense of identification with the 18th century, is independent of any intellectual appraisal of Rome on my part. I know damn well that Roman culture was infinitely inferior to its Hellenic source, & can even understand Spengler's passionate indictment of the Republica . . . . yet not for a second can I emotionally grasp any human event anterior to 500 A.D. except through Roman eyes. (*Letters to C. L. Moore and Others*)

Lovecraft's 1927 nightmare is hardly the only example of how *DRN* is darkly reflected in some of his weirder and more horrific conceptions; the poem is at least as important for the ways it fed his "love of the strange and fantastic" as it is for influencing his materialist thought. Joshi suggests as much when, noting that Lucretius is "the dominant literary influence on the [cosmic] central section" of "The Poe-et's Nightmare" (1916), he points to a crucial connection between their poetics: "although Lucretius does not find terror but only awe and wonder and majesty in the contemplation of infinite space, both poets see in the vastness of the cosmos a refutation of human self-importance" (SM 231).

Joshi goes on to claim that the fact that this poem precedes Lovecraft's reading of Dunsany by three years points to the conclusion that his cosmicism was not literarily influenced but taken first from his study of astronomy in 1902 and then from his early readings in the atomic philosophy of Democritus, Epicurus, and Lucretius, tempered by nineteenth-century advances in biology, chemistry and astrophysics (SM 231).

That Joshi describes Lucretius's influence not as "literary" here, but instead philosophical, despite his recognition of Lucretius' aesthetic centrality above, is likely influenced by Lovecraft's own numerous statements to this effect. In order to appreciate how interconnected these domains of influence are, however, it is first necessary to look more closely at Lovecraft's own statements about, and philosophical engagements with, *DRN*.

"Abstract Truth": *DRN* as Philosophical Influence

Rediscovered in the late fifteenth century, *DRN* had a decisive influence on early modern thought and culture. Its influence on English literature and philosophy became pervasive by the seventeenth century, which saw two English translations of the complete poem, Thomas Creech's (published 1682) and Lucy Hutchinson's (written in the 1650s but not published completely until the twentieth century). More crucially, many of its ideas were disseminated through the work of poets and philosophers as different from one another as Newton and Burton, Milton and Hobbes, Gassendi and Rochester. Lucretius remained widely read in literary and philosophical circles throughout Lovecraft's beloved eighteenth century and was often referred to by Lovecraft's Augustan idols Addison, Swift, and Pope (the last of whom earned the nickname "The English Lucretius" after publishing his didactic poem *An Essay on Man*). By Lovecraft's day, many other complete English translations of the poem were available.[1] Lovecraft, however, appears not to have been particularly influenced by any of these translations; as Joshi notes, he "read Lucretius in Latin" and "owned Jacob Bernays's Teubner edition of 1879" (*IAP* 318).

Lovecraft refers to Lucretius as "one of the greatest thinkers of all time" and has particular praise for the degree to which his atomic materialist picture of the world anticipates aspects of contemporary physics and biology. Lovecraft writes, "the majority of his conclusions accord well with the thought of the most advanced scientific thought of today, though some of them have sources as old as Democritus" (*CE* 2.26). With this claim Lovecraft falls prey to a tendency Alison Sharock identifies as widespread since the eighteenth century, as many "critics are, only semi-consciously, prejudiced in Lucretius' favour because of the high standing of scientific rationalism in the modern imaginary, although there is little connection beyond the vocabulary (admittedly an important qualification) between ancient and modern atomic theory" (2). Nevertheless, Lovecraft was in excellent company in holding this opinion. Albert Einstein begins his introduction to Hermann Diels's 1924 German verse translation of *DRN* both by acknowledging the striking parallels between Lucretius' atomism and that of contemporary physics and by characterizing Lucretius' ideal modern reader in terms that sound uncannily like Lovecraft's self-perception:

> The work of Lucretius will exert its charm upon anyone who is not utterly engrossed in the spirit of our times, but rather feels himself to be a spectator to the present day, and particularly to the intellectual focus of his contemporaries. One sees here how a man who is gifted with interests in biology and theory, who is full of living feelings and thoughts, who is independent, can regard the world. (435–36)

Perhaps the sense of being "a spectator to the present day" which Einstein evidently shared with Lovecraft partially reinforces Lovecraft's own

---

1. Including John Mason Good's verse translation (1805), which I elsewhere argue had tremendous importance for Poe, John Selby Watson's prose translation (1851), William Ellery Leonard's verse translation (1916; there are some striking parallels between Leonard and HPL, including their scorn for literary modernism, their peculiar anxieties, and their close connections to August Derleth, who was among Leonard's Wisconsin literary and social circle) and W. H. D. Rouse's prose translation (1924, which remains the standard Loeb edition to this day).

claim, in a 1931 letter to Frank Belknap Long, that one need only "analyse [Einstein's] 'cosmic religion' [to] see if it differs a whit from my own aesthetic of impersonal but non-conscious order!" (SL 3.300–301). Lucretius' apparent pertinence to developments in contemporary physics and cosmology was also an inspiration for the poet and professor William Ellery Leonard, who prepared the first complete American English-language verse translation of the poem, publishing it in 1916. In an endnote appended to the first instance of his use of the term Cosmos in translating part of Lucretius' opening Hymn to Venus (*DRN* 1.21), Leonard justifies his lexical choice by writing:

> In Greek, a technical term of that Stoic philosophy to which Lucretius was opposed; but in English fairly equivalent to the Epicurean "natura rerum," through the associations of the word with Spencer's "Cosmic Philosophy" and with modern materialism. (4)

Lucretius' avoidance of the Greek word cosmos is informed by its teleological connotations, but Leonard suggests that these connotations need no longer apply given the term's adoption by modern materialist thinkers. Lovecraft seems to have shared Leonard's view in this respect, as his adoption of the term cosmicism to characterize his own philosophical sensibility suggests. Indeed, Lovecraft's cosmic vision, following from Lucretius', is radically opposed to teleological assumptions about the natural world. Joshi writes:

> The central tenet in what Lovecraft called his "cosmic indifferentism" is mechanistic materialism. The term postulates two ontological hypotheses: 1) the universe is a "mechanism" governed by fixed laws (although these may not all be known to human beings) where all entity is inextricably connected causally; there can be no such thing as chance (hence no free will but instead an absolute determinism), since every incident is the inevitable outcome of countless ancillary and contributory events reaching back into infinity; 2) all entity is material, and there can be no other essence, whether it be "soul" or "spirit" or any other non-material substance. Lovecraft evolved these ideas through a lifelong study of ancient and modern philosophy, beginning with the Greek Atomists (Leucippus and Democritus), their followers Epicurus and Lucretius (whose belief in free will Lovecraft was forced to abandon), and such modern thinkers as Ernst Haeckel, Thomas Henry Huxley, Friedrich Nietzsche, Bertrand Russell, and George Santayana. Lovecraft's metaphysical views seem to have solidified around 1919, when he read Haeckel's *The Riddle of the Universe* (1899; English translation 1900) and Hugh Elliot's *Modern Science and Materialism* (1919). (SM 30)

Lovecraft's claim in the 1922 essay "A Confession of Unfaith" that by this point he had "ceased [his] literal adherence to Epicurus and Lucretius, and reluctantly dismissed free-will in favour of determinism" (CE 5.148) through what Joshi calls "his absorption of the great trilogy of Nietzsche, Haeckel, and Elliot, who all unite on the issue" (IAP 329) both shows the degree to which his thought prior to this point conformed wholly to his understanding of Lucretius' exposition of Epicurus, and suggests the degree to which the Roman Epicurean continued to influence him, albeit in a less "literal" way. Despite rejecting Lucretius' analogy between the atomic *clinamen* (unpredictable swerve of atoms) and human free will (what contemporary readers might be tempted to call a "quantum woo"), however, Lovecraft continues to stress in his letters that Lucretius is among the materialist thinkers who most shaped his own philosophical views. For example, in 1927 he writes:

> The world and all its inhabitants impress me as immeasurably insignificant, so that I always crave intimations of larger and subtler symmetries than these which concern mankind. All this, however, is purely aesthetic and not at all intellectual. I have a parallel nature or phase devoted to science and logic, and do not believe in the supernatural at all—my philosophical position being that of a mechanistic materialist of the line of Leucippus, Democritus, Epicurus and Lucretius—and in modern times, Nietzsche and Haeckel. (SL 2.160)

Lovecraft's not entirely consistent self-distancing from his Epicurean philosophical roots can be better understood in light of a few key passages from Elliot's *Modern Science and Materialism*. Initially, like Einstein, Leonard, and an earlier Lovecraft, Elliot emphasizes the continuities between Epicurean materialism and its modern scientific counterpart. He writes:

> Scientific materialism warmly denies that there exists any such thing as purpose in the Universe, or that events have any ulterior motive or goal to which they are striving. It asserts that all events are due to the interaction of matter and motion acting by blind necessity in accordance with those invariable sequences to which we have given the name of laws. This is an important bond of connection between the materialism of the ancient Greeks and that of modern science. Among all peoples not highly cultivated there reigns a passionate conviction, not only that the Universe as a whole is working out some pre-determined purpose, but that every individual part of it subserves some special need in the fulfilment of this purpose. Needless to say, the purpose has always been regarded as associated with human welfare.

> The Universe, down to its smallest parts, is regarded by primitive superstition as existing for the special benefit of man. (120)

Elliot goes on to emphasize the differences between classical materialisms and modern scientific materialism along a number of lines. He states that

> They agree in declaring the uniformity of law; they agree in denying the doctrine of teleology; they agree that all existences are of a material character. But they disagree in their treatment of the alleged spiritual and unseen world. The ancient materialists believed to a certain extent in an unseen world; they believed even in the existence of souls. They asserted their materialism only by the theory that these entities were material in character. Democritus conceived the soul as consisting of smooth, round, material particles. The scientific materialist of today does not believe in any separate existence of this kind whatever. (144)

Lucretius characterized the soul as formed from subtler, more elastic atomic materials than the body, and while Lovecraft obviously rejects the Epicurean conception of the soul philosophically, he notably follows Poe in exploring such ideas in his fictions, including "From Beyond" and "The Colour out of Space." Even more importantly for Lovecraft's reception of Lucretius, Elliot argues against the idea, expressed in DRN's analogy between the *clinamen* and volitional activity (DRN 2.216-93), that there is "an indeterminate factor in human behaviour." Elliot claims:

> Such a belief is indeed only consonant with a profound ignorance of humanity. If indetermination was true, we could not reduce human conduct to rules as we do; we could not embody it in formulas or geometrical curves; statistics would afford no basis for arguing from the past to the future. The more we study, the more industriously we collect statistics, the more deeply we analyze motives and factors, the more accurately are we able to forecast the behaviour of men in bulk. Without this laboriously accumulated knowledge, of course men were bound to believe in an indeterminate element; for then nothing was prophesiable, all was as fickle and arbitrary as the winds of heaven. But as the knowledge increases, the fickleness vanishes; human conduct falls, like all other natural events, into a recognized and regular system. In proportion to our knowledge and analysis of the past, we can prophesy the future; and if we can never attain absolute accuracy, the reason is that, as with the winds, we can never co-ordinate the whole of the factors engaged, we can never attain to a perfect knowledge of the past. (120)

In other words, indeterminacy for Elliot (and for Lovecraft and, insofar as he objected to the quantum theory due to its probabilistic dimension, Einstein) exists only as an epistemological, and not an ontological, condition. One might also assume this to be true of the proto-Enlightenment textual universe of *DRN*; after all, the poem's didactic thrust is that, once we fully embrace and explore Epicurean principles, we will be able to move beyond the mythic and teleological conceits we previously clung to as methods of explaining an otherwise recalcitrant and terrifying reality, and discern the laws that actually order the universe.

However, there are some grounds for reading Lucretius' atomistic universe as one that is not only non-teleological, but also fundamentally indeterminate, in the sense of that term rejected by Elliot and Lovecraft. Darryl Lehoux has recently argued for such an interpretation, claiming that Lucretius "uses blindness to describe the motions of atoms. The most common modern reading of this metaphor is to translate *caecus* as something like 'unseen', thus drawing attention to the fact that atomic processes happen below the visual level." Lehoux argues, however, that there is much more to Lucretius' phrasing than meets the eye; "there is another, ethical layer to the blindness" Lucretius ascribes to atoms," one that draws "our attention to the way atoms follow laws of motion unflinchingly"; in other words, deterministically. Lehoux stresses that

> anti-teleology is underscored repeatedly ... by Lucretius' description of atoms as *caecus*. To follow the common English translation in reading this (only) as 'unseen' rather than 'unseeing' would be to miss one of the most important and jarring aspects of atomic physics when pitted against the common Stoicizing physics of Lucretius' day, where divinity plays central and active roles in the cosmos. (147)

Lehoux's reading of *DRN* makes Lucretius' vision seem more akin not to the ultimately predictable mechanistic materialist world of Lovecraft's philosophical perspective, but to the chaotic and unpredictable reality that seethes below the ordered surface of one of his fictions:

> If *caeca* is meant to underscore the invisibleness of the atoms only, it makes little sense insofar as there are no eyes around to see them anymore anyway. Instead, I think it makes more sense to see him as painting a dramatically bleak picture of the intentional and teleological emptiness of the universe: atoms flitting about randomly, moving without purpose, following their own laws of motion, but to no end whatsoever. (148; see *DRN* 1.1109–10)

Glenn Most is another recent interpreter of *DRN* to emphasize the nucleus of indeterminacy in the poem; he goes on to characterize this as a key component that unifies Lucretius' literary aesthetics with his philosophy. Most describes *DRN*'s vivid poetic language, its description of vast scalar shifts, and its relentless rhetorical disruptions of its own mythical loci as aspects of "the Lucretian sublime," a sublimity that "posits the irrelevance of the gods and the fundamental randomness and meaninglessness of the universe" (249-50).

While it could be argued that recent readings of the poem including Most's and Lehoux's are colored by a postmodern appropriation of quantum indeterminacy as much as earlier interpretations were by Christian theology or mechanistic materialism, it nonetheless allows us to see that there may be, whether consciously or otherwise, something more fundamental than the concept of free will at stake in Lovecraft's partial rejection of Lucretius. While Lovecraft claimed to be untroubled by the "meaninglessness" of the universe, its prospective *randomness* is another story. Consider Lovecraft's reaction upon being introduced to Einstein's theory of relativity:

> My cynicism and scepticism are increasing, and from an entirely new cause—the Einstein theory. The latest eclipse observations seem to place this system among the facts which cannot be dismissed, and assumedly it removes the last hold which reality or the universe can have on the independent mind. All is chance, accident, and ephemeral illusion—a fly may be greater than Arcturus, and Durfee Hill may surpass Mount Everest—assuming them to be removed from the present planet and differently environed in the continuum of space-time. There are no values in all infinity—the least idea that there are is the supreme mockery of all. (SL 1.231)

The letter's combined sense of giddy liberation and disturbed dread is echoed by a number of Lovecraft's fictional protagonists as they come face to face with weird phenomena. For example, Wilmarth in "The Whisperer in Darkness" describes his mingled fear and desire when faced with the possibility of shaking

> off the maddening and wearying limitations of time and space and natural law—to be linked with the vast *outside*—to come close to the nighted and abysmal secrets of the infinite and the ultimate—surely such a thing was worth the risk of one's life, soul, and sanity! (CF 2.505-06)

As Joshi points out regarding "Notes on Writing Weird Fiction":

> Such a thing sounds rather appealing; and the interesting thing is that the utterance exactly parallels Lovecraft's own views as to the function of weird fiction: "I choose weird stories because ... one of my strongest and most

persistent wishes [is] to achieve, momentarily, the illusion of some strange suspension or violation of the galling limitations of time, space, and natural law." (SM 148)

"Strange and Fantastic": *DRN* as Aesthetic Influence

While I don't wish to go so far as to suggest that Lovecraft's conception of cosmic fiction was consciously based on *DRN*, it certainly echoes the poem's focus and highlights the degree to which *DRN* constitutes an *avant-la-lettre* example of what Lovecraft considered to be the weird and the cosmic in literature. At the least, Lovecraft's conception of weird fiction serves as a useful critical lens through which to read Lucretius' poem. Lovecraft's view of rationality's gradual triumph over superstition is often phrased in terms redolent of Lucretius' re-appropriation of the epic poem. For example,

> The crude human animal is ineradicably superstitious, and there is every biological and historical reason why he should be. An irreligious barbarian is a scientific impossibility. Rationalistic conceptions of the universe involve a type of mental victory over hereditary emotion quite impossible to the undeveloped and uneducated intellect. (SL 2.310; see also Joshi, SM 34)

Lovecraft's phrasing aptly echoes Lucretius' characterization of Epicurus as a rational conqueror who has trampled dread *Religio* beneath his feet (*DRN* 1.62-79). Yet Lovecraft also offers another way of viewing the "hero" of Lucretius' epic poem with his conception of weird fiction. In "Some Notes on Interplanetary Fiction," he insisted that "the true hero" of such fiction "is not any human being, but simply a *set of phenomena*" (CE 2.179). This conception can be productively applied to *DRN*, which, aside from the remote and implacable Epicurus and the occasional cameo by mythic and historical figures including Iphigenia and Hercules, features no human characters at all. This deepened its appeal to Lovecraft, and powerfully influenced his literary ideals. As he writes in a late letter,

> Individuals and their fortunes within natural law move me very little. They are all momentary trifles bound from a common nothingness toward another common nothingness. Only the cosmic framework itself—or such individuals as symbolize principles (or defiances of principles) of the cosmic framework—can gain a deep grip on my imagination and set it to work creating. In other words, the only "heroes" I can write about are *phenomena*. (SL 5.19; see Joshi, SM 261)

For despite Lucretius' deliberate adaptation of the heroic epic genre in *DRN* and his valorization of Epicurus as the superhuman conqueror who vanquishes the evils of ignorance, fear, and superstition through philosophy, the responses of several centuries of modern readers emphasize that it is the sublime representations of atoms and void, and of the manifold forms that arise from them, that are the "true hero" of the poem. In Glenn Most's words,

> atomistic void is [...] the protagonist, and [...] is repeatedly presented in larger-than-life settings. But more than anything else, void, put centre-stage, comes to stand for itself and to gesture towards the nature of sheer vacuity and its irresistible compulsions. (248)

It is this compelling *horror vacui*, as much as the marvelous allure of undirected *natura*, that modern readers have tended to respond to in Lucretius' poem. And it is this undercurrent of the poem, arguably more powerful than its liberating message and paean to the virtues of Epicureanism, that infiltrates and shapes Lovecraft's cosmic tales. Consider one of his more famous quasi-mythic creations, Azathoth. Lovecraft first describes this entity (which notably exists, like the Epicurean deities, in an intercosmic space) in his 1926-27 novella, *The Dream-Quest of Unknown Kadath*:

> [O]utside the ordered universe [is] that amorphous blight of nethermost confusion which blasphemes and bubbles at the center of all infinity—the boundless daemon sultan Azathoth, whose name no lips dare speak aloud, and who gnaws hungrily in inconceivable, unlighted chambers beyond time and space amidst the muffled, maddening beating of vile drums and the thin monotonous whine of accursed flutes. (CF 2.100)

That Azathoth is intimately connected with Lovecraft's anxieties about sub-atomic indeterminacy is even more strongly suggested by its later description in "The Whisperer in Darkness" as "the monstrous nuclear chaos beyond angled space" (CF 2.521). Banished by Lovecraft beyond the "ordered universe," amid a cosmic version of the drums and flutes that accompanied the worship of the Magna Mater in *DRN* (2.598-620), Azathoth embodies everything Lovecraft's philosophy rejects. It is uncertainty incorporated (amorphous, confused, boundless) but perversely also purposiveness incarnate (at least so its title and hungry gnawing suggests), precisely that pairing of volition with indeterminacy that Lovecraft abhorred in his otherwise beloved *DRN*. Azathoth is an Epicurean deity without the anthropomorphization that *DRN* so powerfully undercuts; its embodiment is, aptly enough, a macro-atomic complex, the chaos of *caeca primordia* magnified. It is also a stark figuration of what Most calls the Lucretian sublime:

> Lucretius's world is one made up entirely and exclusively of atoms and void which interact with one another according to no principle other than that of sheer chance; the gods exist, to be sure, but they are far too busy enjoying their interplanetary leisure to be bothered with the causal or moral ordering of our world or of any other one. Thus the gods certainly exist, but there is no divine providence and no providential ordering of the world: the world is as it is not because the gods wanted it to be that way, but only because of the random collisions of atoms with one another. (248)

The distorted echo of the Epicurean deities audible in the unspeakable name of Azathoth suggests another vital way that Lovecraft adapted Lucretian poetics. Recognizing an essential aspect of Lovecraft's weird fictions that had been partially obscured by their reception over half a century of critic-fans, including Derleth, who tended to reify and codify Lovecraft's mythos-figures into some kind of hierarchy, David E. Schultz has pointed out that Lovecraft in effect creates an "anti-mythology" (see IAP 1055) with them. This anti-mythologizing tendency has a potent precursor in DRN. Writing of the poem's opening hymn to Venus, Wilson explains that this passage is

> to be sure, paratheology, not theology. Epicurus' own theory of religion was not straightforward, but it was often read as offering a kind of conventionalist account of religious truth. Cicero explained that Epicurus 'alone perceived . . . that the gods exist, because nature herself has imprinted a conception of them on the minds of all mankind . . . [T]heir existence is therefore a necessary inference, since we possess an instinctive or rather an innate conception of them.' The Epicurean gods were, however, remote, corporeal, and unconcerned with human welfare, and in their perfection they were deemed to feel neither anger with men, nor affection for them. Lucretius was more explicit in supposing that the gods are only images, 'visions of divine figures of matchless beauty and stupendous stature,' that appear to men in their dreams and reveries. Perhaps these images correspond to happy material beings existing in the intercosmic spaces, he allowed, but if so they take no account of us and have no power over us. (8)

This paratheological opening presages the argumentative drift of the entire poem. As James I. Porter explains, "The entire thrust of the atomistic critique of nature was in a sense Kantian (proto-Enlightenment) in spirit: its aim was to demythologize nature, to liberate mankind from blinding superstition and to render nature susceptible of dispassionate scientific (rational) analysis" (180). Both Monica Gale and Philip Hardie similarly point out the "predatory" nature of myth in Lucretius; in Gale's words, he "exploits mythological themes and images, while ostentatiously rejecting the myths themselves" (5). The most striking example of this is the shift from the lengthy, sensual incantation to the goddess Venus, identified as a life-giving earth-mother, that opens the first book of the poem (*DRN* 1.1–50) to the explicit attack Lucretius mounts on religious devotion with the second book of the poem. Along with the sacrifice of Iphigenia, Lucretius singles out the cult of the Magna Mater with particular scorn, for those who deify and worship the earth fundamentally misunderstand both nature and divinity (*DRN* 2.646–50).

Lucretius' contrast of deluded *Religio* with both the Epicurean conception of divinity and the brute, material reality of the earth is echoed throughout many of Lovecraft's fictions. In one example, as if in acknowledgment of Lucretius' influence, Lovecraft has the unfortunate narrator of "The Rats in the Walls," de la Poer, retrogress through an ancestral chain that includes at least one ancestor who worshipped Cybele/Athys, the "Magna Mater."

Perhaps most important, though, is the way that *DRN*'s poetics of classical materialist speculation, its fascination with entropy and disintegration, its vivid processions of objects and entities defamiliarized from their typical human sensory apprehension, and its relentless portrayal of human life as merely a transient concatenation of atomic particles shaped Lovecraft's fictional worlds, and the alien objects and beings that inhabit them. According to Jeffrey Andrew Weinstock, Lovecraft's things

> exhibit agency, they intermesh with the human, they prompt reconsiderations of where the line between human and nonhuman actually falls, and compel a reconsideration of the place of human beings in the universe. But in Gothic narrative such as Lovecraft's, the awesome plenitude of the alien everyday becomes a source of horror as, rather than elevating objects, human beings are reduced to things, demoted to matter that doesn't really matter in the larger scheme of things. (76)

Philosopher Graham Harman has influentially turned Lovecraft into a kind of latter-day Epicurus, declaring Lovecraft "an intellectual hero" for the way his writings exemplify "the rejection of everyday common-sense to which speculative realism aspires." Harman's "new" version of materialist speculation mines Lovecraft's writings much the way Lovecraft mined Lucretius' (171). In Fred Botting's words,

> As Harman develops his philosophy of objects, things become increasingly weird, multifaceted and unclassifiable, neither solid nor strictly bound to notions of matter. Like Lovecraft, it evinces a materiality beyond phenomenally registered terrestrial forms, whether in the architecture of hidden cities or in the mineralogical form of artefacts left on the globe as signs of prehistorical habitation. Matter is understood in broader terms, with alien creatures in "The Shadow Out of Time" (1936), for instance, being identifiable only as living things shaped as 'semi-elastic' matter or of a materiality that refuses to be defined. (295)

Surely a large, and so far insufficiently considered, part of Lovecraft's appeal for contemporary speculative realist and speculative materialist philosophers is due to his own lifelong immersion in Lucretian poetics. Lovecraft's writings, rather than inventing the language of speculative materialism, effectively translated it from the Latin of one of his greatest influences.

That this has so far gone unremarked by scholars is a striking irony. Even more striking is that Lovecraft himself seems to have been unaware of the degree to which the classical text that was a vital early source of his rationalist, cosmic philosophy also flowed into the irrational aesthetics of the weird fiction that he is more widely remembered for. In doing so, DRN offered Lovecraft exactly what he sought from weird fiction; a "momentary suspension" of the "galling limitations of space and time." Given this, it is poetic indeed that Lucretius' text would serve, in Lovecraft's often-recounted dream of 1927, as a vehicle to transport him back through time. It is even more poetic that, when he arrived there, Lovecraft would find, swarming like *primordia caeca* below the surface of his nostalgia-gilded ancient Rome, an unpredictable force that seemed to obey no known natural laws.

Works Cited

Botting, Fred. "More Things: Horror, Materialism and Speculative Weirdism." *Horror Studies* 3, No. 2 (2012): 281-303.

Einstein, Albert. "Introduction to Diels' Translation of Lucretius." Trans. Amy Vail. *Classical World* 82, No. 6 (1989): 33-34.

Elliot, Hugh. *Modern Science and Materialism*. London: Longmans, Green & Co., 1919.

Gale, Monica. *Myth and Poetry in Lucretius*. Cambridge: Cambridge University Press, 1994.

Harman, Graham. "The Road to Objects." *Continent* 3 No. 1 (2011): 171–79.

Joshi, S. T. *A Subtler Magick: The Writings and Philosophy of H. P. Lovecraft*. Gillette, NJ: Wildside, 1996. [SM]

Lehoux, Daryn. "Seeing and Unseeing, Seen and Unseen." In *Lucretius: Poetry, Philosophy, Science*, ed. A. D. Morrison and Alison Sharrock. Oxford: Oxford University Press, 2013.

Lovecraft, H. P. *Letters to Alfred Galpin*. Ed. S. T. Joshi and David E. Schultz. New York: Hippocampus Press, 2003.

———. *Letters to C. L. Moore and Others*. Ed. David E. Schultz and S. T. Joshi. New York: Hippocampus Press, 2017.

———. *Letters to Robert Bloch and Others*. Ed. David E. Schultz and S. T. Joshi. New York: Hippocampus Press, 2015.

Lucretius. *On The Nature of Things*. Trans. W. H. D. Rouse and Martin F. Smith. Cambridge, MA: Harvard University Press, 1992.

———. *Titus Lucretius Carus: Of the Nature of Things*. Trans. William Ellery Leonard. London: J. M. Dent; New York: E. P. Dutton, 1916.

Most, Glenn W. "The Sublime, Today?" In *Dynamic Reading: Studies in the Reception of Epicureanism*. Oxford: Oxford University Press, 2012.

Porter, James I. "Lucretius and the Sublime." In *The Cambridge Companion to Lucretius*, ed., Stuart Gillespie and Philip Hardie. Cambridge: Cambridge University Press, 2007.

Sharrock, Alison. "Introduction." In *Lucretius: Poetry, Philosophy, Science*, ed., Daryn Lehoux, A. D. Morrison, and Alison Sharrock. Oxford: Oxford University Press, 2013.

Weinstock, Jeffrey Andrew. "Lovecraft's Things: Sinister Souvenirs from Other Worlds." In *The Age of Lovecraft*, ed., Carl Sederholm and Jeffrey Andrew Weinstock. Minneapolis: University of Minnesota Press, 2016.

Wilson, Catherine. *Epicureanism at the Origins of Modernity*. Oxford: Oxford University Press, 2008.

Reordering the Universe: H. P. Lovecraft's Subversion of the Biblical Divine

René J. Weise
Independent Scholar

Widely known for writing pulp fiction tales of ritualistic necromancy, nightmarish dream-visions, and tentacled extraterrestrials too terrifying to cast one's eye upon, American author Howard Phillips Lovecraft amassed knowledge from countless sources and regularly relied on them as founts of inspiration to bolster and expand his own work. However, though a committed and vociferous atheist, he was not immune to the pervasive influence of the Bible. Indeed, much of his particular brand of horror known as "weird fiction" is rife with scriptural allusions. Cognizant of the Bible's inevitable impact on his work, he seems to have employed an ingenious literary tactic, ostensibly warping the theological influence to meet his own ends. Through calculated parodic subversion and atheistic negation, Lovecraft conceives a paradigm shift of the Biblical Divine and deliberately manipulates religious tropes to expose the flaws and weaknesses of an inconsistent dogma and its deity. Through a narrowly focused lens of comparative theological analysis, two key biblical influences Lovecraft thus manipulated can be correlated to his pantheon of Great Old Ones and Other Gods. First, the Old Testament as a monstrous text introduces both Leviathan and the Lord God as its predominant chaos monsters in parallel with Lovecraft's subversive entity Cthulhu. Second, Lovecraft's treatment of the New Testament's Holy Trinity displays his parodic intentions with his interstitial Other Gods Azathoth, Nyarlathotep, and Yog-Sothoth representative of the Lord God, Jesus Christ, and the Holy Spirit.

    In his critical essay "Supernatural Horror in Literature," first published in 1927, Lovecraft acknowledges a great many authors and texts that influenced the horror genre and his own writing and strikingly notes that "the horror-tale is as old as human thought and speech themselves," recognizing the elements of his own weird fiction as "an ingredient of the earliest folklore of all races . . . in the most archaic ballads, chronicles, and *sacred writings*" (CE 2.85; emphasis added). Though Lovecraft admits that he is heavily influenced by "Celtic and Teutonic . . . mystical inclinations," he additionally mentions the similarly stimulating and "very flourishing . . . branch of weird literature . . . of the Jews" (CE 2.99–100). As a devotee of Lord Dunsany, on multiple occasions Lovecraft calls attention to the King James Bible and emphasizes its rhetorical and lyrical influence on Dunsanian prose poetry (CE 2.121). In his 1920 essay "Literary Composition," Lovecraft's advice to young writers is point-blank: "An excellent habit to cultivate is the analytical study of the King James Bible. For simple yet rich and forceful English, this masterly production is hard to equal . . . [I]t is an invaluable model for writers on quaint or imaginative themes" (CE 2.41). For its literary influence, the Bible was certainly instrumental to the creation of Lovecraft's fictional universe. However, he did not inadvertently allow biblical allusion to seep into his work. As a man who bluntly denounced religion and its effects on humanity, Lovecraft thought it "*damned unlikely* that anything like a central cosmic will, a spirit world, or an eternal survival of personality exist" (SL 4.57).

Lovecraft's stark atheism should not be repudiated or ignored when analyzing his fiction. Instead, one should come to realize that he possessed a deeply rooted reason for manipulating biblical tropes. As author Jason Colavito notes, Lovecraft set out to "relocate the transcendent not in the spirit realm but in the material cosmos" ("Primitivism"). However, he does not seem to be mirroring or inverting these religious tropes; rather, he seems to be *subverting* them to encourage their stylistic effects upon the reader and then to artfully challenge the underlying thematic principles they propose.

Outlining his thoughts on the emergent genre of weird fiction, Lovecraft identifies it as having a "certain atmosphere of breathless and unexplainable dread of outer, unknown forces" and states that "the one test of the really weird is this—whether or not there be excited in the reader a profound sense of dread, and of contact with unknown spheres and powers" ("Supernatural Horror in Literature" 28). Just as the price of knowledge is the birth of human suffering in the Judeo-Christian tale of Adam and Eve, the weird tale's thematic utilization of uncovered truths enforces this mythological tradition as its "protagonist[s] discove[r] a great secret about the cosmos and . . . [are] forced to come to terms with an intrusion of vast, cosmic forces into [their] everyday reality, often with mind- and soul-shaking results" (Colavito, *Fear* 175-76). However, the torment of cosmic discovery is only the beginning. For Lovecraft, true weird fiction exemplifies the spectacle of cosmic *fear*, and his work not only emulates this concept but also proposes the concept of cosmic *indifference*, a cynical negation of dogmatic religious assumptions.

Where Chaos Monsters Reside: The Old Testament as a Monstrous Text

Though its monotheistic objective demanded the editing and even removal of its mythological inheritance of cosmic conflict, the Old Testament failed to eradicate all references to a battle between divine forces, particularly between the Lord God of Israel and the chaos monster of pre-creation known as Tiamat the dragon—more widely identified as Rahab or Leviathan. The echoes of this creature and its conflict with the Lord God can still be traced, particularly in the canonical books of Job, Isaiah, and Psalms, in the apocryphal book of 4 Ezra (also known as 2 Esdras), and in the pseudepigraphical books of 2 Apocalypse of Baruch and 1 Enoch. Revelations from these texts as to the origin, purpose, and nature of Leviathan seem to mirror those proposed by Lovecraft with his infamous monstrosity, the alien deity Cthulhu, first introduced in his short story "The Call of Cthulhu" (1926) and considered one of the Great Old Ones—a part of Lovecraft's pantheon of cosmic gods. This unmistakable link between Leviathan and Cthulhu has been keenly noted by Timothy K. Beal (179-91). However, the extent to which Lovecraft subversively appropriates Leviathan is perhaps more comprehensive than previously imagined. With Cthulhu, Lovecraft appears to be positing a world where the corporeal chaos monsters reign free, unchecked by higher deities of any divine order or form.

Leviathan versus Cthulhu

In the Old Testament, Leviathan is described as a terrifying sea monster, a "crooked serpent ... that [is] in the sea" and an improbable mixture of mythological proportions, unlike any known species, an animal able to spout smoke from its nostrils and fire from its mouth that possesses vicious teeth, armored scales, and cannot be caught, slain, or bargained with except by the Lord (*KJV* Isaiah 27:1; Psalms 18:8; Job 41:1-4, 14-17).

Weapons and armor are useless against Leviathan: "That sword . . . cannot hold: the spear, the dart, nor the habergeon. He esteemeth iron as straw, [and] brass as rotten wood. The arrow cannot make him flee: slingstones are turned with him into stubble. Darts are counted as stubble: he laugheth at the shaking of a spear" (Job 41:26–29). Cthulhu's aquatic attributes bear an uncanny resemblance to those of the biblical chaos monster and, just as strikingly, Lovecraft's Old One physically emerges as an inexplicable mixture of biological and mythological features, as seen in the description of its detailed effigy: "The figure . . . represented a monster of vaguely anthropoid outline, but with an octopus-like head whose face was a mass of feelers, a scaly, rubbery-looking body, prodigious claws on hind and fore feet, and long, narrow wings behind" (CF 2.31). It is significant that both of these sea monsters are definitively corporeal beings of flesh and blood and bone or, in the case of Cthulhu, the equivalent thereof—the Old One having a shape though not of matter as humans understand it but rather of an unidentified plasticity that can re-form itself. Furthermore, there are a multitude of these monstrosities. Cthulhu is just one of many similar species (with its "hordes," the Cthulhu spawn) and just one of many Old Ones. Likewise, in the pseudepigraphical Apocalypse of Abraham, Leviathan is referred to "in the plural" as the parent of "a single monstrous species" (Whitney 67).

Whence do these monstrosities originate? Though Cthulhu's origins are clearly extraterrestrial, having "seeped down from the stars while the young earth was still half-formed" ("The Mound" [CF 4.182]), Leviathan should not be dismissed as merely one of the Lord's oceanic creatures. In fact, its roots are more similar to Cthulhu's than would be easily identifiable from surface analysis of its biblical appearances. Leviathan resides in the "great and wide sea," but its mythological origin—its *original* location—is profound in nature and implication (Psalms 104:26). Though the canonical Bible de-emphasizes this great sea dragon's significance, apocryphal and pseudepigraphical texts allow the story a full telling. Leviathan was not always a creature of the earth's oceans; instead, after defeating the monster, the Lord "gavest [Leviathan] the seventh part, namely, the moist" or "where the waters were gathered" (4 Ezra 6:52, 47). In fact, this divine allocation of the oceans for Leviathan "appear[s] . . . [in] three texts of the Second Temple Period": 4 Ezra, 2 Apocalypse of Baruch, and 1 Enoch (Whitney 31). However, before the Lord engaged Leviathan in pre-creation warfare, its whereabouts were far more cosmic. According to 1 Enoch, "the dwelling-place of Leviathan ... is 'the depths of the sea above the springs of the waters' ... allud[ing] to the 'fountains of the deep' mentioned in Genesis 7:11.... Hence, the abode of Leviathan lies at the very source of the sea ... upon or over the abyss" (52-53). This abyss refers to the waters of pre-creation that were already present before the Lord began forming the earth and all within it: "And the earth was without form, and void; and darkness [was] upon the face of the deep. And the Spirit of God moved upon the face of the waters" (Genesis 1:2). It is only when "*ruah elohim*, 'the breath of God,' moves over 'the abyss,' *tehom*" that the onset of creation truly begins (Mobley 20). What *exactly* were these pre-existing waters, this abyss? They can be traced back to the biblical near-exclusion of Tiamat the chaos dragon, having been rendered toothless in the monotheistic adaptation of the ancient Babylonian conflict-myth that the Hebrews adopted. Tiamat "appears in Genesis, not as a personified serpent, but as instead *tehom*, its Hebrew cognate that means 'the abyss,'" and three Old Testament passages (Job 26:7-14; Psalms 74:12-17, 89:5-14) contain analogous elements of this buried chaos battle mythology (Mobley 20; Creach 19). However, this primordial abyss was not of earth, for the Lord "divide[d] the waters from the waters" (the earth's waters from the cosmic waters) with a firmament or barrier against "the amorphous chaos [of pre-creation], the *tohu wabohu*, the 'wild and waste'" (Genesis 1:6; Mobley 20). Therefore, both Cthulhu's *and* Leviathan's origins are in the cosmos outside our ordered universe and, just as Leviathan was defeated by the Lord and cast to the earth's waters, Cthulhu was defeated and ultimately trapped "in his dark house in the mighty city of R'lyeh under the waters" (*CF* 2.38) as it sank in the southern Pacific Ocean due to prehistoric geological upheaval.

Regarding their power and strength, Leviathan and Cthulhu are approximately matched, though the thematic function of their monstrous dominance differs. Leviathan appears to have a divine purpose, since the Lord allows it to remain in His creation despite having defeated it, and part of this purpose may simply be as a testimonial—evidence of the Lord's cosmic superiority, "a sublime force that reflects God's overwhelming aspect" (Asma 65-66). Certainly, the canonical Old Testament utilizes the mythology of Leviathan in this fashion, highlighting how the Lord has already humbled the monster through defeat in battle and can easily restrain its massive force again (Job 41:1-34; Isaiah 27:1, 51:19; Psalms 74:13-14). On the other hand, Cthulhu represents no god's ultimate supremacy; it is its own deity. Lovecraft purposefully instituted this subversive deviation from the theological norm, crafting Cthulhu as a god but insisting upon its material and not spiritual actuality. The disordered universe from which Cthulhu originates is potentially quantifiable, if humans had such intellectual ability, and its sunken city of R'lyeh is a tangible reality, though "the *geometry* of the . . . [city] [i]s abnormal, non-Euclidean, and loathsomely redolent of spheres and dimensions apart from ours" (CF 2.51). Cthulhu is an abomination that humans are not meant to understand, as the harrowing reaction to its physical appearance attests: "The Thing cannot be described—there is no language for such abysms of shrieking and immemorial lunacy, such eldritch contradictions of all matter, force, and cosmic order. A mountain walked or stumbled. God!" (CF 2.53). Crucially, though, Cthulhu is merely one of many such formidable beings in the physical, *not heavenly* Lovecraftian cosmos.

The Lord as a Worldly Chaos Monster

When Leviathan lost its divine status due to the monotheistic adaptation of its origins and position, it attained physical incorporation in the strictly worldly creation and, in doing so, retained its cosmic status only through amalgamation with the Lord. Leviathan is not simply "God's monster accomplic[e] . . . but represent[s] the more chaotic and frightening visage of God" (Asma 64). When dualistic thinking was expurgated from the Bible, the Lord was in many ways forced to adopt the attributes of the defeated chaos monster. As a combination of diverse personalities (the Lord *yahweh*, God *'elohim*, and the chaos dragon Tiamat), by necessity, the Lord wholly holds Himself accountable for the presence of evil in the world: "*There is* none beside me. I *am* the LORD, and *there is* none else. I form the light, and create darkness: I make peace, and create evil: I the LORD do all these *things*" (Isaiah 45:6-7; Miles 29-30, 89; Frost 19). By adopting the dragon into His own persona, an aspect of the Lord consequently *becomes* a chaos monster. Like Leviathan, the Lord is capable of great worldly destruction and is physically undefeatable by humankind.

As both a deity and a worldly presence, Cthulhu shares some of the Lord's qualities and characteristics. The Old One has devout followers, a cult consisting of both humans and other extraterrestrial beings that "had always existed and always would exist, hidden in distant wastes and dark places all over the world" (CF 2.38). Maintaining devotion to Cthulhu often requires appeasement through blood sacrifice, as does devotion to the Lord in countless Old Testament passages such as Exodus 20:24, 29:10-31, and Leviticus 1:2-17 ("The Mound" [CF 4.187]). Additionally, as with the Lord (for example, in Genesis 15:1, 28:10-17, 37; 1 Kings 3:5), Cthulhu communicates to its disciples through dream-visions. As posed by Robert M. Price, Lovecraft's envisioning of the Old One's rising may indeed represent "a satire on real apocalyptic faith" (*H. P. Lovecraft* 49). However, while Cthulhu may evoke qualities of the Lord as a *worldly* chaos monster capable of great earthly destruction, it is Lovecraft's truly extra-dimensional Other Gods who represent Him as both an *otherworldly* chaos monster and a divine triumvirate beyond all human knowledge and understanding.

The Lord as an Otherworldly Chaos Monster

As a chaos monster, the Lord represents what German theologian Rudolf Otto would term a *monstrum tremendum*—meaning a material message from the divine, "related to the verbs *monstrare* ('show' or 'reveal') and *monere* ('warn' or 'portend')"—the corporeal incarnation of his spiritual concept of *mysterium tremendum*, a religious presence "that brings on a stupefying combination of fascination and terror, wonder and dread . . . 'something . . . whose kind and character are incommensurable with our own, and before which we therefore recoil in a wonder that strikes us chill and numb'" (Beal 6-7). This numinous experience is where religion and horror meet face-to-face in an aweful and paralyzing display of incomprehensible otherness that, for Lovecraft, *is* the experience of cosmic fear under the strain of cosmic indifference, an experience that inevitably results in either madness or death—though, in Lovecraft's universe, "Death brings no appeasement. . . [as] [i]t in no way allows the story to conclude . . . [because] cosmic fear continues to expand" (Houellebecq 32). The Lord as representative of otherness transcends morality, and Otto recognizes that "'the *'ēmāh* of Yahweh ("fear of God") . . . [is] a terror fraught with an inward shuddering such as not even the most menacing and overpowering created thing can instill'" (Sax 95-96; Cardin 299). The "fear of God" has very little to do with righteousness; instead, the holiness of the Lord "'implies power even more than it implies moral goodness'" (Cardin 300).

When considering the Lord, specifically as personified in the Old Testament books of Job and Isaiah, scholars have argued that He does seem to operate at times through a form of cosmic indifference—not unlike that depicted by Lovecraft's interstitial monstrosities. Roger Schlobin convincingly makes the case that the Book of Job functions as "a prototype of horror" in which "there is no moral order" (24, 28). Job is tormented by an unapproachable and unfathomable deity who, aside from a threatening display of absolute power that ostensibly works in effect as a divine ruse, offers no explanation for His sadistic actions and is ultimately indifferent to any human requests for moral justification. The Lord of Job irrefutably qualifies as not only a mythological chaos monster but also as an archetypal *horror* monster; indeed, He is "so evil that good is either unknown or has no impact on [Him] . . . [and His] natur[e] [is] incomprehensible to the epistemolog[y] of [His] victi[m]" (Schlobin 30). Significantly, while enduring the anguish cast upon him from the Lord, Job laments his own birth, entreating Leviathan be summoned to consume the day he was born and end the Lord's torture before it even begins (*KJ2000* Job 3:8). At this point, Leviathan appears more endurable than the Lord, and the notion of Leviathan as the *lesser evil* when compared with the Lord isn't confined to the Book of Job alone.

Though the Book of Job is undeniably the most intense depiction of the Lord as operating outside any standard of ethics, the Book of Isaiah similarly fails to uphold His moral goodness. The prophetic nature of Isaiah, specifically chapters 24 and 34, depicts an utter destruction of earth wrought by the Lord and a violent return to a state of primordial chaos—these events taking place *after* He has defeated Leviathan as if to "sav[e] the world from the archetypal chaos monste[r] only to *become* a chaos monster who, in his unopposed power, outdoes the othe[r] at [its] own horrific game" (Cardin 297-98). The Book of Isaiah is violently bursting at the binding with the Lord's apocalyptic threats to obliterate the known creation and, in a wrathful frenzy of bloody carnage in chapter 24, states:

> Behold, the LORD maketh the earth empty, and maketh it waste, and turneth it upside down, and scattereth abroad the inhabitants thereof. The land shall be utterly emptied, and utterly spoiled: for the LORD hath spoken this word. . . . Therefore hath the curse devoured the earth, and they that dwell therein are desolate: therefore the inhabitants of the earth are burned, and few men left. . . . Fear, and the pit, and the snare, *are* upon thee, O inhabitant of the earth. . . . The earth is utterly broken down, the earth is clean dissolved, the earth is moved exceedingly. (Isaiah 24:1, 3, 6, 17, 19)

Isaiah 24 does not stand as the only such threat. Chapter 34 depicts a similar scenario:

> For the indignation of the LORD is upon all nations, and his fury upon all their armies: he hath utterly destroyed them, he hath delivered them to the slaughter. Their slain also shall be cast out, and their stink shall come up out of their carcases [sic], and the mountains shall be melted with their blood. And all the host of heaven shall be dissolved, and the heavens shall be rolled together as a scroll: and all their host shall fall down. . . . The sword of the LORD is filled with blood. . . . For *it is* the day of the LORD'S vengeance. . . . The streams thereof shall be turned into pitch, and the dust thereof into brimstone, and the land thereof shall become burning pitch. It shall not be quenched night nor day; the smoke thereof shall go up for ever [sic]: from generation to generation it shall lie waste; none shall pass through it for ever and ever. (Isaiah 34:2-4, 6, 8-10)

The horror inherent in Isaiah is that of cosmic fear. It is the knowledge that at any time for any reason—or for no reason at all—there are monsters that can completely eradicate any or all established laws of the ostensibly ordered cosmos. It is the realization that humans are pathetically vulnerable to these forces and are, in fact, perpetually kept in the dark as to the nature and timing of their intentions (Cardin 295-96). In "The Dunwich Horror" (1928), Lovecraft reveals the forthcoming earthly apocalypse to be instigated by the Old Ones' re-establishment in similar biblical prose:

> "The Old Ones were, the Old Ones are, and the Old Ones shall be. Not in the spaces we know, but *between* them, They walk serene and primal, undimensioned and to us unseen. [. . .] They shall break through again. [. . .] They walk unseen and foul in lonely places where the Words have been spoken and the Rites howled through at their Seasons. The wind gibbers with Their voices, and the earth mutters with Their consciousness. They bend the forest and crush the city, yet may not forest or city behold the hand that smites. [. . .] Their hand is at your throats, yet ye see Them not. [. . .] Man rules now where They ruled once; They shall soon rule where man rules now. [. . .] They wait patient and potent, for here shall They reign again." (CF 2.434)

Interstitial Entities and the Psychology of Horror

Noël Carroll formed a theory of horror from a perspective in accordance with developmental psychology, and it can readily be applied to both the Lord of Job and Isaiah and Lovecraft's extraterrestrial deities. Carroll's "category jamming" posits that, after animals' (including humans') cognitive classification system is established in order to make sense of real-life experiences with various objects and entities, "any subsequently strange unclassifiable encounter produces fear in the knower ... [and this] [c]ategorical mismatch [or category jamming] makes the knower very uncomfortable" (Asma 184). Carroll identifies monsters as belonging to this interstitial space, thus prompting our fear of them due to our inability to accurately cognitively classify them. The Lord is one such interstitial entity. He is dangerously enigmatic, repeatedly contradictory, and beyond our ability to comprehend, at once being both a source of blessing and comfort *and* a source of terror and devastation. The Bible often refers to the inscrutability of the Lord, that "*there is* no searching of his understanding" and that "his greatness *is* unsearchable," but this explanation for His incongruity doesn't genuinely offer any sense of *relief* from His potential as a source of cosmic fear (Isaiah 40:28; Psalms 145:3). The Lord, especially as a chaos monster, remains unclassifiable and an archetype for Lovecraft's most terror-provoking otherworldly monstrosities: the Other Gods.

A Parody of the Trinity Doctrine: Azathoth, Nyarlathotep, and Yog-Sothoth

The Book of Job signifies the definitive breakdown of moral order—according to André Lacocque, "'the total collapse of meaning'" (Schlobin 30). It is from this type of religious and philosophical collapse that Lovecraft, scientific materialist and atheist that he was, likely found the most significance. Subversion of the Bible came easily to him, especially since books like Job explicitly present an inconsistency of religious dogma. Lovecraft had merely to apply a subverted lens, and religion could shift to a much more consistently rational philosophy such as existentialism or even nihilism.

As with Cthulhu, Lovecraft was first and foremost interested in establishing his monstrous deities as *physical*, albeit incomprehensible entities. The same remains true for his creation of the Other (outer) Gods, a race of extraterrestrial deities distinct from and arguably more powerful than the Great Old Ones who reside past "the gates of a monstrous cataract wherein the oceans of earth's dreamland drop wholly to abysmal nothingness ... through the empty spaces toward other worlds and other stars and the awful voids outside the ordered universe" (CF 2.112). The Other Gods can be associated as residing *deep within* the Old Testament's abyss, the *tehom* or primordial waters. Their abode is "in the spiral black vortices of that ultimate void of Chaos" (CF 3.269), "the Last Void which is outside all earths, all universes, and all matter" (CF 3.288). It is within this "formless central void" (CF 2.113) that one finds Lovecraft's nightmarish parody of the New Testament's Holy Trinity, the prevalent Christian concept established in 381 with the Nicene-Constantinopolitan Creed that identifies the Father Almighty (the Lord God), the Son of God (Jesus Christ), and the Holy Ghost (Holy Spirit) as a Trinity of three entities co-existing eternally and from the same substance (Wilhelm, "Nicene Creed"). In Lovecraft's universe, "the monstrous nuclear chaos" (CF 2.521) Azathoth can be identified with the Lord God while its "soul and messenger" Nyarlathotep (CF 2.101) resembles Jesus Christ and Yog-Sothoth, the "All-in-One and One-in-All of limitless being and self," (CF 3.300) can stand for the Holy Ghost. Again, Lovecraft seems to desire not merely an *inversion* of the Trinity's attributes (for example, a "satanic" reversal) but rather a *subversion* of the Trinity's being, calling into question the very notion of divinity in an inscrutable universe.

In the Name of the Father . . .

Known as the "blind idiot god," Azathoth is established within Lovecraft's universe as "Lord of All Things" (CF 3.471). Unlike the Lord God, he does not seem cognizant of his surroundings or of his sovereignties, being identified as a "mindless entity . . . which rules all time and space from a curiously environed black throne at the centre of Chaos" (CF 3.255). Lovecraft's narrative poem *Fungi from Yuggoth* (1929-30) identifies Azathoth as "muttering" in the darkness "things he had dreamed but could not understand" that therewith would be brought into being, these "aimless waves whose chance combining / Gives each frail cosmos its eternal law" (AT 89). Azathoth is a creator deity but is utterly unconscious of and indifferent to what he creates. He "gnaws hungrily in chaos," (CF 2.112) though is kept placated by "the muffled, maddening beat of vile drums and the thin, monotonous whine of accursed flutes" (CF 2.111) as played by his minions, a "flopping horde of mindless and amorphous dancers" (CF 3.471). This imagery conspicuously calls to mind the Lord's own "multitude" of angels worshipping him in heavenly song and twists it into something vaguely unsettling (Isaiah 6:3; Luke 2:13-14). With an

Almighty Father like Azathoth, there seems very little hope for redemption or even *purpose* in an otherwise meaningless life.

. . . and of the Son . . .

Referred to as "the crawling chaos," (CF 2.101) Nyarlathotep is identified as the traveling "avatar" of Azathoth—a sort of mobile element of chaos 3.476). He is able to "put on the semblance of men, the waxen mask and the robe that hides" (CF 3.487) in order to walk amongst humanity without his true horrific visage being discernible. His oft-repeated human appearance is that of "a tall, slim figure with the young face of an antique Pharaoh . . . [dressed in] prismatic robes and crowned with a golden pshent that glowed with inherent light" (CF 2.204). Lovecraft's writings about this entity often read like prophecies or visions of his past or future arrivals to earth. Nyarlathotep is extraordinarily charismatic, the "mellow tones" of his voice "rippl[ing] [with] mild music" and his eyes "sparkl[ing] [with] capricious humour" (CF 2.204).

Though some scholars have argued that Nyarlathotep represents an Antichrist figure as opposed to a Christ figure, his characterization within Lovecraft's subverted Divine allows for no such dualistic interpretation (Price, "Higher Criticism" 60). Biblically, the Antichrist is described as a "man of sin" and a "false prophet" whose sole purpose is to deceptively sway the masses and "exalteth himself above all that is called God, or that is worshipped; so that he as God sitteth in the temple of God, shewing himself that he is God" (2 Thessalonians 2:3-4; Matthew 24:24). The Antichrist "is a liar . . . that denieth that Jesus is the Christ . . . [and] denieth the Father and the Son" (1 John 2:22). Simply put, for there to be an Antichrist there must first be a Christ; his very role demands this theological binary. Within Lovecraft's artificial cosmic (dis)order, no such binary exists.

As a Christ figure, Nyarlathotep first arrives during "a season of political and social upheaval . . . out of Egypt" (CF 1.202) in mimicry of Joseph and Mary's flight into Egypt in the Gospel of Matthew which states: "[Joseph] took the young child [Jesus] and his mother [Mary] by night, and departed into Egypt: [a]nd was there until the death of Herod: that it might be fulfilled which was spoken of the Lord by the prophet, saying, Out of Egypt have I called my son" (Matthew 2:14-15). Upon his arrival "into the lands of civilisation," Nyarlathotep "g[ives] exhibitions of power which sen[d] his spectators away speechless . . . [and] swel[l] his fame to exceeding magnitude" (CF 1.203). Unlike Jesus, however, the crawling chaos' "exhibitions of power" are not medical miracles, exorcisms, or resurrections; instead, they are scientific demonstrations of "electricity and psychology" that cause "throngs [to] pres[s] around, frantic for his commands, / [b]ut leaving, could not tell what they had heard" (CF 1.203; AT 88). Lovecraft's keen acknowledgment of scientific discoveries as the modern "miracles" is evident in Nyarlathotep's mythology, as well as a pointed commentary on Jesus' own linguistic ambiguity often found in the gospels that causes his disciples to either question whom he is addressing or what his message is even about (Luke 12:41, 9:45, 18:34).

Furthermore, Jesus and Nyarlathotep share the same apocalyptic future upon their re-arrival to earth: Jesus' world-shattering second coming as revealed in the Gospels of Mark (13:8-37), Matthew (24:4-51), and Luke (17:22-37) and Nyarlathotep's own return when "from the sea a noxious birth beg[ins] . . . [t]he ground [is] cleft, and mad auroras rol[l] [d]own on the quaking citadels of man," leading the way for "[t]he idiot Chaos [Azathoth] [to] bl[o]w Earth's dust away" (AT 89). Nyarlathotep is not a sacrificial savior of humanity; he is its doom. In Lovecraft's universe, there is no room for deliverance from sin or, more accurately, from the cosmic indifference his subversive trinity represents.

. . . and of the Holy Ghost

Recognized as "the gate . . . the key and guardian of the gate" (CF 2.434), Yog-Sothoth, "the ultimate animating essence of existence's whole unbounded sweep" (CF 3.300), can be equated with the Holy Ghost. This being is the portal through which one might enter the central void (or *tehom*), but it is also the personification of a "limitless MIND" (CF 3.302) that knows no bounds and communicates "in prodigious waves that sm[i]te and bur[n] and thunde[r]" (CF 3.300), calling the Pentecost to mind: "And suddenly there came a sound from heaven as of a rushing mighty wind . . . [a]nd there appeared unto them cloven tongues like as of fire, and it sat upon each of [the disciples] . . . [a]nd they were all filled with the Holy Ghost" (Acts 2:2-4).

The omniscience of Yog-Sothoth is fully encompassed in "Through the Gates of the Silver Key" (1932-33), in which the protagonist (and, arguably, alter ego of Lovecraft himself), Randolph Carter, gains access to this being and experiences "a flood of knowledge and explanation which open[s] new vistas ... and prepare[s] him for such a grasp of the cosmos as he had never hoped to possess" (CF 3.302). Similarly, in the Gospel of John, the Holy Ghost is summoned as "the Comforter ... whom the Father will send in [Jesus'] name ... [who] shall teach you all things, and bring all things to your remembrance" (John 14:26).

Various stylistic and thematic attributes of Yog-Sothoth are likewise shared with the Holy Ghost. The invisibility of Yog-Sothoth is repeatedly mentioned, as is the invisibility of the Holy Ghost also identified "because [the world] seeth him not, neither knoweth him" (John 14:17). Moreover, Yog-Sothoth acts as a conduit of cosmic procreation, impregnating a mortal woman who then births a gruesome abomination that is analogous to Jesus, a crucial biblical correlation made by James Egan, who "pointed out that the birth of Wilbur and his brother 'satirically parallels the Immaculate Conception of Christ'" and therefore allowed further identification of Yog-Sothoth with the Holy Ghost: "And the angel answered and said unto [Mary], the Holy Ghost shall come unto thee, and the power of the Highest shall overshadow thee: therefore also that holy thing which shall be born of thee shall be called the Son of God" (Cannon 87; Luke 1:35). In addition, Robert M. Price and Donald R. Burleson present a similar reading, the latter of whom suggests that when the Whateley twins are "viewed ... as a single character ... [they] possess the mythic/archetypal qualities of the questing hero" ("Biblical Bits" 5; *Disturbing the Universe* 124). Indeed, Burleson's analysis of "The Dunwich Horror" presents an indisputable comparison in which he describes the twins' narrative as closely fitting the eight stages of the monomyth, the narrative foundation of all mythic heroes—including Jesus ("The Mythic Hero" 208-11).

Though the earlier correlation posited between Jesus Christ and Nyarlathotep poses no contradiction to Burleson's thesis, it does offer an addendum. Both parallels to the Christ story serve to underscore Lovecraft's subversive manipulation of religious tropes. Just as the Lord is an amalgamation of personas and identities, so too is Jesus. The gospels "give the impression of unity and coherence," but Jesus' various depictions are apparent throughout the New Testament (Fredriksen 7). As Price himself attests, though there may not have been a single-origin speculative mythology behind Jesus' biblical portrayal, *multiple* origins seem to have "flowed together with other Jesus images" to create the multifaceted persona that Christianity has dogmatized (*Deconstructing Jesus* 85). Jesus is seen as both fully human and fully divine, a status so seemingly contradictory that it was officially addressed by the Council of Chalcedon in 451 and explained through the theological doctrine of the hypostatic union, "which declared that in Christ the two natures, each retaining its own properties, are united in one subsistence and one person" (Pace, "Hypostatic Union"). This coexistence of humanity and divinity freely allows for parallel theses. While the Whateley twins jointly represent Jesus' corporeal role of mythic hero and "Son of God," Nyarlathotep wholly embodies his more transcendent characterization as the messenger or "Word of God"—the eschatological prophet of the Lord and His divine personification during the impending apocalypse (Mark 1:1; Luke 1:35; John 20:31; John 1:14; Revelation 19:13; Revelation 1:5-8).

Cosmicism: Anticlosure and a Philosophy of Chaos

Stylistically and thematically, Lovecraft's pantheon bears striking resemblances to the biblical entities it emulates, but the similarities between the Bible and Lovecraft's work do not end with these alone. Structurally, the Bible functions just as Lovecraft's stories do, both laying the foundation for the "terror tale" with the use of what David Heller calls "anticlosure" or horror's "'refus[al] to end'" in which "the reader finds himself torn between ... readings, unable to settle ... this unresolved tension keep[ing] him in a state of permanent terror and prevent[ing] him from ever reaching a satisfactory state of mind regarding the work" (Cardin 309-10). The presence of anticlosure can be found in the contradictory nature of the Bible and of the Lord Himself, haunting readers throughout the ages with mysteries that can never satisfactorily be solved. Anticlosure can also be found, dramatized, in nearly every story Lovecraft wrote. His protagonists are more often than not rendered insane due to their literal or metaphorical acts of "reading"—either of forbidden texts such as the dreaded *Necronomicon* or of a situation that is eternally incomprehensible and ultimately ineffable.

Though H. P. Lovecraft gained aesthetic inspiration from sacred and mythological writings such as the Bible, he seems to have knowingly sought a subversion of their proposed theologies. The literary philosophy known as "cosmicism" developed by Lovecraft insists upon an amoral vision of the cosmos, his pantheon of deities therein representing nothing more than humanity's insignificance in the larger scheme of existence and our inability to comprehend the universe fully. Divinity is stripped from his cosmic gods, and what is left is even less penetrable than dust; it is the primordial chaos from which we all emerged. Indeed, both humanity's origins and its prospects remain as clouded and nebulous as those of Lovecraft's most blasphemous of horrors.

Works Cited

Asma, Stephen T. *On Monsters: An Unnatural History of Our Worst Fears*. Oxford: Oxford University Press, 2009.

Beal, Timothy K. *Religion and Its Monsters*. New York: Routledge, 2002.

4 Ezra (2 Esdras). King James Bible (Apocrypha). 1611 Edition. University of Virginia Library Electronic Text Center. 1995.

The Book of Enoch. The Apocrypha and Pseudepigrapha of the Old Testament. Ed. R. H. Charles and Joshua Williams. Oxford: Clarendon Press, 1913.

The Book of Enoch. Trans. R. H. Charles, 1906. [Nampa, ID]: Northwest Nazarene College, 1995.

Job. The Holy Bible, King James 2000. Ed. Robert A. Couric. *Bible Hub*, 2014.

Burleson, Donald R. *Lovecraft: Disturbing the Universe*. Lexington: University Press of Kentucky, 1990.

———. "The Mythic Hero Archetype in 'The Dunwich Horror.'" In *A Century Less a Dream: Selected Criticism on H. P. Lovecraft*, ed., Scott Connors. Holicong, PA: Wildside Press, 2002. 206-13.

Cannon, Peter. *H. P. Lovecraft*. Boston: Twayne, 1989.

Cardin, Matt. "Gods and Monsters, Worms and Fire: A Horrific Reading of Isaiah." In *Dark Awakenings*. Poplar Bluff, MO: Mythos Books, 2010.

Carroll, Noël. "Horror and Humor." *The Journal of Aesthetics and Art Criticism* 57, No. 2, Aesthetics and Popular Culture (Spring 1999).

Colavito, Jason. *Knowing Fear: Science, Knowledge, and the Development of the Horror Genre*. Jefferson, NC: McFarland, 2008.

———. "Lovecraft, Aliens, and Primitivism." *Jason Colavito Blog*. Jason Colavito, 21 March 2012.

Creach, Jerome F. D. *Violence in Scripture*. Louisville, KY: Westminster John Knox, 2013.

Fredriksen, Paula. *From Jesus to Christ: The Origins of the New Testament Images of Jesus*. 2nd ed. New Haven, CT: Yale University Press, 2000.

Frost, Stanley Brice. *Old Testament Apocalyptic: Its Origins and Growth.* London: Epworth Press, 1952.

Houellebecq, Michel. *H. P. Lovecraft: Against the World, Against Life.* Trans. Dorna Khazeni. San Francisco: Believer Books, 1991.

Joshi, S. T. *The Unbelievers: The Evolution of Modern Atheism.* Amherst, NY: Prometheus Books, 2011.

Lovecraft, H. P. *Against Religion: The Atheist Writings of H. P. Lovecraft.* Ed. S. T. Joshi. New York: Sporting Gentlemen, 2010.

Miles, Jack. *God: A Biography.* New York: Vintage, 1995.

Mobley, Gregory. *The Return of the Chaos Monsters and Other Backstories of the Bible.* Grand Rapids, MI: William B. Eerdmans, 2012.

Pace, Edward. "Hypostatic Union." In *The Catholic Encyclopedia*, Vol. 7. New York: Robert Appleton Co., 1910.

Price, Robert M. "Biblical Bits in Lovecraft." In *Lovecraft and Influence: His Predecessors and Successors,* ed., Robert H. Waugh. Lanham, MD: Scarecrow Press, Inc., 2013. 3-10.

———. *Deconstructing Jesus.* Amherst, NY: Prometheus Books, 2000.

———. "Higher Criticism and the *Necronomicon*." In *A Century Less a Dream: Selected Criticism on H. P. Lovecraft,* ed., Scott Connors. Holicong, PA: Wildside Press, 2002. 58-68.

———. *H. P. Lovecraft and the Cthulhu Mythos.* Mercer Island, WA: Starmont House, 1990.

Sax, Boria. *Imaginary Animals: The Monstrous, the Wondrous, and the Human.* London: Reaktion Books, 2013.

Schlobin, Roger. "Prototypic Horror: The Genre of the Book of Job." In *Semeia 60: An Experimental Journal for Biblical Criticism (Fantasy and the Bible),* ed., George Aichele and Tina Pippin. Atlanta: Society of Biblical Literature, 1992. 23-38.

Whitney, K. William. *Two Strange Beasts: Leviathan and Behemoth in Second Temple and Early Rabbinic Judaism.* Ed. Peter Machinist. Winona Lake, IN: Eisenbrauns, 2006.

Wilhelm, Joseph. "The Nicene Creed." In *The Catholic Encyclopedia,* Vol. 11. New York: Robert Appleton Co., 1911.

Resisting Cthulhu: Milton and Lovecraft's Errand in the Wilderness

Marcello Ricciardi
St. Joseph's College

In many ways, the American wilderness was the birthplace of the Weird. Faye Ringel speaks of the first Puritans arriving in the New World and encountering the Native American, the dark Other (7-9), who became the paradigm for all that is diabolical and mysterious. Our colonial ancestors trekked across a rugged frontier removed and remote from the civilities of European culture, fostering the emergence of witchcraft, which, if not transferred from England, at least found a healthy renaissance in this remote, desolate corner of the world, and, of course, psychoprojecting all the werebeasts, water serpents, and ghostly entities that excited the popular imagination at the time.

In this context American literature was born, a hauntingly puritanical Gothic phenomenon that has its roots in American colonialism and which undergoes a rich consummation under the dark auspices of Hawthorne and Melville. Lovecraft clearly demonstrates all these proclivities and inherits his own peculiarly puritanical cosmic consciousness, which is the inheritance of the Michael Wigglesworths and Jonathan Edwards of colonial literature. Perry Miller aptly speaks of the Puritans' errand into the wilderness (i-ix), the agonistic attempt to establish a New Jerusalem, a New Israel that will definitively establish the Kingdom of God on earth and usher in the Second Coming. From Puritan literature up until the American Renaissance, the American literary identity is heavily indebted to the archetypal image of the New Adam, as noted by R. W. B. Lewis (1), a Trahernian man who seeks to erect a Paradise in the Wilderness, psychodramatically as well as topologically.

In this respect, of all English poets Milton, ironically, is the most American, an observation made by nineteenth-century American writer

Margaret Fuller. Such a pronouncement may seem a bit anachronistic at first, but Milton is the purest and most ascetic of English poets in his aspiration to transcend *to* or at least transition *from* a nationalistic to a universal mode of monomythic consciousness, seeking, like the American Puritan, to raise his own "Eden ... in the waste Wilderness" (7), as he pronounces at the opening of Book I of *Paradise Regained*. For Milton, there was no Matter of Britain to spark his poetical imagination, no Nine Worthies, Arthurian romance, chivalric quest, or dramatic Henriad to applaud. Whereas Dante's *Divine Comedy* always keeps the reader in mind of medieval Italy, Milton's epic tragedies are as removed and remote from Tennysonian British nationalism as the Puritan poets were from the Cavaliers. In fact, as George Sensabaugh aptly reminds us in *Milton in Early America*, the Puritan settlers crossed over to the New World with their two most prized possessions—the English Bible and the poetry of Milton (4-16). Yes, Shakespeare came along too, and, as always, was poet premier on and off the continent, but it was Milton who lit the spark for a new national consciousness, a new missionistic undertaking, much like Adam and Eve venturing forth out of Eden at the end of *Paradise Lost*, with wandering steps and a new world before them (11.648), or like Christ in *Paradise Regain'd* overcoming the Tempter in the wilderness in order to inaugurate his great mission of salvation for all mankind. Milton provided the Puritan psyche with a monolithic and megalomaniacal sense of high vocation (without Milton there probably would have been no Ahabian Satan), unlike Shakespeare's problematic and, at times, protean sense of purposeless morality.

I would like to argue for Milton and Lovecraft as desert poets in the ancient tradition of the desert fathers. Both sought a sense of spiritual isolation, a removal from the quotidian concerns of secularity, and both purposely sought an active engagement with those dark forces that threatened to ravage the human psyche. Their prose and poetry seem to be a variation of St. Athanasius' epic on the life of St. Antony of the desert, a gladiatorial wrestling match with invasive diabolical hordes of non-human entities infesting inner and outer space. Prophetically, Milton both anticipates invasion literature as well as perfects the captivity narrative. Milton's Hebraic consciousness as another David seeking to bring down a Goliath, or as a Jacob wrestling with the Angel of the Lord, is all part of his Mosaic, Abrahamic, and Messianic identity, another founder and deliverer of a renegade people in need of liberation, and which is much closer to the early

American spirit than the Shakespearean ethos could ever be.

For Lovecraft, such an enterprise is part of his Puritan heritage as well, yet doomed to failure: in the Lovecraftian world resistance is ultimately futile, but not without its own sense of interior merit and self-resistance. In Milton's autocosm an Eden can be raised in the wilderness, psychologically if not geographically, a hard lesson the Puritans themselves would soon learn and one in which old man Milton would as well with the failure of the Good Old Cause and the imminent restoration of Charles II. In that respect, Milton as English Puritan perfectly coalesces with his American brethren. Lovecraft's heroes encounter the very same American wilderness replete with entities, enigmas, and malevolent presences; but the struggle to reclaim that open bit of space and sanctify it, redeem it from the abyss as Milton does interiorly and as the Puritans attempted exteriorly, is always fruitless and ends in either despair-ridden defeatism or in a momentary deferment of engagement with Rudolf Otto's *mysterium tremendum* (12).

Lovecraft cannot fully interiorize Puritanical self-ascendency and psychical victory in the wake of certain defeat in the same way that Milton can, nor can he come out of the scathing interior inferno whole but undiminished, shivered but steadfast. However, in a letter to Frank Belknap Long, Lovecraft does defend the Puritanical aesthetical ethos when he admits that Puritans "unconsciously sought to do a supremely artistic thing—to mould all life into a dark poem" and in that respect "these Puritans were truly marvellous" (St. Armand 17). As a result, for there to be a "Profane," St. Armand concludes, "there must exist a Sacred. Thus aberration is the quintessence of Decadence and, with Lovecraft, this aberration is at the same time Puritanical and cosmic, transforming a shudder at the overstepping of ordinary moral limits into a galactic terror at the subversion of the natural chronometers of Time and Space" (26). Consequently, the Philistian Dagon that Milton's Samson inevitably overthrows by being overthrown himself and thereby releasing the Israelites from their captivity is the very same Dagon that ultimately hurls the Lovecraftian narrator out a window to his horrific end but without the benefit of both a private and public salvific liberation. Samson's descent is his ascent, whereas the Lovecraftian protagonist's descent results only in his definitive demise. Two agons with two very different outcomes.

To speak, therefore, of Milton and Lovecraft as desert poets is to speak of a patristic tradition of self-imposed isolation, spiritual agons, and interiorized psychomachias of heart and mind. Self-immolation is the hallmark of all meaningfully authentic mystical encounters and engagements with the self, leading, ideally, toward the promise of higher and altered states of consciousness. As noted earlier, the exemplar of the wilderness warrior is St. Antony of Egypt, whose legendary battles against the infernal fiend are heroically memorialized by St. Athanasius. Antony, whose entire life, like St. Paul's, was a series of incessant combats against the world, the flesh, and the devil, but primarily against the devil, in many ways set the standard as to what constitutes monastic or hermetic soldiership. Following in the tradition of St. John the Baptist and the Old Testament prophets, the desert monk is like the voice of one crying out in the wilderness, a herald for radical interior change bent on achieving deeper levels of being and communion with oneself, with others, and with the Absolute, preparing the way and making straight the crooked path—the exemplar, of course, being Christ, inverting the false hierarchy of satanic value in lieu of a celestial scale of ascent. And the desert prophet is nothing less than an oracular voice, a man on a mission possessing a heightened sense of vocation, a divine calling. He sees the world not merely as it *was* or *is* but as it *should be*, endowed with telescopic vision that encompasses past, present, and future realities simultaneously, intuitively aware, to cite Cotton Mather, of the invisible world surrounding him but surpassing sensory perception (210-14).

Flannery O'Connor soberly speaks of the prophetic figure in literature and in life as one who seems to "carry an invisible burden and to fix us with eyes that remind us that we all bear some heavy responsibility whose nature we have forgotten.... But to the eye of the general reader, these prophet-heroes are freaks. The public invariably approaches them from the standpoint of abnormal psychology" (861). John Keel, himself scrutinized as a rationally suspect prophetical voice of all things conspiratorial, macabre, and maleficent, and outcast heir of Milton, Lovecraft, and Charles Fort (themselves strange purveyors of their own occult or prophetic knowledge), would interpret any and all such invisible visibilities as altered states of consciousness that tap into the Superspectrum with all its electromagnetic anomalies defying space and time—extraterrestrials, ultraterrestrials, and seventh towers notwithstanding (193-94). The desert poet-prophet also learns to see himself not only as he truly is, but as he aspires to become.

Milton and Lovecraft both relentlessly espouse such convictions of reality, each committed to a supernal vision of human destiny and identity—

albeit on two diverging ends of the cosmic spectrum, divine consummation as adeptly evinced in *Paradise Lost, Regain'd*, and *Samson Agonistes* versus infernal conflagration as consummately realized in "The Call of Cthulhu." But in the midst of such aridity, which is either the prelude to repeated rebirth or perpetual death, illumination or darkness, and neither mutually exclusive, the desert is also a place of purification, of sanctification, a period of time for trial and testing. As Milton reminds us in *Areopagitica*:

> He that can apprehend and consider vice with all her baits and seeming pleasures, and yet abstain, and yet distinguish, and yet prefer that which is truly better, he is the true warfaring Christian. I cannot praise a fugitive and cloistered virtue, unexercised and unbreathed, that never sallies out and sees her adversary, but slinks out of the race where that immortal garland is to be run for, not without dust and heat. Assuredly we bring not innocence into the world, we bring impurity much rather: that which purifies us is trial, and trial is by what is contrary. (728)

The very divine flame of unrequited love that fuels the fires of psychological torment and self-loathing—in other words, hell—is the very same flame of adoration and self-abnegation that impels the prophet to seek first the kingdom and forsake the baubles of the world. "I know your method of studying to be so arranged," Milton writes to his close friend Charles Diodati, "that you frequently take breath in the middle, visit your friends, write much, sometimes make a journey, whereas my genius is such that no delay, no rest, no care or thought almost of anything, holds me aside until I reach the end I am making for" (Diekhoff 53)—Milton's own unique rendition of what Christ says in the Gospel of Luke, "Tell that fox that I drive out demons and cure the ill and on the third day I shall be perfected" (13:32). Primal simplicity, commitment to interior truth, and otherworldly visitations impel the desert father, and it is this very same simplicity and commitment to the primacy of supernal living that compelled both Milton and Lovecraft to seek newer, other, and stranger worlds, worlds familiarly unfamiliar, removed, yet not remote from the Neoplatonism that informs the cosmologies of both Lovecraft and Milton where interstellar realities are both the other and the same. Milton's Archangel Raphael explains it best to Adam when attempting to translate celestial discourse into terrestrial idioms: "[Though] what if Earth / Be but the shadow of Heav'n, and things therein / Each to other like more than on Earth is thought?" (*PL* 5. 574-76).

Milton frequently speaks of himself as a poet-prophet bent on a high vocation and awaiting the fulfillment of his destiny, a premise exhaustively explored by critics. But this does not negate Milton's sense of aloneness, his solitariness in inhabiting an alien world, his sense of psychic if not historical displacement. Although Dante is typically seen as a poet of exile, expelled from his native homeland and forced into literal banishment, Milton's sense of dislocation is no less severe. Whereas Lovecraft sees his beloved Providence as his creative impetus and then proceeds to transform topographical space into something that approximates the mental landscape of his mind, figuratively terraforming historical terrains into alien vistas, Milton, in lieu of geographical relocation or transmutation, inhabits a totally aetheric space, allowing him to undergo a hermeneutical and hermetic journey of self-transcendence and self-dejection—much like Dante traversing his own diabolical and celestial hierarchies of the mind.

Nowhere is this more clearly stated than in Milton's familial lamentations:

> I am accustomed in very frequent grieving over my own lot: the sense, namely, that those whom the mere necessity of neighbourhood, or something else of a useless kind, has closely conjoined with me, whether by accident or by the tie of law, they are the persons, though in no other respect commendable, who sit daily in my company, weary me, nay, by heaven, all but plague me to death whenever they are jointly in the humour for it, whereas those whom habits, disposition, studies, had so handsomely made my friends, are now almost all denied me, either by death or by most unjust separation of place, and are so for the most part snatched from my sight that I have to live well-nigh in a perpetual solitude. (Diekhoff 61)

John Milton, trapped in a world he never made.

In *The Exorcist*, the demon Pazuzu is probably right when he accuses Father Merrin of being proud, but he is also at the same time wrong, since he doesn't know that Merrin spent all that time in the desert learning humility. Blatty's Merrin reminisces at the beginning of the novel about how at one time he wouldn't have been able to love a certain kind of man (4). Milton, like Merrin, like the French Jesuit philosopher, paleontologist, and priest Teilhard de Chardin on whom Merrin is based, like Thomas Merton who spoke of constantly becoming a new man (247-48), and like all the desert fathers preceding him, flees to the desert to escape a false sense of self, a false sense of entitlement, and a false sense of ego, and to learn in their place lowliness, meekness, and transparency—and, judging from his complaint about his familial relationships, Milton, at thirty-nine years of age, is still very far from being perfected.

Although Lovecraft is consistently viewed as an outsider artist, a term appropriated by Thomas Ligotti, Lovecraft as monastic artist suggests the inhabitation of an inner space unmolested by and immune to sociopolitical as well as intrusively cultural conditioning. "Lovecraft," according to Donald Tyson in his controversial biography, "had for many years been living the life of an ascetic.

> He had withdrawn from society, avoided crowds, spent most of his time in solitary study, and ate only enough food to keep his body functioning. He neither smoked or drank, and his sexual life was nonexistent. In effect, he was living the life of a virtuous medieval monk without the burden of religious dogma. It is possible that this ascetic lifestyle, coupled with sexual abstinence, awoke in Lovecraft spontaneous spiritual manifestations of the body that are recognized in various Eastern religious and philosophic disciplines. (84)

Milton, too, in his youth, sought to fulfill the promise of a biblical heritage. His early poems speak of his refraining from imbibing the fruit of the vine, in favor of the clear elixir of water, the true tonic for a prospective epic poet, but also in keeping with his archetypal pattern hero Samson who was bound to fulfill his Nazarite covenant by abstaining from the grape as well as by keeping his locks unshorn. Milton, like his Adam and archangels, kept his hair at shoulder-length as well. Milton and Lovecraft's *asceticism* was closely knit to their *aestheticism*, each voluntarily inducing (or in Milton's case involuntarily with respect to his blindness) some form of sense deprivation in order to achieve an altered state of consciousness, a potential catalyst that could trigger a heightened sense of interior awareness.

Paul Roland posits an alternative approach to understanding Lovecraft's self-professed secularism and scientific materialism: "Although he proclaimed himself a rationalist and professed disbelief in the supernatural, Lovecraft entertained the idea that writers and artists can develop an acute—even psychic—sensitivity to other realities or dimensions through the development of their imagination and so be able to access the symbolic landscape of these inner worlds of the psyche in which their fears could take on form—fears which were to haunt him throughout his brief, unhappy life" (52). I believe what is significant to note here with Tyson and Roland's approach is that Lovecraft's desire to escape from the constrictive perimeters of the visual spectrum of reality is imaginal in nature, Lovecraft himself having no inner propensity to remove himself from his familiar/familial social environs, much like Milton inhabiting his biblical paradigms while remaining very much an Englishman dictating *Paradise Lost* in his garden—his Englishness never devolving into Britishism. One cannot help but think of T. S. Eliot's attestation in *Four Quartets* of being here and elsewhere simultaneously, where time and timelessness, space and place beautifully coalesce: "Here, the intersection of the timeless moment / Is England and nowhere. Never and always ("Little Gidding" 52-53).

Paradoxically, but not surprisingly, Lovecraft and Milton both were reputed to have convivial personalities, gracious and courteous to friends and respected acquaintances alike, but both curiously removed and detached from both themselves and from the daily exigencies of life—ironically, common attributes of the saints—being *in* the world but not *of* it, to quote the Gospel maxim (John 15:19), keeping their inner and truer selves at arm's length from the contagions of communal and familial living. Lovecraft's hauntingly opaque declaration of love to his wife Sonia—"'No, my dear . . . if you leave me I shall never marry again. You do not know how much I appreciate you'" (Roland 238), as well as Milton's elusive admission to his third wife—"'God have mercy Betty, I see thou wilt p[er]forme according to thy promise in providing mee such Dyshes as I think fit whilst I live, and when I dye thou knowest that I have left thee all'" (Lewalski 537), though not as banal as Shakespeare's gifting his second-best bed to his wife, suggests men more than half in love with an ideal, but little less than half in love with an all too perishing reality of failed possibilities, diminishing realities, and languishing mortalities—"what to make of a diminished thing" (*The Oven Bird* l. 14), in the hauntingly dark Frostian refrain. One foot in this world and one in the next, one on land and one in sea, neither Wedding Guest nor Mariner—in many ways the perfect prerequisite for both the mystic and interior monastic, living in time but outside of it, occupying multiple tiers of reality, visible and invisible, belonging to all ages, but anachronistically remaining in none—a biographical and poetical prefiguration of T. S. Eliot's own spiritual conundrum and pilgrimage in his *Four Quartets*.

Although Miltonic and Lovecraftian narratives involve a wrestling with diabolical presences, a close engagement, no quarter given encounter with outer monstrosities laying siege to the protagonists' physical and psychical life, it should be noted that an agonistic escalation also unfolds in the chronological progression and maturation of both Milton and Lovecraft's literary development—the outer darkness, although still all encompassing, can be resisted and a temporary respite obtained.

Beginning with Dr. Willett's successful exorcism of the spirit of Joseph Curwen in *The Case of Charles Dexter Ward*, to Dr. Henry Armitage's equally successful excisory incantation against Wilbur Whateley's twin brother in "The Dunwich Horror," to Henry Akeley and his dogs' valiant, but doomed, resistance under siege in "The Whisperer in Darkness," to Joseph Mazurewicz in "The Dreams in the Witch House," who, regardless of his psychological predispositions, does comprehend the efficacy of the crucifix in keeping Keziah Mason at bay, leading up to "Through the Gates of the Silver Key," where various avatars of Randolph Carter inhabiting multitudinous multiverses beyond space and time serve as guardians of the galaxies, to "The Haunter of the Dark," where the townsfolk keeping a candlelit vigil are proactively and prayerfully besieging the diabolically infested former Church of Starry Wisdom, Lovecraft's protagonists adopt a more adversarial attitude in the face of incalculable odds. Representatively, in a 1928 letter to August Derleth, Lovecraft admits that while writing "The Dunwich Horror," "I found myself psychologically identifying with one of the characters (an aged scholar who finally combats the menace) toward the end" (cited in *IAP* 718). Lovecraft has come a long way from the futility of human resistance since "The Call of Cthulhu."

So, too, with Milton, from his elegy "Lycidas," where Edward King becomes a guardian oceanic spirit, the demiurgic protector of the shore after his own untimely demise at sea, to the Lady in *Comus* who though successful in abstaining from Comus' sensual inducements in the woods, must still rely upon Sabrina, an agent of divine grace, to release her from her captivity, to the great epic *Paradise Lost* where we witness *God for man*, releasing Adam and Eve from the shackles of despair in the promise of a future Messiah, to the even greater epic, at least in Milton's estimation, of *Paradise Regain'd*, where *God as man*, through psychic engagement with the adversary, much like Algernon Blackwood's occult detective John Silence— minus the godhood—overcomes the source of all Evil and fortifies human resistance against any future diabolical threat of incursion, to Milton's own final pronouncement on self-realization, the tragedy *Samson Agonistes*, where *God in man* assists the biblical Hercules in triumphing over his own desert despair and win, to quote Milton's God from *Paradise Lost*, "the easier conquest" (6.37) against Philistian yoke. God the Father *for* man, God the Son *as* Man, and God the Holy Spirit *in* man epitomize Milton's triadic, triumphant, and Trinitarian poetics.

Ironically, after *The Dream-Quest of Unknown Kadath*, the Lovecraftian protagonist, as noted before, seems more determined, more committed and resilient. There seems to be a growing sense of deliberate and purposeful orientation against the encompassing shadows, either by particular mentoristic sages who rise to the occasion or by the citizenry themselves, as in Lovecraft's last tale, "The Haunter of the Dark." Defeat does not seem so imminent nor the protagonists so desperate; there is a respite, a lull in the storm, temporary, but tenable. Darkness may have the final say, but a rising crescendo of resistant voices attempts to drive out and away cacophonies from beyond or below the stars. Lovecraft is incrementally and progressively approximating something akin to the heroic. It may not be Robert E. Howard's vision of stolid, atavistic, defiant primitivism, Solomon Kane excluded, but it does echo a measured, tempered, and intelligently interior line of demarcation where the Lovecraftian, much like the Miltonic hero, must take a stand. "Standing" is the Miltonic mantra in all his poems from the Lady in *Comus* to the angel Abdiel in *Paradise Lost* to the Christ in *Paradise Regain'd* to the imprisoned blind champion in *Samson Agonistes*: to stand—not meaning merely to deliver but to be delivered, not *waiting for*, but *awaiting what will* come next, keeping oneself in a constant state of vigilant readiness.

At the end of the 1951 version of *The Thing from Another World*, journalist Ned Scott broadcasts a warning: "Tell the world. Tell this to everybody, wherever they are. Watch the skies everywhere. Keep looking. Keep watching the skies." Milton utters the same admonishment at the opening of Book IV of *Paradise Lost*, "O for that warning voice" (1), as he bears witness to Satan's furious descent to earth and imminent invasion of the planet. Lovecraft replicates his own cosmic infiltration when he has Dr. Armitage observe: "Things like that brought down the beings those Whateleys were so fond of—the beings they were going to let in tangibly to wipe out the human race and drag the earth off to some nameless place for some nameless purpose" (CF 2.466). "But of that day or that hour no one knows," enjoins Mark's Christ. "Take heed, watch, for you do not know when the time will come. . . . And what I say to you I say to all: Watch" (13:32-37). Following the Gospel injunction, Milton and Lovecraft both supremely understood the efficacy of standing and watching.

Perhaps, after *The Dream-Quest of Unknown Kadath*, Lovecraft's bifurcated hero self-achieved some sense of cohesion, some unified synthesis, reconciling both the conscious and unconscious aspects of his psyche, resulting in a retreat from passive surrender to the inevitable and forward movement towards self-mastery, self-transformation, and, ultimately, toward authentic self-discovery. Milton, too, aspires to such self-integration and psychic equilibrium in his Satan/Son dichotomy, Melville with his Ahab/Ishmael counterforce, and Conrad with his Marlow/Kurtz-Jim archetypes. "Whatever universal masterpiece of tomorrow may be wrought from phantasm or terror will owe its acceptance rather to a supreme workmanship than to a sympathetic theme," Lovecraft concludes in "Supernatural Horror in Literature." "Yet who shall declare the dark theme a positive handicap? Radiant with beauty, the Cup of the Ptolemies was carven of onyx" (96). Historical evidence suggests that the Cup of the Ptolemies most likely belonged to the Holy Roman Emperor Charlemagne and was converted into a Christian chalice during the Middle Ages. Perhaps, in the end, Lovecraft, like Milton and his Puritan ancestors, found, at the completion of his errands, his own Grail in the wilderness.

Works Cited

Athanasius. *The Life of Antony and the Letter to Marcellinus.* Trans. Robert C. Gregg. New York: Paulist Press, 1980.

Blatty, William Peter. *The Exorcist.* New York: Harper & Row, 1971.

Diekhoff, John S., ed. *Milton on Himself: Milton's Utterances upon Himself and His Works.* London: Cohen & West, 1965.

Eliot, T. S. *Four Quartets.* New York: Harcourt, 1971.

Frost, Robert. *The Poetry of Robert Frost.* Ed. Edward Connery Lathem. New York: Holt, Rinehart & Winston, 1969.

Keel, John A. *The Eighth Tower: On Ultraterrestrials and the Superspectrum.* San Antonio: Anomalist Books, 2013.

Lewalski, Barbara K. *The Life of John Milton: A Critical Biography.* Oxford: Blackwell, 2000.

Lewis, R. W. B. *The American Adam.* Chicago: University of Chicago Press, 1959.

Lovecraft, H. P. *The Annotated Supernatural Horror in Literature.* Ed. S. T. Joshi. 2nd ed. New York: Hippocampus Press, 2012.

Mather, Cotton. "The Wonders of the Invisible World." In *American Sermons: The Pilgrims to Martin Luther King Jr.* New York: Library of America, 1999.

Merton, Thomas. *The New Man*. New York: Farrar, Straus & Cudahy, 1961.

Miller, Perry. *Errand into the Wilderness*. New York: Harper & Row, 1964.

Milton, John. *Complete Poems and Major Prose*. Ed. Merritt Y. Hughes. Englewood Cliffs, NJ: Prentice-Hall, 1957.

The New Oxford Annotated Bible. Revised Standard Version. Ed. Herbert G. May and Bruce M. Metzger. New York: Oxford University Press, 1971.

O'Connor, Flannery. "The Catholic Novelist in the South." In *Collected Works*. New York: Library of America, 1988.

Otto, Rudolf. *The Idea of the Holy*. Oxford: Oxford University Press, 1950.

Ringel, Faye. *New England's Gothic Literature*. Lewiston, ME: Edwin Mellen Press, 1995.

Roland, Paul. *The Curious Case of H. P. Lovecraft*. London: Plexus, 2014.

Sensabaugh, George F. *Milton in Early America*. Princeton, NJ: Princeton University Press, 1964.

St. Armand, Barton Levi. *H. P. Lovecraft: New England Decadent*. Albuquerque, NM: Silver Scarab Press, 1979; rpt. Providence, RI: WaterFire Providence, 2013.

The Thing from Another World. Dir. Christian Nyby. RKO, 1951. Film.

Tyson, Donald. *The Dream World of H. P. Lovecraft: His Life, His Demons, His Universe*. Woodbury, Minn: Llewellyn Publications, 2010.

"The Discriminating Urban Landscapist": Tradition and Innovation in the Architectural Writings of H. P. Lovecraft

Connor Pitetti
Stony Brook University

All the side streets around this section have finely quaint colonial vistas to offer the discriminating urban landscapist.
—Lovecraft to Annie E. P. Gamwell, 17 September 1927

As to the whole general question of the beauty of ancient towns—I suppose it's a bit involv'd, but surely no more so than the question of all forms of beauty ("The Waste Land", for example) which are more or less subtle and lacking in universal obviousness.
—Lovecraft to Frank Belknap Long, 26 January 1924

"The only really lovely places in America, architecturally speaking," H. P. Lovecraft wrote in a letter to his longtime correspondent Elizabeth Toldridge, "are certain old villages which progress has left behind" (*ET* 145).[1] These kinds of simplistically nostalgic proclamations appear frequently in Lovecraft's nonfictional writings on architecture. Discussing urban renewal projects in his hometown of Providence, R.I., in a letter to his aunt, Lillian D. Clark, for example, Lovecraft claimed that he was "unable to take pleasure or interest in anything but a mental re-creation of other & better days," and goes on to say that to "avoid the madness which

---

1. Work on this essay was made possible through the generous support of the S. T. Joshi Endowed Research Fund. Thanks are due to Christopher Geissler and the staff of the John Hay Library at Brown University and to Kate Wells and the staff of the Providence Public Library for their assistance with the research.

leads to violent suicide" he had no choice but to "cling to the few shreds of old days & old ways which are left to me" (9 August 1925).[2] Descriptions of old buildings and urban landscapes often act in these writings as catalysts for extended fantasies of escape from the modern world, in much the same way that the antiquarian heroes of Lovecraft's fiction slip from the appreciation of ancient artifacts into fantastical encounters with ancient realities. In another letter, Lovecraft writes that a sightseeing trip in Philadelphia has allowed him to "take leave of the modern world, & plunge out into the red brick 18th century" (16 November 1924). Similarly, Lovecraft's descriptions of encountering new construction and modern landscapes often preface impassioned denunciations of twentieth-century decadence, consumerism, and superficiality.

But these explicit expressions of nostalgia for a lost past are often complicated by the fact that they appear alongside enthusiastic accounts of modernizing innovation. In the same letter to Toldridge in which he opposes progress and loveliness, for example, Lovecraft also claims that the construction of modern skyscrapers has "saved" New York from the aesthetic degradations of the nineteenth century by giving the city an "an exotic & fairylike appearance" (*ET* 145). He was particularly enamored of John Howells and Raymond Hood's American Radiator Building, which he described in a letter to Lillian as a "black & gold Dunsanian skyscraper" (4–5 November 1924). High praise indeed from a lifelong fan of the Irish fantasist! Elsewhere, he makes a similar claim about Providence, concluding a rhapsodic description of the city's "archaic, village-like quality" with the observation that it has become "even more magical now that we have tall buildings ... to light up & suggest enchanted cliff cities of Dunsanian mystery" (letter to E. Hoffmann Price, February 1933). This for-

---

2. Extracts of this letter were published in *SL*, but the passage quoted here does not appear in that volume. When choosing extracts for publication, Derleth and Wandrei focused (for obvious reasons) on passages in which HPL discusses his fiction, his circle, his philosophy, and concrete details of his personal biography. I have cited published editions of the correspondence wherever possible, but this essay draws on the many pages of architectural descriptions that appear in letters written while HPL was traveling (and especially in letters to his Aunt Lillian), and these passages are, for the most part, among those that have never appeared in print.

ward-looking aspect of Lovecraft's architectural discourse reaches something of an apogee in the letter to Frank Belknap Long from which my second epigraph is taken, where Lovecraft equates the urban antiquarian's aesthetic pleasures to those of a reader of that most notoriously avantgarde of all modernist poems, T. S. Eliot's *The Waste Land* (SL 1.282).

Lovecraft's writings about architecture are, in other words, characterized not by a naïve and escapist nostalgia, as he himself often claimed, but by a tension: throughout this work he is visibly striving to balance his explicit desire to defend and reclaim America's cultural heritage with his often implicit but no less significant acknowledgment of the power of modern ideas and technologies to produce new forms of architectural beauty and value. A similar duality is, of course, apparent throughout his work. Timothy Evans speaks, for example, of the "antiquarian" and "cosmic" sides of Lovecraft's relationship to folklore, describing his commitment to accuracy in the preservation and transmission of traditional folk narratives and his wild innovation on those narrative models in the construction of his own stories. Tracy Bealer identifies a similar ambivalence in Lovecraft's views on race, arguing that in "The Shadow over Innsmouth" Lovecraft struggled to reconcile his nostalgia for a lost (and imaginary) racially pure America and his fascination with the possibilities for change and development inherent in the prospect of a racially mixed future (44). Robert H. Waugh, who described Lovecraft as "a divided man" who "knew that he was divided" (220), has argued that tensions such as those Evans and Bealer describe constitute the key to Lovecraft's entire oeuvre; Waugh finds in these ambivalent dualities "the center of Lovecraft's moral vision" (226). Despite its ubiquity in his work and thought, however, this Janus-like ambivalence about the relative value of the old and the new is particularly marked in Lovecraft's writings on architecture.

Perhaps the unique nature of architectural modernization forced Lovecraft to take developments in in this field seriously in ways that were not demanded of him by, for example, literary modernism. He could dismiss Joyce's *Ulysses* or Eliot's *Waste Land* as theoretically important but aesthetically uninteresting because the existence of these modern masterpieces did not keep him from enjoying the eighteenth-century writers he preferred, but he could not take the same disinterested stance toward a modern town planning proposal that demanded the destruction of older buildings to make way for its innovations. It is in Lovecraft's architectural writings, accordingly, that we find some of his most sustained and explicit attempts to reconcile the transformative potential of new technologies and new ideas with his desire to preserve traditional cultural forms. In what follows I examine two such attempts—a late essay on Roman and American architecture, written in 1934, and the newspaper pieces Lovecraft contributed to the debate over the construction of the new Providence County Courthouse in the late 1920s. Reading these pieces alongside the theoretical writings of the architect Le Corbusier, a contemporary of Lovecraft's and an influential theorist of modernist aesthetics, my analysis contextualizes Lovecraft's more extreme statements concerning architecture and modernism. My readings show that far from rejecting modernization, Lovecraft advocated a transformative modernist art practice that avoided the excesses of both modernist iconoclasm and conservative preservationism by identifying innovation itself as a tool that could be used to protect and enrich the cultural tradition.

"Common Sense in Art Forms": Lovecraft and the Theory of Architecture

Lovecraft's most extensive theoretical discussion of tradition and innovation in the arts appears in the essay "A Living Heritage: Roman Architecture in Today's America." The bulk of this essay consists of a history of classical architecture and its role in the development of American vernacular styles, but it is prefaced by a theoretical polemic on the state of art in the early twentieth century.[3] This preface reaches beyond the purported topic of classical influence and meditates on the role of tradition and novelty in artistic production and consumption more generally. "A chair," Lovecraft writes here, "is *not*, in essence, simply a 'sitting machine.' A house is *not* merely a 'living machine'" (CE 5.121). In addition to performing the practical functions for which they are designed, Lovecraft argues that chairs and houses—and by extension other architectural and decorative art objects—play a less well-defined but no less important role in the emotional and psychological lives of their users. "By

---

3. The main historical section of the essay, written at the request of Maurice W. Moe, never appeared in print during HPL's lifetime; the theoretical prefatory section was published in the amateur journal the *Californian* in the summer of 1935.

corresponding in greater or lesser degree with our naturally ingrained and traditional images . . . of what a chair and house ought to be," he writes, such objects create a sense of stability and familiarity, allowing us to orient ourselves in a recognizable world. These familiar objects thus literally sustain human lives, supporting us in "the pitiful struggle of the ego against that ineluctable change which means decay and engulfment in the illimitable dark" (CE 5.121).

Several years before composing this essay Lovecraft had written that "tradition means nothing cosmically, but it means everything locally & programmatically because we have nothing else to shield us from a devastating sense of 'lostness' in endless time & space. Nowadays we can't believe as our forefathers did, but we can share some of their instinctive feelings toward the daily scenes around them, so that a sort of comfortable placement in the invisible cosmic pattern will seem . . . to be provided for us" (SL 2.357). In this later essay, he argues that one of the functions of the decorative and architectural arts is to provide this comfortable sense of being securely situated in a comprehensible world. Paintings, poems, and other forms of fine art serve a similar purpose, he suggests, as long as they correspond in some recognizable way with accepted ideas of what a painting or poem "ought to be."

Taken on its own this is an extremely conservative position, in which art serves not to interrogate or challenge the social status quo but to reinforce it. But Lovecraft complicates the conservative logic; one of the rhetorical projects of "A Living Heritage" is to present the apparently antithetical projects of innovation and preservation in art and culture as not only compatible but mutually supportive. "Naturally," he writes, "every new age has additions, subtractions, and modifications to make to its inherited art traditions. No one argues in behalf of a rigidly static art . . . New objects are invented and old ones are altered, thus providing constant opportunities for reworking and expanding our familiar structural forms" (CE 5.124). Acknowledging that without innovation traditional forms will become moribund and lose their power, he also insists that without the grounding in tradition that ensures familiarity, innovative cultural and artistic forms will be ineffective or alienating.

Lovecraft explicitly opposes this carefully ambivalent position to what he describes as the "modernistic" aesthetics of his contemporaries (CE 5.120). The "tragic fallacy" of twentieth-century art, he argues, lies not in its commitment to innovation, but rather in its failure to recognize the emotional and existential value of the familiar, and thus in its corresponding failure to embrace the adaptation of inherited forms as the most legitimate form of innovation. "According to the pedlars of these [modernist] theories," he writes, "all art ought to be divorced completely from tradition and from earlier art-forms. Each age, they assert, ought to express itself in its own fashion and with its own materials; ignoring the modes of expression dictated in other ages by other modes of life, and existing only to fulfil an utilitarian function." He characterizes modernism in art as a kind of reckless and willful iconoclasm: modernists, he wrote, "hate the known" (CE 5.120).

As a summary of modernist aesthetics this is obviously a gross oversimplification (a point S. T. Joshi registers when he describes the opening section of "A Living Heritage" as "a somewhat intemperate condemnation of 'functionalist' art and architecture" [CE 5.139]). Much of modernist art is best understood as a critical reaction to and condemnation of the social, political, and technological changes associated with modernization; many modern artists turned to innovative aesthetic strategies as a way of addressing their sense of having lost some vital connection to the social past or to tradition. Such attempts often involved a rejection of certain older practices and values as obsolete or antiquated, but rarely were they simply iconoclastic attempts to destroy and replace traditional culture. Given that Lovecraft does not acknowledge the complexity of modernist responses to modernity in "A Living Heritage," it is tempting to read the position he theorizes in this essay as basically reactionary. His protest that he is not arguing for "a rigidly static art" can easily be written off as a rhetorical move meant to make a deeply conservative rejection of change seem less rigid; it is particularly easy to dismiss the essay in this fashion when one reads it in the context of Lovecraft's swooning over "old villages which progress has left behind" and his repeatedly proclaimed desire to "cling to the shreds of old days."

But Lovecraft's flattening of the modernist movement into a one-dimensional anti-traditionalism here seems to have been intended polemically, and "A Living Heritage" does offer a compelling critique of the most iconoclastic and extreme tendencies of modernist avant-gardism. In particular, Lovecraft seems to have been taking aim at the ideas of the Swiss architect Le Corbusier, who had declared in the influential 1924 manifesto *Vers une architecture* that "a house is a machine for living in" and that "a chair has no soul; it is a machine for sitting in" (*Towards* 107, 142). Le

Corbusier quite explicitly argued that the implication of this "machinic" view was that a repudiation of tradition was a necessary precondition for successful modern art. Beauty and value, he argued, were products of the optimization of functional utility, and adherence to traditional aesthetic standards and forms could only impede the artist in his search for ever purer and more efficient forms. In the context of architecture and urban planning, Le Corbusier went even further, arguing that older structures should be torn down and replaced by their more perfect successors. "Our world, like a charnel-house," he wrote, "is strewn with the detritus of dead epochs. The great task incumbent on us is that of making a proper environment for our existence, and clearing away from our cities the dead bones that putrefy in them" (City 244).

This conviction that modernity demanded a clean break with tradition reached its apotheosis in the "Plan Voisin," Le Corbusier's radical proposal to modernize Paris by bulldozing the historic city center and replacing its narrow streets, old houses, and picturesque wrought iron with a grid of 400-foot-wide highways, sixty-story skyscrapers, and austere glass and steel façades. This plan was never carried out, of course, and was in its very extremism always something of a polemical caricature of itself, but the functionalist justification for a wholesale demolition and replacement of urban landscapes which it epitomizes was immensely influential, and much of twentieth-century town planning practice took its cue from Le Corbusier's slash-and-burn rhetoric.[4]

It is difficult to imagine two theories of urban life more starkly at odds

---

4. Details of the Plan Voisin were published in Le Corbusier's 1925 collection of town-planning essays, *Urbanisme*, which was translated into English as *The City of To-morrow and Its Planning* (1924); *Vers une architecture* was published in English in 1927 as *Towards a New Architecture*. It is thus entirely possible that HPL read these books, or at least knew of them through one of his correspondents. It is difficult to explain why he did not cite Le Corbusier in "A Living Heritage," especially given the oblique but clear reference to the Swiss architect's ideas in HPL's rejection of the idea of machines for sitting and living in. But while it is impossible to say with certainty which of Le Corbusier's writings HPL had read, it is clear that he was aware of the architect and his work (although he seems to have been misinformed as to his nationality); in a letter to Toldridge written on 26 February 1932, HPL notes that "the greatest advocate of modernistic building & city-planning is the Frenchman Le Corbusier" (*ET* 205). Many thanks to Donovan K. Loucks for bringing this passage to my attention.

than those of Le Corbusier and H. P. Lovecraft. For the Swiss architect, cities of narrow streets and old houses were so undesirable as to be moral evils: "they use up our bodies, they thwart our souls," he lamented; "their degradation wounds our self-esteem and humiliates our sense of dignity" (*City* xxi). For the American author, on the contrary, narrow streets and old houses were one of the very few things capable of nurturing the body, uplifting the soul, sustaining self-esteem, and helping humanity in our endless struggle to maintain our dignity before "the illimitable dark." "A town of broad streets," he wrote to Frank Belknap Long, "and straight lines and right angles cannot have the highest appeal, because it is so clearly geometrical and artificial that we cannot read in it any gradual growth from its natural site" (*SL* 1.282). Such a city lacks, in other words, that sense of the familiar which Lovecraft believed was necessary to stabilize psychological life. "What makes a town really lovely and fascinating," he continues, "is the quaint irregularity which links it to its geographical location—the suggestions of hill and dale, river and shore—and to the continuous history of its inhabitants—the marks of original settlement, slow expansion, and development in channels and directions determin'd by the topography of the site and aspirations and genius of the people" (*SL* 1.282). Here Lovecraft offers a more nuanced account of beauty in urban architecture than is to be found in his sweeping denunciation of progress in the letter to Toldridge quoted above; Lovecraft suggests that progress and change are part of what makes a town lovely, and that beauty derives from our ability to see a city's history recorded in its physical form. It is not progress as such that destroys beauty, then, but only those forms of progress which threaten to efface this record. This letter to Long thus suggests the same middle path between conservative traditionalism and radical innovation articulated theoretically in "A Living Heritage." With the example of Le Corbusier's extreme (and extremely influential) rejection of all attempts to hold onto the past as a foil, it becomes clear that Lovecraft's cautious acknowledgment of the importance of innovation in that essay should not be dismissed as a rhetorical defense of conservative antimodernism, but rather taken at face value as an attempt to theorize an art practice capable of reconciling the seemingly mutually exclusive goals of preservation and innovation.

In the following section, I turn to a case in which Lovecraft articulated this idea of a middle path between enthusiasm for the new and love of the old not as a theoretical abstraction, but in the form of concrete suggestions about a specific construction project. Lovecraft had no formal training in architecture; his knowledge of the subject was entirely that of an autodidact, derived from extensive reading and his famously exhaustive first-hand surveys of American and Canadian cities. It is not surprising, then, that most of his architectural writings consist of descriptions of the various buildings and cities he visited. Only very rarely did Lovecraft venture beyond the descriptive and offer prescriptive comments about building and urban design, and it was even more rare for him to do so publicly. One of the few occasions on which he entered into a public debate and offered specific suggestions about the construction, demolition, and preservation of real buildings was during the construction of the Providence County Courthouse in the late 1920s. There was nothing more important to Lovecraft than his beloved hometown in Rhode Island; his impassioned statement of identity with the city, "I am Providence," is well known (CE 4.30). Given that the construction of the new courthouse was a major event in the civic life of Providence, and that it profoundly transformed the appearance and atmosphere of the city as a whole, it is perhaps not surprising that this project moved Lovecraft to adopt a more active mode of architectural writing. Lovecraft's participation in the debates over the Courthouse project provide a uniquely concrete example of the middle path between avant-garde iconoclasm and conservative preservationism that he theorized abstractly in "A Living Heritage."

"Save the Old Brick Row": Lovecraft and the Practice of Architecture

Le Corbusier's renovatory plan for Paris was extreme, but the problems he was proposing to solve were real. The populations of many major urban centers grew rapidly in the nineteenth century as a result of industrialization and a general demographic boom resulting from improved healthcare technologies, and in the early twentieth century Paris was far from being the only city in the world struggling to meet the many challenges this rapid growth had created. Lovecraft's birthplace was one of these cities. Incorporated in 1824 with a population of approximately 15,000, a century later Providence could boast nearly a quarter of a million residents. In 1910 there were no officially registered apartment buildings in the city, the streets were lit by gaslights, and the steeple of the First Baptist Church was the tallest structure in town; in 1918, twenty-eight apartment buildings were listed in the Providence Directory, nine thousand electric lights had been installed on the streets, and a modern skyscraper in the stepped New York style dominated the skyline (Cady 89). Within Lovecraft's own lifetime, in other words, the city that he so often described as a timeless survival of the vanishing American past was actually undergoing a series of radical evolutions.

Among the many expansion and modernization projects the city was forced to undertake as a result of its rapid growth was the construction of a new courthouse. This project took ten years to complete, from the establishment of a planning committee in 1923 to the dedication of the new building in 1933. It involved a drastic reworking of one of the city's oldest colonial neighborhoods, the Market Square area between the east bank of the Providence River and the foot of College Hill—not terribly far from the house at 454 Angell Street where Lovecraft was born, and scarcely a stone's throw from the house at 66 College Street where he spent his final years. Plans and drawings were published as they developed in the *Providence Journal*, where they became ongoing topics of debate in the editorial pages. Lovecraft was a regular reader of the *Journal*, and his letters from this period are full of worried speculation about the courthouse. "It is no light matter," he wrote to Lillian, "to decide on something which will be linked to the city's aesthetic scheme for better or for worse throughout an indefinite futurity!" (5 March 1926). He was pleased with the proposed courthouse itself; the Providence firm of Jackson, Robertson, & Adams had designed a monumental steel-framed modern structure, but had modeled its exterior on the distinctive red brick façades and white gables of Providence's old Georgian-style houses, and had broken its mass into a series of tiered wings that emulated the silhouettes and skylines of the colonial city.

The choice of a site for the new building, however, was an ominous one for a lover of Providence antiquities. The new courthouse was to cover an entire block to the east of Market Square, containing two of the oldest structures in the city: the Brown & Ives counting house, commonly known as 50 South Main, and the Stephen Hopkins house, both dating from the first half of the eighteenth century. The Hopkins house in particular was important from an antiquarian point of view; a ten-term Rhode Island governor, a signer of the Declaration of Independence, and the first chancellor of Brown University, Hopkins was a central figure in the history of both the city and the nation. In 1926 Lovecraft wrote to

Lillian that "the news that the Stephen Hopkins house is really coming down [to make way for the courthouse] desolates me immeasurably!" (6 April 1926).[5] Despite his anxiety over the fate of these venerable antiques, however, Lovecraft did not enter the public debate around the courthouse project for another three years, and when he did finally speak up he did so in defense of some structures of a rather less remarkable pedigree.

Lovecraft's contribution to the courthouse debate took the form of an editorial entitled "Retain Historic 'Old Brick Row'" in the 24 March 1929 edition of the *Providence Sunday Journal*, and a poem, "The East India Brick Row," published in the same paper on 8 January 1930. In these pieces Lovecraft argued for the preservation of three blocks of warehouses between South Main and South Water Streets, immediately to the west of the courthouse site. Fronting onto the Providence River, these warehouses had for many years been part of the bustling commercial heart of the maritime city, busy with international trade. In the second half of the nineteenth century, however, shipping firms began to move their operations to new docks on the drained marshland across the river, and by the time of Lovecraft's editorial the old brick row had fallen into neglect. Official plans called for the entire area to be razed, leaving an open park that would extend from the front of the new courthouse to the river. Lovecraft strongly opposed these plans, insisting in his editorial that Providence was "singularly lucky in possessing this quaint, characteristic waterfront at our advanced stage of civic growth," and arguing that the park proposal was tantamount to an attempt to render Providence indistinguishable from the modern metropolis of Boston (MW 511).

Lovecraft was not the only person opposed to the city's plans for the warehouses; the John Hay collection includes a typed letter to the editor of the *Journal* signed by his good friend James Morton which reproduces the text of Lovecraft's own editorial almost exactly. Nor was it only friends who supported his efforts. A week after his editorial appeared, the *Journal* published a short note from another reader in support of Lovecraft's position: "refreshing indeed was it to read in last Sunday's Journal," writes B. of Pawtucket, "the article by H. P. L. advocating the preservation of the

---

5. In recognition of its historical importance, the Hopkins House was eventually moved rather than torn down. It is now maintained as a house museum and is open to the public.

historic 'Old Brick Row'" ("Historic Buildings" 5); Lovecraft also noted in a letter to Toldridge that his poem about the warehouses was "favourably received, & won me a very pleasant letter from the editor" (January 1930).

But there seems never to have been any real doubt as to what the fate of these buildings would be. An open plaza had always been part of the proposed courthouse design, and drawings in the *Journal* from as early as 1924 show the area occupied by the old brick row cleared and planted with trees. As the editors of the local Providence magazine the *Netopian* put it, "as one views the simple architecture of the buildings, and the beauty they lend to the skyline of the waterfront of Providence, it seems rather regretful that they must come down; but Progress is always ruthless" (11). Lovecraft disagreed, protesting that those in favor of demolition "take a very superficial view in considering a permanent landscape for this focal, historic meeting-place of bay and hill" (MW 511). Elsewhere he allowed himself some stronger language: "May misfortune, leprosy, radium-poisoning, remorse, time-table slavery, sudden death, and everything else pursue the criminals who are destroying this loveliest legacy of old days—pursue them, & all their posterity even unto the time of great Spenglerian collapse!" (JFM 212).

The most striking thing about Lovecraft's choice of the old brick row as his point of entry into the courthouse debate is the fact that these warehouses, all relatively recent replacements for older wooden structures destroyed in the "Great Gale" of 1815, were not particularly notable either historically or architecturally. This suggests that Lovecraft's interest in them was not fundamentally historical in nature, but rather aesthetically motivated; he was interested in the warehouses, in other words, not because they were old, but because they looked old. In the poem "The East India Brick Row," he describes the warehouses as "links that join us to the years before," but the connection to the past that he finds in them is not a specific link in a chain of historical narrative—not the direct connection to a specific history that Charles Dexter Ward finds in the old Curwen house, for example. The history Lovecraft finds in Water Street is more ambiguous, a matter of general suggestion rather than specific reference. The warehouses are "symbols," he says in his poem; the "ghosts" of the Providence docks that they conjure up are "faint and distant," "half-heard," "murmurs," a matter of "phantom and dream" (AT 307-8).

Someone with Lovecraft's facility for antiquarian research could, of course, have linked these buildings to specific owners and businesses; the

Netopian article quoted above, published only a few months before Lovecraft's poem, cites records on the old brick row going back to 1650 (7). But this is not the approach Lovecraft chose to pursue in his poem; instead of historical narrative, he gives an impressionistic catalogue of the objects stored in the warehouses ("Bales from Bermuda, towers of Malay teak; / Satins and spices from the Yangtse's mouth") and the sounds heard outside of them ("Lapping of waters, and the half-heard creak / Of ropes and spars"). In the poem's final line he speaks of the warehouses offering "some vital thing" that the viewer "cannot name" (AT 307–8). This "vital thing" that is left unnamed in Lovecraft's poem would seem to be analogous to the "naturally ingrained and traditional images" that he argued are evoked by familiar art objects in "A Living Heritage"; these otherwise unremarkable warehouses were important, in other words, because they were part of what made Providence recognizably itself.

One of the ways in which the warehouses rendered the city recognizable was by contributing a certain structural density to the streetscape. When the courthouse was built and 50 South Main was demolished, the loss of this old building was a sore blow to the antiquarian; but in and of itself the loss of any one small building could produce no very great change in the atmosphere or aesthetic of the city as a whole. Replacing the three long blocks of the old brick row with a park, on the other hand, would change the atmosphere of the entire Market Square area. The characteristic feel of pre-automotive cities like colonial-era Providence is largely a product of densely clustered buildings and complex networks of narrow streets. The old brick row created this effect in the Market Square area by hemming South Main Street into a narrow channel at the foot of the hill and opening up a network of alleys on the east side of the street. On Water Street, meanwhile, the old brick row formed the most visible face of the neighborhood when approached from the west. Simply by virtue of its size and centrality, the old brick row shaped the experience of anyone who visited Providence. Tearing these buildings down would be a sore blow not because it would involve the loss of an antiquarian treasure but because it would erase a familiar feature of the city, one of the things that made Providence unique. As articulated in his poem, then, Lovecraft's argument against demolition rests not on an investment of value in the past as such, but rather on an investment in the familiar atmosphere of the Market Square neighborhood that these structures helped to define.

Similarly, the argument Lovecraft makes in his editorial in favor of preserving the familiar atmosphere of the city does not hinge on the nostalgic claim that the traditional is inherently valuable, but rather on a pair of superficially paradoxical propositions regarding the nature of urban development: he suggests, first, that successful modernization of the Market Square area depended upon the preservation of the neighborhood's traditional atmosphere, and, secondly, that that atmosphere itself could best be preserved and enhanced through the implementation of modernizing changes. The new courthouse, which is still in use today, is in many ways a very modern structure, but the massive and technologically up-to-date building is dressed in the architectural detailing of traditional eighteenth-century Providence, and its designers have been praised for their successful integration of the new structure into the historical neighborhood. It was precisely because of the courthouse's successful imitation of traditional architecture, Lovecraft argued, that it was necessary to save the old brick row, as "no other building or buildings, and no open landscape development, could compare with this old row as a frame for the tall, white-belfried newcomer" (MW 514). On its own, the courthouse is just a clever imitation of colonial American design, but if it were to take its place within a densely built colonial neighborhood the imitation would "derive . . . an additional grace and mellowness" (MW 513). Conversely, the faux-historical courthouse would produce a "harmony with the old brick row" and give the old warehouses "an improved scenic position" (MW 514, 515). Here, then, Lovecraft has turned both the conservative and the avant-garde arguments on their heads; the old brick row is, in his account, neither a precious remnant of a disappearing world that is threatened by the forces of change, nor is it an outmoded obstacle to be swept away in the name of progress. Instead it becomes a co-conspirator with the modern courthouse: together, they had the potential to be more than either could be on its own, a sort of composite architectural time machine "bridging the years between the early maritime Providence and the modern metropolis" (MW 514).[6]

---

6. Nor was HPL's ambition simply to save everything he could from the wrecking crews; he advocated for the demolition of several old structures in the neighborhood that were either in an irrecoverable state of disrepair or aesthetically at odds with the overall Georgian style of the Market Square area, arguing that the removal of these antique buildings would amplify the aesthetic consistency of the courthouse and

More radically, Lovecraft advocated an extensive renovation of the old brick row itself, involving a thorough synthesis of traditional and modern building practices. Recognizing that the city no longer had any need for the warehouses in the capacity for which they had been originally designed, he suggested that they be adapted to changing circumstances rather than condemned as obsolete; specifically, he proposed using them to house a new Hall of Records, as the insufficient size of the building previously used for this purpose was one of the original justifications given for the entire courthouse project. By blocking off the alleys that bisected the brick row and opening up the internal walls, Lovecraft argued, "as large a continuous structure as desired can be made of the venerable warehouses, linked where the gaps occur." The newly inter-connected complex would then be gutted and fitted with "floors, partitions, and stacks of modern fireproof construction" (MW 515). The result would be a complex hybrid, a shell of early nineteenth-century brick marked with regular bands of new construction and wrapped around a modern core of steel and reinforced concrete. This creative adaptation of the city's existing infrastructure would satisfy the developer as much as it would the preservationist; in it, Lovecraft wrote, "the grace of the ancient walls and roof-line would remain, and the ends of practicality prosper without loss to quaintness and tradition" (MW 515). Most importantly, the old brick row would continue to serve as a familiar reminder of the city's past while participating in the life of the evolving city in the present, evoking "ingrained and traditional images" while accommodating Providence's changing needs.[7]

Given that he was willing to see the old brick row gutted and transformed, it seems fair to say that Lovecraft's objection to the planned demolition was not an objection to progress as such, but to the iconoclastic idea that the new must necessarily be pursued at the expense of the familiar. As a project of wholesale demolition and replacement the courthouse threatened to erase the familiar aesthetic atmosphere of Providence, but Lovecraft argued that if it was handled with care, as a managing of the

---

warehouses.

7. HPL does not mention how very appropriate it was that he proposed this complex palimpsest of a building be used as a repository for the city's records; this usage would add yet another layer of historical complexity, with the old-new structure literally containing the archive that represents the history of Providence.

city's architectural resources, then the project could be developed in a way that not only maintained but actually enhanced that atmosphere. His proposal for the old brick row is thus not anti-modern at all—or rather, it is only as anti-modern as the artistic novelties proposed by other modernist innovators who sought new means of protecting and revitalizing enervated cultural traditions. Rejecting both the desire for a new version of Providence and the attempt to preserve an older Providence, Lovecraft advocated for a transformation that would allow the city to become something new without ceasing to be what it had once been. Citing the practical, aesthetic, and cultural benefits of development that works with rather than replaces existing building stock, Lovecraft's old brick row proposal is a concrete example of the practice of traditionally sensitive innovation that he described theoretically in "A Living Heritage." In these texts, architecture triggers neither an escapist turn toward the past nor a headlong flight into the future, but instead acts as a site upon which modern historical subjects must try to produce a livable present through the active management of their cultural legacy.

Lovecraft failed, in the end, to save the old brick row, and no trace of the warehouses remain in what is today Providence's Memorial Park. Shortly after the demolition had been completed, he wrote in a letter to Toldridge that "[m]odernity, in the main, is an *amplification* rather than *negation* of the past" (ET 159). For Lovecraft, the demolition of the old brick row represented not only the loss of an irreplaceable piece of the American tradition, but the squandering of an opportunity to create the modern American future. For readers today, his efforts to save these warehouses remain a striking illustration of his attempt to develop a modern art practice that was both suited to the future and worthy of the past.

Works Cited

Bealer, Tracy. "'The Innsmouth Look': H. P. Lovecraft's Ambivalent Modernism." *Journal of Philosophy: A Cross-Disciplinary Inquiry* 6, No. 14 (Winter 2011): 44–50.

Cady, John Hutchins. *The Civic and Architectural Development of Providence, 1636–1950*. Providence: The Book Shop, 1957.

Evans, Timothy H. "A Last Defense Against the Dark: Folklore, Horror, and the Uses of Tradition in the Works of H. P. Lovecraft." *Journal of Folklore Research* 42, No. 1 (2005): 99–135.

"Historic Buildings Are Priceless Asset to City." Letter. *Providence Sunday Journal* (March 1929): 5.

Le Corbusier (Charles Édouard Jeanneret). *The City of To-morrow and Its Planning*. Trans. Frederick Etchells. 1924. Mineola, NY: Dover, 1987.

——. *Towards a New Architecture*. 1927. Mineola, NY: Dover, 1985.

Lovecraft, H. P. *Letters to Elizabeth Toldridge and Anne Tillery Renshaw*. Ed. David E. Schultz and S. T. Joshi. New York: Hippocampus Press, 2014. [ET]

——. *Letters to James F. Morton*. Ed. David E. Schultz and S. T. Joshi. New York: Hippocampus Press, 2011. [JFM]

——. *Miscellaneous Writings*. Ed. S. T. Joshi. Sauk City, WI: Arkham House, 1995. [MW]

Waugh, Robert H. "Landscapes, Selves, and Others in Lovecraft." In *An Epicure in the Terrible: A Centennial Anthology of Essays in Honor of H. P. Lovecraft*, ed., David E. Schultz and S. T. Joshi. 1991. New York: Hippocampus Press, 2011. 230–55.

"The Passing of Some Hundred-Year-Old Waterfront Landmarks." *Netopian* (November 1929): 7–11.

Tentacles in the Madhouse: The Role of the Asylum in the Fiction of H. P. Lovecraft

Troy Rondinone
Southern Connecticut State University

On 12 May 1903, G. Alder Blumer, head of the American Medico-Psychological Association, gave a presidential address filled with foreboding. Modern asylums, he explained, could not stem the rising tide of "defectives" (17). He advocated stricter marriage laws and tougher immigration laws. At a lecture a few years earlier, Blumer had gone so far as to praise the ancient Scottish tradition of burying alive unfit children and their mothers. He'd noted, "from the point of view of science the cruel and remorseless Scot was more advanced than his descendants of our day" (quoted in Dowbiggin 1997, 84). Blumer's views were not anomalous. Rather, they were the advanced, educated opinions of a well-respected doctor. When he said all these things, he was superintendent of Butler Hospital for the Insane. Located about a mile and a half from H. P. Lovecraft's home, Butler would be the place where both of Lovecraft's parents ended their days.

For Lovecraft, Butler was a dark place. In fact, in the early twentieth century the very word "asylum" had so many unhappy connotations that psychiatrists had started changing the name of their institutions to "hospitals" (Rothman 319-20). Overcrowding, rough treatments, bizarre therapies, and an overall lack of standardization wreaked havoc on scientific pretense. Fiction was not kind either. Starting with Poe's 1845 short story "The System of Dr. Tarr and Professor Fether," asylums were regularly described as places where the sane become crazed, where society is inverted, and where liberty is negated (Poe 359-76). While Lovecraft had personally visited Butler Hospital on numerous occasions, his experience with that institution was only that of a traveler through its beautiful gardens. He never set foot inside, even in his mother's last days (*IAP* 306). This is important. Lovecraft's knee-jerk fear reflected not just his own worry about the madhouse but also that of the broader culture.

This essay will explore the asylum in the fiction of H. P. Lovecraft. Employing historian David S. Reynolds's definition of cultural biography, I aim to "fit" Lovecraft into his literary and historical milieu, digging into the deeper, wider conversation between America's imaginary of the asylum and its place in Lovecraft's tales (Reynolds 9). The insane were stigmatized in the early twentieth century, their troubles commonly linked to racial backwardness and evolutionary decline. Lovecraft employed common referents of madness, scientific pessimism, and Social Darwinism to build his fictional asylums, and each of these areas will be explored in turn.

A couple of caveats before I proceed. This essay is not intended to be an exhaustive review of *all* asylum references in the work of Lovecraft. I focus mainly on key stories such as "The Call of Cthulhu," "The Whisperer in Darkness," "Beyond the Wall of Sleep," *The Case of Charles Dexter Ward*, "The Thing on the Doorstep," and "The Shadow over Innsmouth." Secondly, it should be clear I am not focusing on *real* mental institutions. I will note historical connections when necessary, but as a cultural historian I am more intrigued by the way art takes some things from life and leaves others in the shadows.

The Tenuous Nature of Sanity

The loss of sanity figures predominantly in Lovecraft. It happens when the mind breaks after glimpsing the unnamable horror of an indifferent, grotesque cosmos. As he notes at the start of "The Call of Cthulhu," our ignorance is really a "merciful thing." It shields us from the truth that would drive us mad. In this tale, the coming of the monstrous god from the sea signals a worldwide panic among certain types of people—namely, the overly sensitive and the racially degenerate. Cthulhu's first victim is Henry Anthony Wilcox, a "dark young man of neurotic and excited aspect" (CF 2.24), who is inspired to create a "shockingly frightful" (CF 2.23) sculpture of the tentacle-headed god. Wilcox is a student at the Rhode Island School of Design and from "an excellent family" (CF 2.25). However, he is also eccentric and prone to "strange stories and odd dreams" (CF 2.25). He loses his mind and is taken into his family's care under the watch of a physician.

Wilcox's experiences, we learn, are part of a much bigger pattern.

People around the world are going insane. Although "New England's traditional 'salt of the earth'" and scientific types are largely unaffected, the "artists and poets" become touched with a temporary madness. One architect, "with leanings toward theosophy," goes "violently insane" and dies as result. A man in London wakes from a nightmare and jumps to his doom. Then there are the religious cultists, the "native unrest" in India, the "Voodoo orgies" in "Hayti," the crazed "Levantines" in New York, and so on. Finally, "so numerous are the recorded troubles in insane asylums, that only a miracle can have stopped the medical fraternity from noting strange parallelisms and drawing mystified conclusions" (CF 2.29-30). The madness lasts only a short while, and Wilcox is able to experience a full recovery.

Madness in "The Call of Cthulhu" is a real, biological thing. It affects the brain and causes people to behave irrationally and suicidally. Writes Lovecraft of Cthulhu, "The Thing cannot be described—there is no language for such abysms of shrieking and immemorial lunacy, such eldritch contradictions of all matter, force, and cosmic order." Two initial witnesses die instantly of fright. Another who escapes "looked back and went mad, laughing shrilly as he kept on laughing at intervals till death found him" (CF 2.54). The terrifying message here is that sanity is a brittle shield, shattered by the fatal knowledge of indescribable terror.

A few other examples will demonstrate Lovecraft's recurrent theme of fragile sanity. In "The Horror at Red Hook," Detective Thomas F. Malone goes on an extended leave of absence after experiencing the horrors of the Beyond. He knows better than to try to relate his experiences: "To hint to unimaginative people of a horror beyond all human conception—a horror of houses and blocks and cities leprous and cancerous with evil dragged from elder worlds—would be merely to invite a padded cell instead of restful rustication, and Malone was a man of sense despite his mysticism" (CF 1.482). In "The Outsider," the protagonist is a ghoul who doesn't realize his true self until he catches his reflection in a mirror. The image drives him nearly mad and he winds up on antidepressants (the "balm" of "nepenthe" [CF 1.272], a drug used to combat sorrow with literary references going back to the Greeks, and which seems to be used in a metaphorical sense here, perhaps even meaning simple forgetfulness of one's own horrid fate).

In "The Whisperer in Darkness," Lovecraft makes clever use of the brittle shield metaphor. In this story, a professor of literature, Albert Wilmarth, communicates via letter with a recluse named Henry Wentworth Akeley regarding an invading extraterrestrial race. This is not *E.T.*;

these beings are intent on mining a metal unavailable on their planet and capturing human brains for cosmic transport, with the ultimate possible goal of human enslavement. Akeley's scientific objectivity convinces Wilmarth that his outlandish story might be true. "The array of vital evidence was damnably vast and overwhelming; and the cool, scientific attitude of Akeley—an attitude removed as far as imaginable from the demented, the fanatical, the hysterical, or even the extravagantly speculative—had a tremendous effect on my thought and judgment" (CF 2.483). But it is an unacceptable truth. At one point Akeley even invites commitment to a mental institution: "They can lock me up in a madhouse if they want to—it'll be better than what the *other creatures* would do" (CF 2.498). Wilmarth recognizes the inevitable result of agreeing with Akeley's views: madness. As he explains,

> what [Akeley] had learned since making his pact with the Outside Things was almost too much for sanity to bear. Even now I absolutely refuse to believe what he implied about the constitution of ultimate infinity, the juxtaposition of dimensions, and the frightful position of our known cosmos of space and time in the unending chain of linked cosmos-atoms which makes up the immediate super-cosmos of curves, angles, and material and semi-material electronic organisation. (CF 2.520)

In the end, Wilmarth finds out firsthand that the aliens are already here. Only it may be too late. Fleeing Akeley's house, the narrator reflects, "The ride that followed was a piece of delirium out of Poe or Rimbaud or the drawing of Doré [. . .] If my sanity is still unshaken, I am lucky" (CF 3.538).

Just as with Poe, for Lovecraft madness was just a short step away from rationality. Also like Poe, Lovecraft trucked in current medical language to lend realism and deepen the horror. For example, variations of the term "neurosis" seem to pop up frequently. An idea popularized by Freud, by the 1920s *neurosis* had seeped its way into American bourgeois culture. Though Lovecraft dismissed Freud overtly (he scoffs at Freud's "puerile symbolism" [CF 1.71] in "Beyond the Wall of Sleep"), he often uses what might be termed "pop Freudianism" in his stories.[1]

---

1. *IAP* 1.469 quotes a letter from HPL to Anne Tillery Renshaw dated 1 June 1921: "Dr. Sigmund Freud of Vienna, whose system of psycho-analysis I have begun to investigate, will probably prove the end of idealistic thought. In details, I think he has

A few words about the rising popularity of Freud in Lovecraft's day can help provide context. The famed analyst's influence in America dates to the end of the nineteenth century, with William James's 1893-94 Harvard lectures on Freud, Breuer's studies on hysteria, and Havelock Ellis's review of *Studies on Hysteria* in 1898. By the time that Freud lectured at Clark University in his only trip to America in 1909, educated men and women were probably acquainted with his thoughts on hysteria and sexuality, as well as concepts like complexes and association tests (though these ideas were more the product of Carl Jung's take on psychoanalysis).

In 1910, broader audiences of specialists were exposed to Freud with the English publication of *Three Essays on the Theory of Sexuality*, in which he shockingly argued that sexuality is not something that arrives with puberty but rather is shaped by erotic infantile experiences. Around 1915, mainstream periodicals started taking notice, and by the 1920s intellectuals helped make his ideas commonplace among the bourgeois (see Dowbiggin 2011). As Frederick Lewis Allen recalled, in the 1920s the "Freudian gospel" had "imbedded itself in the American mind after being filtered through the successive minds of interpreters and popularizers and guileless readers and people who had heard guileless readers talk about it" (85).

According to S. T. Joshi, Lovecraft might not have read any of Freud's works firsthand, but he probably would have been familiar with his ideas through magazine articles and discussions (*IAP* 469). A few textual examples reveal Lovecraft's conversance with Freudian concepts. In "The Thing on the Doorstep," for example, he gives us a bizarre oedipal situation. Asenath Waite, a strong-willed woman, suffers from both hereditary insanity and a strong desire to be a man. She marries weak-willed Edward Derby and dominates him, taking control of his body. It turns out, however, that she is in fact a receptacle for her wizard father Ephraim, who supposedly died insane. So now we have a daughter, currently occupied by her father, who wants to be her husband, so she can fully realize him/herself. Freud theorized that girls, once they discover that they have no penis, feel "castrated" and become consumed with jealousy. They overcome this "penis

---

his limitations; and I am inclined to accept the modifications of Adler, who in placing the ego above the eros makes a scientific return to the position which Nietzsche assumed for wholly philosophical reasons." On the rising influence of Freudian ideas and words in the 1920s, see Douglas 123-29.

envy" by replacing their longing for a member with an intimacy with their father and, ultimately, a desire for a child and a husband. In Asenath's case, her "romance" with her father makes them a single being, one still capable of male envy. Interestingly, Lovecraft uses a classic pop-Freudian term in noting that husband Edward Derby "transferred his dependence from the parental image to the new and stronger image" (CF 3.331). Edward's "transference" is metaphorical; his wife's is literal. Adding one more layer—the implicit sexism in Freud's analysis of the female psyche—Lovecraft tells us that Asenath "wanted to be a man—to be fully human—that was why she got hold of him" (CF 3.339). Here Lovecraft implies that Edward's maleness is the reason why Ephraim needs his body. It will lift him above the semi-humanity of Asenath's Second Sex. It's not necessary to snoop about Lovecraft's library to see that he was culturally conversant with Freud's controversial ideas.

In "The Shadow out of Time," Lovecraft provides his most extended treatment of pop mind science. In this story, the main character Professor Nathaniel Wingate Peaslee is tossed out of his own body, while an alien occupies him for five years. During this time his odd behavior makes him "a mild celebrity among the psychologists," an example of a person with a "secondary personality" (CF 3.367). Later, to discover what happened, Peaslee makes use of "psychologists, historians, anthropologists, and mental specialists of wide experience, and by a study that included all records of split personalities from the days of daemoniac-possession legends to the medically realistic present" (CF 3.374). He wonders if he suffered "a special type of delusion afflicting those who had suffered lapses of memory" (CF 3.376). Was his "subconscious mind" trying to "fill up a perplexing blank with pseudo-memories" (CF 3.376)? The "alienists" ultimately decide that he did not suffer "true insanity," but rather part of that class of "neurotic disorders" that Lovecraft's fellow East Coast intelligentsia often incorporated into their conversations. Of course science is wrong. Peaslee will ultimately "prove" his sanity by discovering a text he wrote as a Yithian many eons ago.

Lovecraft appears to be fairly up-to-date in terms of mental hospital commitment procedure. In "The Thing on the Doorstep," Edward Derby has a breakdown that, even if supernatural in causation, reflects the sort of agitation that could get a person committed. Derby "suddenly shrieked and leaped up from his chair with a look of uncontrollable fright" and proceeded to rant about his "brain" (CF 3.349). His "frenzy" dulls into a kind of catatonia, and though his friend tries to give him more time to regain his senses, he continues experiencing "frightful seizures" (CF 3.350). Derby is a man of wealth, so his personal "doctor, banker, and lawyer" are all consulted before two additional "specialist colleagues" (CF 3.350) of his family physician are contacted. They find him to be insane and he is incarcerated in the Arkham Sanitarium.

Commitment typically involved one or more specialists agreeing on a course of asylum confinement. In "The Thing on the Doorstep" Lovecraft is careful to record the details of a manic break followed by the vigilant evaluation of medical specialists. After a time, Derby appears to be sane and the protagonist, Daniel Upton, is brought in to help him re-enter society. At this point Daniel realizes two things: one, that the man in the asylum *is* "sane," and two, that he is *not* Edward. The truth of soul transference makes it clear that the possessed Edward must be killed, and so Daniel shoots him dead in the "madhouse."

Lovecraft knew that the asylum had negative connotations that kept people from sending loved ones there. In "The Colour out of Space," a New England country family decides to keep its deranged mother out of the "county asylum" so long "as she was harmless to herself and others" (CF 2.100). The wealthy parents of Henry Wilcox in "The Call of Cthulhu" similarly seem to decide that home care is better for their manic son. When folks can't be kept in the attic, the Arkham Sanitarium awaits.

The Limits of Science

The asylum was supposedly a place where patients received treatment and cured their madness. Yet the reality was far sadder. As Lovecraft learned firsthand, for many the asylum was a place to die. His father's "paralysis" (probably neurosyphilis) could not be reversed at Butler Hospital. The asylum could not even prevent death by nervous exhaustion. In the case of his mother, who was committed to Butler for "traumatic psychosis" due to "an awareness of approaching bankruptcy," death came following a botched gall bladder surgery (summary of doctor record, quoted in *IAP* 130). The asylum, in both Lovecraft's life and the lives of many others, was an abattoir.

Statistically, the reality of mental institutions was very dispiriting. Between 1903 and 1933 the number of patients in mental hospitals grew from 143,000 to 366,000. Most of the insane were warehoused in massive hospitals containing over 1,000 beds. The largest such place, the Georgia State Sanatorium in Milledgeville, housed over 10,000 by 1950 (Burns 38). Patients experienced atrocious patient-to-doctor ratios, bombardments of opiates, dubious treatments, and general neglect. People sent to mental hospitals were often in a bad physical state. In New York State, 20 percent of admittees between 1910 and 1920 were in the final stages of syphilitic paresis, and 87 percent of these expired in the hospital, typically within four years (Grob 125-26; Shorter 53-59). (Lovecraft's father lasted a little over five years.)

Another common diagnosis was *dementia praecox*. Coined by Emil Kraepelin, this term referred to symptoms of derangement afflicting young adults. Later called "schizophrenia," dementia praecox was familiar enough that Lovecraft used it in *The Case of Charles Dexter Ward* (CF 2.305), where a mind doctor is trying to diagnose young Mr. Ward. Ward is actually mad because his body is occupied by the ancient evil wizard Joseph Curwen.

Lovecraft has others condemned to the asylum for similar supernatural reasons. Edward Derby in "The Thing on the Doorstep" is committed because he is resisting mind transference. Joe Slater in "Beyond the Wall of Sleep" is confined because an alien occupies his body. An unnamed "business or government man" winds up "crazy and is out at Danvers" (CF 3.165) for noticing something fishy in Innsmouth. Then there are zombies like Dr. Allan Halsey in "Herbert West—Reanimator," who "beat its head against the walls of a padded cell for sixteen years" (CF 1.302) before being rescued by its fellow undead, to wreak havoc on the living.

As Lovecraft knew firsthand, the asylum could be a hopeless place, and doctors there could only quarantine, not cure. *The Case of Charles Dexter Ward* begins with an extended discussion of a missing patient at "a private hospital for the insane near Providence, Rhode Island" (CF 2.215). Ward is placed there after his "mere eccentricity" turns into "dark mania" (CF 2.215). The physicians are baffled by his case. Physiological signs point to an illness not recorded, "in even the latest and most exhaustive of treatises" (CF 2.216).

The fundamental insufficiency of mind medicine moves the plot along in *Charles Dexter Ward*. Figuring out just when Ward lost his faculties forms a series of narrative signposts. Just when did Ward *really* go insane? Apparently a whole team of psychiatrists debate this point. The "more academic school of alienists" think he lost his mind early in his investigations of his demonic relative Curwen. The "slightly less" (CF 2.300, 286) group date it later, following Ward's European trip that ends in strange sounds coming from his attic laboratory. It is Dr. Marinus Bicknell Willett, the family physician, who is most accurate. He finds that Ward still has "balance" and a regular physiological makeup when he returns from Europe, though he "could never reach the young man's inner psychology" (CF 2.287). But Dr. Willett can't help noticing that the youth is looking more and more like the portrait of Curwen on the wall. Eventually he learns that Ward's body is occupied by Curwen, and he is forced, like the protagonist of "The Thing on the Doorstep," to kill the creature in the asylum.

In the end, Dr. Willett transforms himself from "solicitous family physician" to "ruthless and implacable avenger" (CF 2.363). Not unlike Dr. Sam Loomis in the film *Halloween*, Dr. Willett realizes the asylum cannot fix some people, and only total destruction will do. He also realizes that some things are best left in the dark. He cannot tell anyone about it because "it is a madness out of time and a horror from beyond the spheres which no police or lawyers or *alienists* could ever fathom or grapple with" (CF 2.364; my emphasis).

In Lovecraft's tales, science offers no means of succor or safety. Rather, it is a flashlight that permits humans to peer into the face of cosmic horror and lose their minds. In stories like "The Colour out of Space," research from local professors from Miskatonic University deepens the mystery of the alien life-form invading New England. In *At the Mountains of Madness* a scientific expedition provides us pages of delicious, nuanced analyses of the Beyond. Ultimately, Lovecraft's oeuvre offers a negative assessment of science. Dr. Willett gives us perhaps the best Lovecraftian summation right before he kills Curwen: "a man can't tamper with Nature beyond certain limits, and every horror you have woven will rise up to wipe you out" (CF 2.365).

Degeneration

Monsters aren't hard to find if you look long enough. In Lovecraft's time, racial science had spawned new heights of monstrous description of the "lesser" races. Books like William Z. Ripley's *The Races of Europe* and Madison Grant's *The Passing of the Great Race* (the latter praised alike by Theodore Roosevelt and Adolf Hitler) brought to readers grotesque descriptions of different peoples with scientific rigor and academic imprimatur (Whitaker 65; Spiro xxi). Ripley, a Sociology professor at MIT, interested himself with brow ridges, noses, lips, cephalic indexes, and other categorizations that led to statements such as, "The aristocracy everywhere tends toward the blond and tall type, as we should expect" (330). In a 1908 *Atlantic Monthly* article, Ripley rued the "great horde of Slavs, Huns, and Jews" that was washing up on our shores, though he ultimately concludes, "in due course of time, even if the Anglo-Saxon stock be physically inundated by the engulfing flood, the torch of its civilization and ideals may still continue to illuminate the way" (759). Criminologist Cesare Lombroso was also very popular, and his influential "criminal anthropology" provided descriptions of physical "abnormalities" that indicated hereditary criminality (1).

Worst of all were the descriptions given by whites of African Americans. Black people had long been treated with violence and disrespect. Now scientists could reference cranial and anthropological studies to "prove" animalistic attributes. The situation reached a new low when the Bronx Zoo put an African named Ota Benga in the Monkey House in 1904, where he briefly lived with an orangutan. The curator thought it would be even more amusing to litter the cage with bones, so he did. Lovecraft's enthusiastic racism fit into a society where some of the brightest minds posited some of the most horrific theories. The director of the American Museum of Natural History, Henry Fairfield Osborn, opened the Second International Eugenics Congress on 21 September 1921 with an address that heartily recommended the sterilization of the unfit. Perhaps the ultimate evidence of the popularity of race science and eugenics was the passage of the Immigration Act of 1924, which used an outdated census to target peoples deemed inferior—Asians, Southern and Eastern Europeans, Jews, and the mentally impaired (Kuhl 38-39).

Growing out of eugenic ideas, insanity was widely believed to be an inherited trait indicative of inferior "breeding." "Mental defectives" were prevented from marrying, segregated off in asylums, and sterilized. Explained urologist William J. Robinson, "Such individuals have no rights. They have no right in the first instance to be born, but having been born, they have no right to propagate their kind." Perhaps it is not so shocking that both the *New England Journal of Medicine* and the *New York Times* defended Hitler's program of sterilizing the insane in the 1930s (Whitaker 58, 64).

Though these trends competed with more progressive notions that saw race in less biological terms, in the marketplace of ideas, American belief tended toward the monstrous (it would not be until after World War II that eugenics got a bad name). Obviously Lovecraft trucked in the harshest of these schools of thought. His well-documented fear of immigrants, Jews, and blacks indicate that "inferior" races spelled horror to him (*IAP* 112). What is pertinent here are the ideas regarding degeneracy that creep into his tales.

Degeneracy theory posited that evolution sometimes went in reverse. According to this line of reasoning, Darwinism operated on two levels simultaneously. On the one hand, those who were fittest survived and prospered. On the other hand, modern civilization had perversely created circumstances that allowed for a march back into primitivism. Psychiatrists and others had for decades worried that civilization itself was a cause of insanity. New "scientific" theories of race encouraged some to think that inferior "germ plasm" could wreak havoc on pure racial stocks, leading civilization into decline. Lovecraft's New York City experience seemed to spark the worst in this line of thought (he once referred to the immigrant neighborhoods there as places of "degenerate gelatinous fermentation" [quoted in Poole 97]). Many during this time believed that insanity was evidence of degeneration. Charles Darwin himself rued the fact that asylums were protecting the "unfit" from natural selection and exacerbating the problem. In *The Descent of Man* (1871) he commented that asylums were an example of "care wrongly directed" leading to "the degeneration of a domestic race" (161–62).

In Lovecraft's stories, degeneration and the asylum connect just as they did in the public mind. Of course, here the supernatural is always involved. In "Beyond the Wall of Sleep," Joe Slater is committed to "the state psychopathic institution." He is described as a "typical denizen of the Catskill Mountain region; one of those strange, repellent scions of a primitive colonial peasant stock whose isolation for nearly three centuries in the hilly fastnesses of a little-traveled countryside has caused them to sink to a kind of barbaric degeneracy, rather than advance with their more fortunately placed brethren of the thickly settled districts" (*CF* 1.72). Here Lovecraft seconds the popular notion that state hospitals were filled with the poor and the degenerate.

The horror in this case is that Slater might not be what he at first seems. He seems capable of imaginings beyond the capacity of an inferior type. Reflects the narrator, "How, I often asked myself, could the stolid imagination of a Catskill degenerate conjure up sights whose very possession argued a lurking spark of genius?" (*CF* 1.77). The dilemma is solved with the help of a kind of mind radio that reveals that Slater is the shell for a cosmic being battling an interstellar force. Slater's human form dies about this point. Says the alien of Joe, "He is better dead, for he was unfit to bear the active intellect of cosmic entity" (CF 1.83). In other words, this degenerate was at once suitable for possession but yet too "unfit" for long-term alien proprietorship. Lovecraft gets it both ways. Joe Slater is an inferior breed who is easily inhabited by an alien, yet his lowliness makes him incapable of sustaining the alien's life force. Eventually the alien goes off to battle with his foe, what humans know as the star Algol. When the narrator tries to explain the truth to the hospital superintendent, he learns that science is not ready for the supernatural. The psychiatrist "assures me on his professional honour that Joe Slater was but a low-grade paranoiac, whose fantastic notions must have come from crude hereditary folk-tales which circulate even in the most decadent of communities" (CF 1.85).

Degeneracy and the asylum combine in other stories as well. In "The Shadow over Innsmouth," the protagonist learns of his horrifying heredity—his ancestors interbred with fish creatures (Deep Ones) and he is slowly showing signs of transformation. He weighs his options. Should he shoot himself as his uncle Douglas did after learning of his racially degenerate fate? Or should he watch the transformation and lose his mind, winding up in a "sanitarium" like his cousin? He ultimately decides to break the cousin out of the "Canton madhouse" and together to live in the sea, "amidst wonder and glory for ever" (CF 3.230). As with "Beyond the Wall of Sleep," in "Innsmouth" Lovecraft capitalizes on fears of degeneracy and its imprisonment in the asylum while simultaneously offering an alternative, otherworldly explanation. Degeneration in this story really hits home—the narrator himself learns he is a hereditary time-bomb.

In Lovecraft's day, family was destiny. The same year he wrote *Charles Dexter Ward* the Supreme Court decided in an 8-1 vote that that the sterilization of the feebleminded was constitutional. In *Buck v. Bell* (1927), the Court heard a case in which a "feebleminded" woman named Carrie Buck was raped and later sterilized by the state of Virginia. Chief Justice Oliver Wendell Holmes, Jr., argued that such degenerates as Buck "sap the strength" of our country. He drove home his argument by reflecting on Buck's family history: "three generations of imbeciles are enough" (quoted in Hall 39). Lovecraft, who personally might have feared for his own family history, provides the genealogy of generations of fish folk in "Innsmouth." As with his other stories, mankind is doomed.

Conclusion: The Asylum and Weird Madness

H. P. Lovecraft lived much of his life in the shadow of the asylum. He didn't like to mention his family connection to Butler Hospital, but he saw fit to use mental institutions regularly in his fiction. In his tales these are places that house those afflicted by dark cosmic forces, where the hopeless lived out their existences under the care of ignorant mind doctors. The options for his committed characters are chillingly limited. Sometimes they escape ("Herbert West—Reanimator"), sometimes they are killed by heroes saving the world (*The Case of Charles Dexter Ward* and "The Thing on the Doorstep"), sometimes they are killed by aliens ("Beyond the Wall of Sleep"), and sometimes they are freed to commune with otherworldly friends (as plotted by the protagonist of "The Shadow over Innsmouth").

Lovecraft built on and expanded commonly held fictional tropes of the asylum. In the footsteps of Poe and others (including even Louisa May Alcott, who used a private madhouse to great effect in her 1863 short story "A Whisper in the Dark"), Lovecraft knew that mental hospitals made perfect horror settings. For earlier writers, family conspiracies were typical causes of commitment. For Lovecraft, the supernatural was always involved.

Reflecting his times, Lovecraft did not feel the need to provide realistic accounts of asylum treatments. Like the contemporaneous *Dracula* plays in which the audience watched long stretches of Dr. Seward's sanitarium without viewing depictions of treatments, Lovecraft gave us simple settings to show the reader that cosmic terror leads to madness, and that madness might land you in a hopeless place. He is ultimately telling us that mankind's odds in the face of the unfathomable are hopeless, too.

But Lovecraft did not merely *use* fictional asylum settings—he *expanded* the literature. In linking madness to otherworldly causation and using scientific descriptors for effect, he created a new sub-genre of asylum fiction—what I shall call "weird madness." By having his asylum inmates incarcerated not because they have been framed but because they actually deserve to be there, even if for reasons unexplainable by mind science, he did not condemn the asylum in the same manner as earlier writers. Rather, he makes it more horrifying because it makes not one whit of difference whether people are incarcerated or not. Mankind can try to help the deranged, but failure is inevitable. Weird madness is never curable and is often fatal.

At the heart of weird madness is a tenor of realism. In Lovecraft's day people were very worried about asylums. Lovecraft capitalized on this despair, as well as the longer history of the fictional asylum, to construct a *new* place. His asylum was inhabited with humans targeted by aliens, dark magic, and bad science. He did not invent the monster who haunts the asylum (I think George Lippard's magical mentalist Ravoni in *The Quaker City* [1844] should hold this honor), but he did give us monstrous, unearthly patients. One strains to find examples of this before Lovecraft. Later writers would liken society to a vast asylum, a place where we are controlled and medically placated, but entirely unwell all the same. Lovecraft sought to make asylums like society too, though in a different manner. For him, both the asylum and civilization represent the delusory hope of scientific control.

Perhaps Lovecraft's most visible impact on the fictional asylum has less to do with any one story but rather with what others did with his writing. The most famous fantastical asylum must be the Arkham Asylum for the Criminally Insane.[2] Sometime home of the Joker and various other DC comic book criminals, this place, which first appeared in 1974, owes a clear debt to Lovecraft. As Jack C. Harris, the later DC editor who first proposed the idea to writer Denny O'Neil, recalled, "what better asylum could there be for such maniacs than Arkham, the dark dwelling of tormented souls from Lovecraft's horrific tales?" (Voger 5). Here villains are incarcerated, often to escape still unwell.[3] In the landmark graphic novel *Arkham Asylum: A Serious House on Serious Earth*, Batman is told that the lunatics have taken over and are holding hostages. Encountering the Joker and friends, the Dark Knight finds that the medical treatment provided at the institution is worthless, and in fact it has made some (like Two-Face) even worse. The villains are deformed and deranged, but also manically celebratory—in short, this is a combination of Poe's cynical social commentary and Lovecraft's biological degeneracy. Eventually Batman must face his own demons, as might be expected from the writer's heavy-handed Jungian symbolism.

Arkham Asylum has become more popular since 1989 when *Serious House* appeared. One finds it in both the Tim Burton and Christopher

---

2. Also known as the Elizabeth Arkham Asylum for the Criminally Insane.

3. For another possible strand of inheritance, note that Julius Schwartz, who had known HPL, was also editor of DC Comics during this period.

Nolan film cycles, not to mention the 2009 hit video game *Batman: Arkham Asylum*. Does it matter to Batman fans the Lovecraftian origin of this weird place? Probably not. But this is not to say it's only just a name. Lovecraft gave us a haunting, hopeless place where people with dark powers are confined but not healed. Neither Dr. Willett nor the Caped Crusader can help.

Works Cited

Allen, Frederick Lewis. *Only Yesterday: An Informal History of the 1920's.* New York: Harper and Row, 1931.

Blumer, G. Alder "Presidential Address." *American Journal of Insanity* 60, No. 1 (July 1903): 1-18.

Burns, Tom. *Psychiatry: A Very Short Introduction.* London: Oxford University Press, 2006.

Darwin, Charles. *The Descent of Man, and Selection in Relation to Sex, Volume 1.* 1871. New York: D. Appleton & Co., 1872.

Douglas, Ann. *Terrible Honesty: Mongrel Manhattan in the 1920s.* New York: Farrar, Straus & Giroux, 1995.

Dowbiggin, Ian Robert. *Keeping America Sane: Psychiatry and Eugenics in the United States and Canada, 1880-1940.* Ithaca, NY: Cornell University Press, 1997.

———. *The Quest for Mental Health: A Tale of Science, Medicine, Scandal, Sorrow, and Mass Society.* New York: Cambridge University Press, 2011.

Grob, Gerald N. *The Mad among Us: A History of the Care of America's Mentally Ill.* New York: Free Press, 1994.

Hall, Kermit L. *The Oxford Guide to United States Supreme Court Decisions.* New York: Oxford University Press, 1999.

Kuhl, Stephan. *For the Betterment of the Race: The Rise and Fall of the International Movement for Eugenics and Racial Hygiene.* New York: Palgrave Macmillan, 2013.

Lombroso, Cesare. *Criminal Man.* Trans. Mary Gibson and Nicole Hahn Rafter. Durham, NC: Duke University Press, 2006.

McCandless, Peter. "Curative Asylum, Custodial Hospital: The South Carolina Lunatic Asylum and State Hospital, 1828-1920." In *The Confinement of the Insane: International Perspectives, 1800-1965,* ed., Roy

Porter and David Wright. Cambridge: Cambridge University Press, 2003. 173-92.

Miron, Janet. *Prisons, Asylums, and the Public: Institutional Visiting in the Nineteenth Century.* Toronto: University of Toronto Press, 2011.

Morrison, Grant, and Dave McKean. *Arkham Asylum: A Serious House on Serious Earth.* 15th Anniversary Edition. New York: DC Comics, 2004.

Poe, Edgar Allan. *The Portable Edgar Allan Poe.* Ed. J. Gerald Kennedy. New York: Penguin Books, 2006.

Poole, W. Scott. *Monsters in America: Our Historical Obsession with the Hideous and the Haunting.* Waco, TX: University of Baylor Press, 2011.

Reynolds, David S. *John Brown, Abolitionist: The Man Who Killed Slavery, Started the Civil War, and Seeded Civil Rights.* New York: Knopf, 2005.

Reiss, Benjamin. *Theaters of Madness: Insane Asylums and Nineteenth-Century American Culture.* Chicago: University of Chicago Press, 2008.

Ripley, William Z. *The Races of Europe.* London: Kegan Paul, Trench, Trübner & Co., 1900.

———. "The Races of the United States." *Atlantic Monthly* 102 (December 1908): 745-59.

Rothman, David J. *Conscience and Convenience: The Asylum and Its Alternatives in Progressive America.* Boston: Little, Brown, 1980.

Shorter, Edward. *A History of Psychiatry: From the Era of the Asylum to the Age of Prozac.* New York: John Wiley & Sons, 1997.

Spiro, Jonathan Peter. *Defending the Master Race: Conservation, Eugenics, and the Legacy of Madison Grant.* Hanover, NH: University Press of New England, 2009.

Torrey, E. Fuller, and Judy Miller. *The Invisible Plague: The Rise of Mental Illness from 1750 to Present.* New Brunswick, NJ: Rutgers University Press, 2002.

Voger, Mark. *The Dark Age: Grim, Great, and Gimmicky Postmodern Comics.* Raleigh, NC: TwoMorrows Publishing, 2006.

Whitaker, Robert. *Mad in America: Bad Science, Bad Medicine, and the Enduring Mistreatment of the Mentally Ill in America.* Cambridge, MA: Perseus, 2002.

Unspeakable Languages: Lovecraft Editions in Spanish

Juan L. Pérez-de-Luque
University of Cordoba, Spain

The goal of the present study is to overview the different translations and editions of H. P. Lovecraft's work that have been published in Spanish during the last eighty years. A chronological approach will be followed, presenting the different editions from the late 1930s until the most recent translations of the author. At the same time, I will pay attention to the editions and translations that have been released not only in Spain, but also in the rest of the Spanish-speaking countries that published meaningful editions of the Lovecraftian fiction.

Surprisingly enough, the first translation into Spanish from a tale by Lovecraft that I have been able to document took place as early as 1939. "The Diary of Alonzo Typer," translated as "El diario de Alonso Typer," was a collaboration between William Lumley and Lovecraft, originally published in the February 1938 issue of *Weird Tales*, and its translation appeared in the first issue of *Narraciones terroríficas*, published in June 1939.

Narraciones terroríficas was a pioneering publication in the Hispanic world. It was one of the first, if not the first, weird fiction magazine/compilation ever published in Spanish, and the historical and logistical circumstances surrounding its birth are worth noticing. The publishing house of this magazine was Ediciones Molino, whose owner, Pablo Molino, had to flee to Argentina with the onset of the Spanish Civil War in 1936. However, the printing and translations of *Narraciones terroríficas* took place in Barcelona, under the supervision of—or, more accurately, completely done by—José Mallorquí, whose own home address appeared in the volumes as contact address, and who was the real creator and engine of the project. Then, the volumes were sent to Latin America and distributed in several countries, namely Argentina, Mexico, and Chile. In fact, it was difficult to find these volumes in Spain, and according to Hassón, even Mallorquí himself did not own any in his personal library ("José Mallorquí" 287).

Mallorquí had two main sources from which he secured the tales to be translated and published: American and British pulp fictions and classic texts. From the American magazines, *Weird Tales* was the one that provided him with more stories. Following Hassón's statement, Mallorquí did not follow a particular sequence when translating and editing from his original sources ("Múltiples rostros" 254). He worked with whatever material he could find, so the contents in *Narraciones terroríficas* do not follow a particular chronological order if compared with *Weird Tales*.

The collection ran for almost thirteen years, and, as I have previously mentioned, "The Diary of Alonzo Typer" was the first Lovecraft text to be included. However, the cover of the issue did not credit him as author, and only William Lumley appeared as the writer. The same happens with the second tale, "The Curse of Yig," which is a collaboration between Zealia Bishop and Lovecraft, in which only the former appears as the author. However, it would not be fair to blame Mallorquí for the omission of Lovecraft's authorship in both stories, since the original *Weird Tales* issues did not include him either.

These are the different texts that can be found through the 76 existing issues of *Narraciones terroríficas*:

#1 "El diario de Alonso Typer" ("The Diary of Alonzo Typer," with William Lumley; Lovecraft not credited), 1939.

#8 "La maldición de Yig" ("The Curse of Yig," with Zealia Bishop; Lovecraft not credited), 1939.

#9 "Ratas en los muros" ("The Rats in the Walls"), 1939.

#10 "Aire frío" ("Cool Air"), 1939.

#34 "Las declaraciones de Carter" ("The Statement of Randolph Carter"), 1942.

It was not until 1946 that the first book entirely devoted to Lovecraft was published in Spanish. The volume, entitled *El que acecha en el umbral* (*The Lurker at the Threshold*), is an edition of the novel purportedly written by Lovecraft and Derleth (both of them are credited as authors), although in fact written almost entirely by Derleth. It was published in Argentina by Molino, the same publishing house that had previously released *Narraciones terroríficas*. However, it was translated in Argentina by Delia Piquérez, following a different editorial policy than the one that was used with the previously mentioned collection.

After this timid start, there seems to be a significant temporal gap until the appearance of new material in Spanish. In fact, the next text did not arrive until 1956. *En el rincón obscuro*, published in Mexico by Populibros La Prensa, collects up to fifteen different horror stories from Lovecraft and other assorted authors, many of them strongly connected with the Lovecraft Circle (such as Derleth, Robert Bloch, Clark Ashton Smith, Robert E. Howard, and Belknap Long). The volume includes the first Spanish translations of two tales by Lovecraft, "The Music of Eric Zann" ("La música de Eric Zann") and "The Outsider" ("El forastero"). The whole volume was translated by Oscar Kaufmann Parra, and the selection and edition was done by Leo Margulies and Oscar J. Friend, two renowned American pulp fiction editors. The book was announced as a collection of "15 spine-chilling tales from nine of the most famous writers of this genre." Needless to say, most of the authors included in the book were still far from famous when it was published. The fact that the selection was carried out by two relevant pulp editors from the United States might lead us to think that the whole volume was possibly a translation of a volume published in the United States. However, I have been unable to find the corresponding English source, and both stories by Lovecraft had been previously published only in *Weird Tales* (in the case of "The Outsider") and in the *National Amateur* (in the case of "The Music of Erich Zann"). So it is quite possible that the Mexican publishing house asked Margulies and Friend for a selection of texts.

One year later, in 1957, a key volume was published in Argentina (with a second edition issued in 1964). *El color que cayó del cielo* is the first volume exclusively devoted to some of Lovecraft's most important tales. It includes four new stories in Spanish: "El llamado de Cthulhu" ("The Call of Cthulhu"), "El color que cayó del cielo" ("The Colour out of Space"), "El que susurraba en las tinieblas" ("The Whisperer in Darkness"), and *En las montañas alucinantes* (*At the Mountains of Madness*).

This particular book is important in several different aspects. To begin with, the content is remarkable. It is the first time that these four major texts by Lovecraft are compiled and translated, all together in a single volume. Secondly, the publishing house, Minotauro (founded two years before in Buenos Aires), will become a key company in the process of dignifying the genres of science fiction and fantasy in the Spanish-speaking world. It is remarkable, for instance, that the cover of the book moves away from the traditional catchy and sensationalist illustrations that traditionally accompanied the genre and pulp publications. It looks much more restrained, if not serious, than the average. This will be the general editorial line in terms of aesthetic sobriety followed by Minotauro right up to the present day. At the same time, it is the first volume that I have been able to find that includes an introductory essay on the author. It was written by Ricardo Gosseyn, who was also the translator of the volume. The piece is a basic account of Lovecraft's life and work that quotes from several of his letters and essays, previously unpublished, and that includes some major misconceptions, such as proposing that the elemental correspondence between some of the alien gods (Cthulhu-water; Hastur-air) was something imagined by Lovecraft, when it was actually a product of August Derleth's fictional universe. The last fact to be considered about this volume is that Minotauro, probably even at the beginning of its existence, was able to give broad distribution to its books, so this volume might have reached many more readers than the previous editions so far mentioned.

In 1961, in Spain, the publishing house Acervo started editing *Narraciones terroríficas* (not to be confused with the other pulp collection that shares the same title), a series of ten volumes that included texts from different worldwide horror writers, from Nikolai Leskov to José Cadalso to Robert Bloch. Volumes 4 (1964: "The Outsider"/"El extraño," "Cool Air"/ "Aire frío," "The Whisperer in Darkness"/"El susurrador en la oscuridad"), 5 (1964: "The Thing on the Doorstep"/"La cosa en el umbral"), 7 (1966: "The Moon-Bog"/"El pantano luna," "Herbert West—Reanimator"/"Herbert West, reanimador," "The Horror at Red Hook"/"Horror en Red-Hook"), and 8 (1968: "The Hound"/"El sabueso") include stories by Lovecraft. They were all translated by Alfredo Herrera and José Maria Aroca, so some of the tales were receiving their second Spanish translation here, since they had been previously published elsewhere. The most remarkable fact about this collection is that it was the first time Lovecraft reached Spain, twenty-five years after the other *Narraciones terroríficas* were sent to South America from Barcelona. The fourth issue mentions that the collection tried to avoid "excessive gruesomeness that would lower the high literary quality, which is the ultimate goal." It is important to remember that Spain was under Franco's dictatorial regime, and that every artistic product was subject of censorship and control, so anything too grisly or terrifying, or slightly heretical, was cut down by censors.

Meanwhile, in 1963 the collection *Cuentos de terror* released new translations of "The Outsider" and "The Rats in the Walls," as well as the first translation of "The Nameless City." The author of these translations was Rafael Llopis, who would soon become a key name for the reception of Lovecraft in Spain, as will be seen below. Just two years later, a translation of "The Shunned House" appeared in the collective volume *Con los pelos de punta*. This book, published in 1965, is the Spanish edition of Groff Conklin's anthology *Twisted*, which was published in the United States in 1962. *Con los pelos de punta* was distributed by Editoral Molino in Latin America.

In 1966, Acervo published the first volume of *Obras escogidas*, a selection of Lovecraft's fiction. Again, José Maria Aroca was in charge of the translation, and he would work with both previously translated and untranslated material. This volume includes nine tales, as well as a short biographical introduction by José A. Llorens Borras. Among them, we can find the first translations of "The Dreams in the Witch House" and *The Case of Charles Dexter Ward*, together with a new version of *At the Mountains of Madness*. A second volume, published in 1974, collects fourteen more stories and also has a brief introduction by Llorens Borras. This selection will be the Spanish equivalent to the Argentinian volume *El color que cayó del cielo*, and it is considered the first compilation of fiction devoted exclusively to Lovecraft's tales that appeared in Spain. The selection covers all the different stages of the author's work, from his early production ("Dagon") to his oneiric tales ("The Silver Key," *The Dream-Quest of Unknown Kadath*), as well as his most Gothic tales ("The Statement of Randolph Carter," "The Tomb") and some of his most relevant stories, such as the three mentioned above. Of the two introductions, the one contained in the second volume is worth noting. Llorens Borras mentions how the collection covers the different stylistic stages of Lovecraft's output, mentioning Lord Dunsany as one of his evident influences. At the same time, the editor seems to struggle with the classification of the Randolph Carter cycle. He considers these stories autobiographical sketches full of personal opinions and ideology. Finally, the introduction to the second volume also puts forward in a very succinct way some issues that will later become central for many scholars, such as Lovecraft's political views or the speculations about his sexual orientation. The books were very successful: the first volume was reprinted in 1975, 1981, 1988, and 1996, while the second volume was reprinted in 1988 and 1998. However, the quality of the edition is average at best, and it contains numerous typographical errors.

Translations of "The Colour out of Space" and "From Beyond" can be found in the volumes III (1964) and VI (1966) of *Antología de novelas de anticipación*, also published by Acervo in Spain. While not being especially remarkable volumes, it is interesting to note that the anthologies had a much more science-fiction orientation than the previously mentioned editions, so at this point it seems clear that there were some difficulties in labeling Lovecraft's oeuvre within a particular genre.

Seix Barral, a major publishing house in Spain, published *At the Mountains of Madness* in 1968, with a new translation by Calvert Casey. In 1969 one of the most relevant Lovecraftian volumes in Spanish was released. *Los mitos de Cthulhu*, edited by Rafael Llopis for Alianza Editorial, would be a cornerstone for the Spanish reception of Lovecraft. Alianza, at the same time, would become one of the leading publishing houses distributing the work of Lovecraft. *Los mitos de Cthulhu* is a collection of tales by several authors, not only Lovecraft. But instead of being unconnected, as used to be the case whenever Lovecraft appeared in previous anthologies, they were all written by members of the Lovecraft circle, and the texts included in the volume constitute a wondrous starting point for those who want to know about the Cthulhu Mythos. The collection is divided in three parts: precursors of the Mythos (with texts by Lord Dunsany, Ambrose Bierce, and Algernon Blackwood, among others), the Mythos (Lovecraft, Frank Belknap Long, Clark Ashton Smith, and Robert Bloch), and the Mythos after Lovecraft (Derleth, Campbell, Bloch, and Juan Perucho).

The translations, by Llopis himself and Francisco Torres Oliver, are probably the most widely circulated ones in Spain, and the best known by most readers. Apart from that, Rafael Llopis includes in the volume an extended essay entitled "Los mitos de Cthulhu," a landmark in Spanish Lovecraft studies. (There is an English translation available in *Lovecraft Studies* issues 27 and 28, 1992–93.) Llopis is perfectly able to contextualize Lovecraft and the twentieth-century horror tale in their time, a period of ongoing changes that frequently alienated the writer. At the same time, the scholar and translator is able to depict a complex human figure with many different façades, from the serious gentleman to the cheerful tourist, from the weird fiction creator to a realist writer who described rural New England in depth, its landscapes and its people. Above all, he is the central figure of the Lovecraft Circle, who was source of inspiration for the other writers included in the volume. Llopis analyzes Lovecraft's philosophical thought, his mechanistic materialism, his old-fashioned ethics, his ideological background, and his taste for the lost past. All in all, Llopis highlights the most relevant features of the writer, both in his life and in his fiction.

The second part of the essay deals with how the Mythos is configured, and Llopis tries to cast light on the different connections between the creatures, gods, places, names, and books that appear in the tales included in the volume. Finally, he studies the later attempts to systematize the Mythos, mainly Derleth's proposals and cosmogony. It can be asserted, without hesitation, that thanks to Llopis and this particular volume, Lovecraft finally landed in the Spanish literary community. To round out the whole volume, a story by Juan Perucho, "A la manera de Lovecraft," was included. It is considered the first Spanish Lovecraftian text published in a major collection. *Los mitos de Cthulhu* is still one of the most popular collections of Lovecraftian fiction, and a cornerstone for both Spanish readers and academics.

From this moment onwards, and coinciding also with the last years of Franco's dictatorship, when the burden of censorship was significantly weaker, there was an enormous proliferation of Lovecraft editions in Spanish that has not yet ended. New translations, anthologies, collections, and editions flourished year after year, the 1970s and 1980s being the most important decades. It would be impossible to pay attention to all the different minor editions and translations that were issued, but some landmarks need to be highlighted because of their particular relevance.

Alianza Editorial, after publishing *Los mitos de Cthulhu*, released a "Lovecraft collection" during the 1970s and early '80s. The collection includes eight books of tales by Lovecraft, two more collecting collaborations with Derleth, the already mentioned *Los mitos de Cthulhu*, and the essay *El horror sobrenatural en la literatura* (*Supernatural Horror in Literature*). Alianza collected most of the fiction of Lovecraft in these books, all of them translated by Llopis and Torres Oliver, and the volumes are still available and are probably the best-known editions in Spain. At the same time, it was the first time a nonfiction work by Lovecraft was translated by a major publishing house, and it happened as late as 1984.

We need to step back to 1979, in order to focus on pulp and amateur publications again. *Blagdaross* was a fanzine edited by a group of teenagers at their high school, led by Alberto Santos Castillo and Pedro Calleja. It was printed using the duplicator device available at their high school, and the first issue consisted of 70 copies. They managed to print eight issues, the last one being released in 1984. Under any other circumstances, *Blagdaross* would not be more than another amateur fanzine, but what is really striking about it is the nature and quality of its contents. It included unprecedented material by Lovecraft and *about* Lovecraft. Actually, the very first issue included, apart from a translation of "The Quest of Iranon" (the first one in Spanish), the essay "El gran americano despreciado" ("The Great American Throw-Away"), by Dirk W. Mosig. It was the first time an academic article on Lovecraft was ever published in Spanish, and it is difficult to imagine how a group of high-school students managed to get the original English versions for their contents. José María Nebreda was in charge of the translations for all the issues, which also included some of their own works as well as poetry and nonfiction by Lovecraft, J. R. R. Tolkien, Ramsey Campbell, Robert H. Barlow, etc. To put the cap on their heroic quest, the last issue included *Fungosidades de Yuggoth*, the first Spanish translation of *Fungi from Yuggoth*, a book of poems that would not get a professional Spanish edition until four years later, in 1988.

In the 1990s, the publishing house Edaf started the process of issuing several volumes collecting Lovecraft's fiction as well as his collaborations with other authors, under the editorial supervision of Alberto Santos, and with José Antonio Álvaro Garrido as translator. At first consisting of eleven volumes, the series would be reissued and expanded in 2003-04 in a new edition of twenty-seven volumes, thematically organized, divided between horror stories, oneiric tales, the Randolph Carter cycle, the Cthulhu cycle, order and chaos, and collaborations. The editions have been widely distributed both in Spain and Latin America, and the books, in paperback, present a renovated image that reminds the reader of modern pulp fictions, with cover artists such as H. R. Giger among others. They are short books (90 to 120 pages), including one to five different stories and, in some volumes, a brief introduction by Alberto Santos.

The publishing house Valdemar is the final stop in the present overview. Nowadays, it is perhaps the most important publisher related to fantasy and horror fiction in Spanish. It is located in Spain, but it distributes also in most of the Spanish-speaking countries. Within its collection "El club Diógenes," from 1994 until 2004, it published six assorted paperback volumes by Lovecraft, including a translation of *Fungi from Yuggoth*. These volumes are still popular and reprinted frequently.

In 2005 and 2007 Valdemar published what has been considered by many readers the definitive compilation of Lovecraft fiction, *Narrativa com-*

pleta, in two deluxe volumes edited by Juan Antonio Molina Foix and translated by Francisco Torres Oliver, José María Nebreda (who, several decades before, was in charge of most of the translations of the previously mentioned fanzine *Blagdaross*), and Molina Foix himself. The volumes include virtually all the narrative fiction written by Lovecraft, including some material and juvenilia previously unpublished in Spanish. The extensive introductory essays by Molina Foix in the two volumes are thoughtful and rigorous. The endnotes are translations, sometimes summarized or slightly adapted, of the notes included in the editions prepared by S. T. Joshi for Penguin Classics. A third volume collecting collaborations and ghostwriting, *Más allá de los eones*, was published in 2013, following the same quality pattern.

What seems quite surprising at this point is that the vast majority of the translations consist only of Lovecraft's fiction and poetry. Just a handful of scattered letters can be found in some magazines, and a few essays he wrote have been also reproduced in minor and amateur publications. None of the writer's nonfictional production has ever been systematically translated and published in Spanish. Considering the relevance that Lovecraft has acquired during the last three decades in the Hispanic world, and the fact that much of the process of compilation has been already done in English by scholars such as S. T. Joshi or David E. Schultz, the lack of Spanish translations of letters and articles seems baffling.

Focusing the attention on the field of academic studies, the landscape is also bleak. Within a small number of books that just repeat over and over again the same worn-out ideas about the writer and his life, just one volume is worthy of mention. *Cuadernos del abismo* was published in 2008 (with a second revised edition appearing a year later), and contains several articles by translators, editors, and scholars related in one way or another to Lovecraft. It is the result of a conference that took place in Madrid in 2007, and it is not a purely academic work, since it also contains some pieces of Lovecraftian fiction. The quality of the articles is uneven, but it is a first step in the academic study of this figure in the Hispanic world. The only biography available in Spanish, apart from the biographical sketches scattered through the different introductions and forewords, is de Camp's *Lovecraft: Una biografía* (*Lovecraft: A Biography*), published by Valdemar in 2002, and translated by Francisco Torres Oliver. The essay *H. P. Lovecraft: Contra el mundo, contra la vida* (*H. P. Lovecraft: Contre le monde, contre la vie*), by the French author Michel Houellebecq, appeared in 2006, translated by Encarna Castejón and published by Siruela.

To sum up, Lovecraft has been a constant presence in the Hispanic shelves since 1939. The first steps were timid, connected with horror compilations produced by minor publishing houses that released poor-quality editions, and there were some periods of inactivity. However, the translation boom arrived in the late 1960s, and it is now experiencing one of its peaks, probably triggered by the recent freeing of copyright in 2007. However, considering how popular his writings are for the average Hispanic reader, there are still important gaps in the market, especially when considering the nonfiction and the worrying lack of academic studies on his life and oeuvre.

Works Cited

Gosseyn, Ricardo. "Prólogo." In Lovecraft's *El color que cayó del cielo*. Buenos Aires: Minotauro, 1957. 7-13.

Hassón, Moisés. "José Mallorquí: Más allá del escritor. *Narraciones terroríficas y Futuro*." In *La novela popular en España 2*, ed., Fernando Martínez de la Hidalga. Madrid: Robel, 2001. 285-91.

———. "Los múltiples rostros de *Narraciones terroríficas*." In *La novela popular en España 2*, ed., Fernando Martínez de la Hidalga. Madrid: Robel, 2001. 251-83.

Joshi, S. T. *The Weird Tale*. Austin: University of Texas Press, 1990.

Lázaro Lafuente, Alberto. "La recepción de la narrativa inglesa de terror en la España de Franco: antologías y colecciones." In *Periphery and Centre IV*, ed., Rubén Jarazo Álvarez and Lidia M. Montero Ameneiro. La Coruña: Universidade da Coruña, 2009. 223-33.

Llopis, Rafael. "Los mitos de Cthulhu." In *Los mitos de Cthulhu*, ed., Rafael Llopis. Madrid: Alianza, 1969. 11-52.

Llorens Borras, José A. "H. P. Lovecraft y su obra." In Lovecraft's *Obras escogidas: Primera selección*. Ed. José A. Llorens Borras. Barcelona: Acervo, 1966. 5-12.

———. "Introducción." In Lovecraft's *Obras escogidas: Segunda selección*. Ed. José A. Llorens Borras. Barcelona: Acervo, 1974. 4-9.

Santos Castillo, Alberto. "Editar a Lovecraft." In *Cuadernos del abismo: Homenaje a H. P. Lovecraft*, ed., David Hernández de la Fuente and Fernando Broncano. 2nd ed. Madrid: Literaturas Comunicación, 2009. 201-6.

Color out of Mind: Correlating the Cthulhu Mythos Universe to the Autism Disorder Spectrum

Lars G. Backstrom
Independent Scholar

"The Outsider," "The Color out of Space," "In the Vault": even though I was only twelve years old there was something in these stories I could relate to, but could not really explain what it was. A few decades later I was diagnosed with Asperger's syndrome (AS), a disorder on the autistic disorder spectrum (ADS). With the intense focus that a person with AS can pursue an interest, I began to read extensively about my condition. Soon enough I started noticing similarities between the worldview in Lovecraft's texts, particularly in the Cthulhu Mythos stories, and the way somebody with AS experiences the world. Given the strong correlation between the texts and my condition, I felt it necessary to write this paper as a tribute to Lovecraft, as a tribute to all those Lovecraft fans who are also on the spectrum, and as a way for those not on the spectrum to understand how people with AS feel and relate to the world.

To the best of my knowledge nobody has ever analyzed the texts of Howard Phillips Lovecraft from the perspective of a person on the ADS. The only similar study that I know of is by Gary and Jennifer McIlwee Myers, *Lovecraft's Syndrome: An Asperger's Appraisal of the Writer's Life* (2015). However, they do their analysis based upon the character of H. P. Lovecraft the author, whereas my essay is based on his stories and the characters within.

My paper will begin with an introduction to AS, followed by a comparison between AS and the worldview in the Cthulhu Mythos universe. I will then take a closer look at three of Lovecraft's better-known stories and show that they can be read as unintended extended metaphors for AS.

Introduction to Asperger Syndrome

AS is a very complex and poorly understood disability (Atwood 52). Part of the ASD, AS is a lifelong disability that affects how people perceive the world and interact with others. Given the scope of this essay, I will only discuss the aspects of the condition that are relevant to the writings of Lovecraft.

AS is sometimes referred to as wrong planet syndrome because those with AS can be compared to an alien trying to understand earthly customs and cultures (Atwood 77). AS in children was first identified in 1944 by Austrian clinician Hans Asperger (cf. Frith 8), but it was not until 1993 that the World Health Organization included AS in the tenth edition of its International Classification of Diseases (Atwood 36). The Adult Asperger Assessment was developed in 2005 by Baron-Cohen et al. (Atwood 49).

Estimates of the affliction rate vary significantly: between one in 68 to one in 33,000 (Atwood 46). There are about three to four times as many males diagnosed with AS than women (Atwood 46; Frith 52). What tends to be noticed are the social limitations, partiality to repetition and ritual, and obsession with obscure interests that accompany AS. However, these are only symptoms, not the condition itself, and they do not represent how people with AS perceive their condition.

Neuro-imaging scans show abnormalities in the brain function of people with AS, most notably in the frontal and temporal regions of the cortex. These regions contain the amygdala (which regulates emotions such as sadness, anxiety, and anger), the cerebellum (which coordinates and regulates muscular activity), and the basal ganglia (a group of structures involved in coordination of movement). Contained within the same regions of the cortex is the executive function, which governs, among other things, the ability to determine good and evil, predict outcomes, and plan, organize and finish tasks (Atwood 234-38).

Theory of mind, that is, the ability to understand thoughts, emotions, and intentions in others—and to some extent within the Asperger person himself—is impaired. Lacking a theory of mind means that it becomes difficult for someone on the ADS to understand that emotions, opinions, and ideas might be based on personal beliefs and not on facts; therefore it is taxing, or sometimes even impossible, for the person with AS to understand the goals of others or to predict their behavior, leading to anxiety and feelings of paranoia (Baron-Cohen et al. 38-39; Cole et al. 2007).

People on the ADS appear to lack the area in the brain that interprets the facial expressions of other people, a symptom called Prosopagnosia (Atwood 130, 327-28; Uddin 4, 6). People with AS also have monotropism, or weak central coherence, meaning that they can excel at paying attention to detail but struggle to understand the whole picture (Atwood 241). Thus an individual with AS sees the world as composed of a myriad of independent bits of data that need to be continuously evaluated and re-evaluated (Frith 103-7, 108-10). A positive side effect of this is that unexpected connections can be made between non-related facts, leading to the creation of novel solutions to problems or the discovery of something new (Atwood 237).

A person on the ADS is often socially awkward. Not only does social interaction involve enormous amounts of often vague and incomplete information that needs to be constantly processed, but, as described above, a person with AS also lacks many of the tools to ease the processing (Atwood 122-23). This often leads to social isolation, alienation, and ultimately bullying (Carley 55-56; Atwood 99). Another common characteristic of people with AS is that they can develop intense special interests (Atwood 172). These fulfill several functions: they provide comfort as an escape from the chaotic outside world, help create understanding of the outside world, provide a sense of identity, and stimulate the creation of an imaginary world that is easier to comprehend (Atwood 182-88).

Persons on the ADS can be hypersensitive in one or more senses, often touch, sound, and light (Atwood 275, 279, 284-85). This easily leads to overstimulation, indecisiveness, anxiety, stress, or even total shutdowns due to the inability to handle the sensory overloads (Atwood 272-73). People with AS tend to have excellent long-term memory and highly developed visual thinking (Atwood 252-53). The downside of this is that they can continuously relive traumatic experiences, something that can lead to post-traumatic stress disorder (PTSD), a condition only previously recognized among soldiers or victims of violence (Atwood 138-39; Carley 87).

Reading Lovecraft's Texts Based on the ADS Experience

After this introduction to AS I will now demonstrate that a way to understand the horror in Lovecraft's stories, and the Cthulhu Mythos universe in particular, is by comparing such stories to how a person with AS experiences the world. To add richness and variety to the comparisons,

I have taken examples of people with AS from several sources as well as examples from my own experience.

My comparisons begin with an early case study in which a patient had been diagnosed as being on the ADS when he was a child. As an adult he described his experiences, summarizing his childhood as being filled with confusion and terror. He lived in a "frightening world where painful stimuli could not be mastered ... everything was unpredictable and strange ... [and] ... he could never predict or understand the behavior of other children" (Frith 103).

As a comparison, the Cthulhu Mythos universe is a place of incredibly strong sensations. Vile stench alone threatens to overwhelm the characters in many stories (Airaksinen 195-97). The mere sight of Great Cthulhu kills two hardy sailors, and what Danforth sees in the mirage in the clouded sky above the city of the Old Ones traumatized him for the rest of his life. Similarly, in the pit in Joseph Curwen's laboratory Dr. Willett sees a creature with outlines that whispered "terrible hints of obscure cosmic relationships and unnamable realities behind the protective illusions of common vision ... [and for a] ... few instants he was undoubtedly as stark mad as any inmate of Dr. Waite's private hospital" (CF 2.235-36). As a child I had always been drawn to passages such as these without really knowing why, but now I understand that I was being drawn to the comparison between the strong sensations experienced by the characters and my own world filled with overwhelming stimuli, which in the narratives of Lovecraft can go completely out of control.

Both the unnamed narrator in "Dagon" and detective Thomas F. Malone are traumatized and disturbed by recurring and intrusive visual memories of their experiences at the monolith (the former) and the police raid at Parker Place (the latter). In modern medical parlance it can be said that they have developed PTSD. Even the unnamed narrator in "Pickman's Model" develops similar symptoms after visiting Pickman's studio in Boston's North End. I myself can get overwhelmed by vivid visual memories of traumatic episodes in my childhood, together with the frightening feelings that accompany them, which I now know were largely due to my undiagnosed AS.

Now consider the opening lines of "The Call of Cthulhu":

> The most merciful thing in the world, I think, is the inability of the human mind to correlate all its contents. We live on a placid island of igno-

rance in the midst of black seas of infinity, and it was not meant that we should voyage far. The sciences, each straining in its own direction, have hitherto harmed us little; but some day the piecing together of dissociated knowledge will open up such terrifying vistas of reality, and of our frightful position therein, that we shall either go mad from the revelation or flee from the deadly light into the peace and safety of a new dark age. (CF 2.21-22)

This passage alone contains most of the major aspects of Asperger Syndrome: the inability to connect facts, the inability to comprehend a complex world, the problem of getting too easily overwhelmed by too much information, and the alienation felt by the person with AS. Even the other beings in the universe are disjointed, and while the characters can identify each of the other beings' parts the general outline eludes them.

The best example is perhaps Great Cthulhu itself:

If I say that my somewhat extravagant imagination yielded simultaneous pictures of an octopus, a dragon, and a human caricature, I shall not be unfaithful to the spirit of the thing. A pulpy, tentacled head surmounted a grotesque and scaly body with rudimentary wings; but it was the *general outline* of the whole which made it most shockingly frightful. (CF 2.23-24)

Another example of a creature whose image is difficult to convey is the dying Wilbur Whateley in "The Dunwich Horror":

It would be trite and not wholly accurate to say that no human pen could describe it, but one may properly say that it could not be vividly visualized by anyone whose ideas of aspect and contour are too closely bound up with the common life-forms of this planet and of the three known dimensions. It was partly human, beyond a doubt, with very man-like hands and head, and the goatish, chinless face had the stamp of the Whateleys upon it. But the torso and lower parts of the body were teratologically fabulous, so that only generous clothing could ever have enabled it to walk on earth unchallenged or uneradicated. (CF 2.438-39)

The characters describing Great Cthulhu and Wilbur Whateley and humanity as a whole are helpless against these beings, which almost always appear in plural (cf. the Old Ones, the Great Race, the Mi-Go, Deep Ones); and what we are left with is that they have knowledge we do not have access to, that it is their universe, and that we are the outsiders (Airaksinen 198-200). If they notice us at all their behavior is similar to that of bullies, i.e., they gang up on us and find us amusing playthings (cf. the ghouls of Boston or the Mi-Go in Vermont). Some humans strike bargains with them: cf. Captain Obed Marsh ("The Shadow over Innsmouth"), Walter Brown and Noyes ("The Whisperer in Darkness"), and the cultists of Cthulhu ("The Call of Cthulhu"). However, the deals are obviously on unequal terms and show similarities to the way people with AS strike bargains with their tormentors to get some form of acceptance (Atwood 82).

Lovecraft fan, author, artist, and blogger Lisa Walker England, a person with AS, writes that what attracts her to Lovecraft is his focus on his characters' relation to their environment and not to one another. Think of Charles Dexter Ward's and Robert Blake's Providence, Pickman's Boston, Danforth and Professor Dyer in the city of the Old Ones, and the crew of the *Emma* in R'lyeh, just to mention a few examples. The localities of Red Hook, Arkham, Kingsport, Dunwich, and Innsmouth and their relation to the main characters are more central to the stories than any relationships between characters, and their architecture and geography are more detailed that any character descriptions in any of Lovecraft's works.

In the Cthulhu Mythos, however, horror does not intrude into a nice and cozy universe where it can be defeated by strong family ties, luck, or human ingenuity, as is the case with most other well-known authors of horror fiction. No, the horror lies in the nature of the universe itself, in which humanity is the aberration (cf. "The Dunwich Horror" and *At the Mountains of Madness*). Lovecraft fan, author, and person with AS Jennifer McIlwee Myers wrote to renowned ADS specialist Dr. Tony Atwood that Lovecraft's texts provide her with a way to deal with her otherness (Atwood 187). What greater sense of otherness can there be with humans being the *Other*?

It is precisely because of their otherness that it is very easy for persons on the ADS to relate to and empathize with the characters in Lovecraft's oeuvre. Such characters tend to be solitary, socially awkward, bookish academics or artists moving in the fringes of society. Charles Dexter Ward obsessively investigates the city of Providence and his genealogy (*The Case of Charles Dexter Ward*)—perhaps as an unconscious attempt to find a place in the world that he will not find among his peers. For his part, Edward Derby is a sensitive, "prodigiously learned" (CF 3.328), and creative author with the "fresh complexion of a child," but socially isolated and shy, leading him to be an incel (involuntary celibate) lacking in contacts, "retarded" in "self-reliance and practical affairs," and not "equal to a struggle in the business or professional arena" (CF 3.326). He has one friend, the architect Daniel Upton, and their friendship is based on mutual interests and shared social isolation. Derby and Upton move in the bohemian and "decadent" group at university, perhaps the only group that accepts them, with Derby imitating their behavior in a manner similar to what a person with AS does without really understanding the meaning (Atwood 27).

Edward Derby shares a social naiveté and an inability to read people and their intentions with Charles Dexter Ward, which leaves them helpless to predators like Joseph Curwen, Edward Hutchinson, and Ephraim/Asenath Waite. Sharing this particular trait is also Walter Gilman, who is a mathematics prodigy with hypersensitive hearing and who only has one real friend: Frank Elwood. Their friendship is based on Gilman helping Elwood with his math homework.

Gilman's isolation and inability to understand the danger he is in leaves him vulnerable to Keziah Mason and Brown Jenkin. His innocent and trusting nature, social isolation, and the fact that he is unable to perceive that these are not nice people by any standards makes Gilman an easy target. Relating this to AS, it is highly likely that Gilman had difficulties understanding non-direct communication. It took me many years to understand that people do not always say what they mean, and that people lie.

Another character that shows strong traits of being on the ADS is Albert Wilmarth ("The Whisperer in Darkness"). He can remember Henry Akeley's letters almost verbatim, but he cannot distinguish which are real and which are forgeries. Neither does he recognize Noyes as an impostor, nor does he recognize that instead of talking to Akeley he is talking to a mask. For his part, Randolph Carter's experiences with dreaming indicate his extremely developed ability to focus, his visual thinking, and excellent memory, traits he shares with the majority of people with AS (Atwood 252–53).

The fate of several of the point-of-view (POV) characters is something people with AS would find intensely frightening. Charles Dexter Ward, Henry Akeley, Nathaniel Wingate Peaslee, and Edward Derby all lose their identities, something a person with AS fears intensely. Since a person with AS has a limited social identity (sometimes none), the loss of personal identity creates intense terror, a terror similar to death, because it is the ultimate loss of self (Lyons and Fitzgerald 753; Airaksinen 201). Other characters are so marked by their experiences that they are unable to share them, and, in any case, their experiences are often so extreme that there are no words in the language to describe them, which is very similar to the difficulties people with AS have describing emotions, even their own (Frith 120–21).

The loneliness and despair experienced by the POV characters in several Lovecraft stories is also something a person on the ADS can relate to (Frith 136). My feelings were of that sort until I met my wife. The two narrators in "The Hound" and "Herbert West—Reanimator" are both dominated by more forceful individuals. It is possible to read homoerotic overtones into these relationships; however, they can also be interpreted as a person on the ADS attaching themselves to a mentor or protector (Atwood 90 and 344). Their loyalty to their friend becomes so strong that it overrides the fact that what they are doing is completely out of bounds. On the other hand, what is Herbert West if not a person on the ADS gone wrong? He is brilliant in one narrow field, but obsessed with achieving perfection with his goal of reanimating the newly dead with no thought of what he is doing is wrong; in fact, the idea never even occurs to him (Wing 175-76; Atwood 334-38).

An Alternative Reading of Three of H. P. Lovecraft's Better-Known Tales Based upon the Asperger Experience

So far I have analyzed the texts and characters of Lovecraft to show how they relate to the experience of a person with AS. I will now focus my attention on three selected texts to demonstrate how they can be read as extended metaphors for AS.

In "The Outsider," the unnamed narrator lives in a dark castle surrounded by an equally dark forest. Tellingly, the perpetual darkness prevents the narrator from getting an overview of his situation. He has no knowledge of other people other than via books, and he has no clear understanding of who he is. He feels trapped and tries to escape by walking into the forest away from the castle; but while there is no boundary in the forest, neither is there any limit. In despair he returns to the known situation in the castle rather than losing himself in the unknown.

Desperate and longing to be with the people he has seen in the books, and who he thinks are like him, he makes another determined effort to attend freedom, and this time he manages to escape. He finds another castle, this one brightly lit and full of merry people, whom he seems to recognize, in joyful celebration. When he tries to join them they reject him. He thought he was like them, but he is not. After a period of despair he embraces his otherness and joins other outcasts and celebrates with them in places unknown to humanity.

Relating this text to AS, the level of shunning experienced by the person with AS is much higher than that of the general population (Atwood 99). Compounding this problem is that people with AS might have difficulties distinguishing who is friendly toward them and who is not, and this is due to the inability to read faces and understand social cues. Like the narrator in the story, I too have joined groups of people considered to be outcasts (back in my days tabletop role-playing gamers) because they embraced my otherness.

In "The Whisperer in Darkness," Henry Wentworth Akeley is a very educated recluse, but with little worldly wisdom. He lives alone surrounded by a wilderness full of mysteries and secrets. This wilderness is the home of strange alien beings that make him, in effect, the alien. His only contact with the outside world is shopping for groceries in nearby towns, and his only companions are his guard dogs. Even though they are a mere utility for him, he really seems to care for them. His friendship with Wilmarth is purely based on a shared mutual interest.

Although Akeley's loneliness is physical, this can be interpreted as the social loneliness experienced by people with AS. Because social competence is impaired, the world is indeed like a jungle full of traps and mysteries. It is much easier to retreat and hate the loneliness than to try to understand a world that does not understand us, a world where many bully us precisely because of our lack of social competence. This is directly tied with the paragraph below.

Akeley is obsessed with the aliens, and this annoys them. They would have left him alone, but now they start attacking him, acting very much like bullies by using their numerical superiority and local knowledge to isolate him and control the situation (Airaksinen 122-23; Atwood 99). The aliens propose that Akeley join them, but it would be completely on their terms. Akeley would not only lose his ability to interact and influence his situation, being subjected to any auditory or visual sensation they wish to impose on him, and he would also completely lose his individual identity, becoming just a helpless brain in a featureless metal cylinder—a true nightmare for a person on the ADS.

In "The Shadow out of Time," Professor Nathaniel Wingate Peaslee experiences a five-year-long period of amnesia. During this time his curious behavior has alienated everybody around him, and he finds himself abandoned by everyone except his youngest son, Wingate Peaslee. During his period of amnesia the professor does not recognize his family or friends; his muscular coordination is faulty; while very strong, he is clumsy and has facial tics; and his language and vocabulary were of a "curiously stilted quality, as if he had laboriously learned the English language from books. The pronunciation was barbarously alien, whilst the idiom seemed to include both scraps of curious archaism and expressions of a wholly incomprehensible cast" (CF 3.366).

All these are well-known symptoms of AS (Atwood 204-6, 262-64, 266-68). The lack of body awareness is also typical of persons on the ADS, indicating that it is a skill that has to be learned (Lyons and Fitzgerald 751-52). Adults with AS sometimes have a strange gait lacking in fluency and efficiency; especially when running, legs and arms do not move in coordination (Atwood 259). As for speech, the pattern might be unusual, lacking in inflection and sometimes rhythmic nature.

During the professor's amnesia he never formed friendships, spending his time with outcasts and gathering obscure information on humanity's society, customs, history, knowledge, and secrets, very much as people on the ADS do when learning to cope with the world surrounding them (Atwood 77-78). The stilted nature of the Asperger person's vocabulary is many times due to the fact that people with Asperger spend an inordinate amount of time reading extensively (on their own) about their favorite topics. AS in children has been sometimes been called "Little Professor" syndrome because of children's extensive vocabulary and penchant to talk endlessly about their favorite subject.

Finally, in recollections and nightmares the professor remembers that an alien from the earth's distant past had switched minds with him, and while the alien spent five years in his body he spent five years in the alien's body. He himself had been surrounded by other aliens and had, curiously enough, gotten along well with them. After being returned to his own body he struggles with distinguishing between the world around him and his intrusive memories, similar to what a person on the ADS often does (Atwood 187).

Conclusion

In this paper I have shown how H. P. Lovecraft's oeuvre, especially the Cthulhu Mythos universe, closely resembles how a person with AS experiences the world. I have also shown how three of Lovecraft's texts, "The Outsider," "The Whisperer in Darkness," and "The Shadow out of Time," can be seen as extended metaphors for AS. The confusion, horror, helplessness, and anxiety the POV characters feel in all these stories closely resemble the everyday experience of a person on the ADS when confronted by the everyday outside world.

A person on the ADS experiences a fragmented, chaotic, and incomprehensible world and has to spend time and effort to put together dissociated, vague, and often contradictory pieces of information to create coherence and understanding. Lovecraft perverts this scenario so that instead of comprehension leading to relief and a possible cause of action, the combination of unexpected conclusions and incredibly strong sensations overwhelm the characters and narrators, ultimately leading them to insanity and oblivion.

A person on the ADS usually suffers from alienation, very much the way the POV characters in the Cthulhu Mythos universe do because of their experiences and knowledge. Finally, Lovecraft did not write about chatty people doing chatty things, but about persons on the fringes of human society, their relation to their environment, and their quest for comprehension. Is this not very much like the life of many a person with AS?

Works Cited

Airaksinen, Timo. *The Philosophy of H. P. Lovecraft: The Route to Horror.* New York: Peter Lang, 1999.

Atwood, Tony. *The Complete Guide to Asperger's Syndrome.* London: Jessica Kingsley, 2007.

"Autism Spectrum Disorder (ASD)." Centers for Disease Control and Prevention. 12 August 2015.

Baron-Cohen, Simon, Alan M. Leslie, and Uta Frith. "Does the Autistic Child Have a 'Theory of Mind?'" *Cognition* 21, No. 1 (1985): 37-46.

Carley, Michael John. *Asperger's from the Inside Out.* New York: Perigee, 2008.

Cole, Livia, Simon Baron-Cohen, and Jacqueline Hill. "Do Children with Autism Have a Theory of Mind? A Non-Verbal Test of Autism vs. Specific Language Impairment." *Journal of Autism and Developmental Disorders* 37, No. 4 (2007): 716-23.

England, Lisa Walker. "What Is It about H. P. Lovecraft?" *Scrappystoryteller.* April 2014. https://scrappystoryteller.com/2014/04/29/what-is-it-about-h-p-lovecraft/.

Frith, Uta. *Autism: Explaining the Enigma.* Oxford: Blackwell, 1989.

Lyons, Viktoria, and Michael Fitzgerald. "Atypical Sense of Self in Autism Spectrum Disorders: A Neuro-Cognitive Perspective." *Recent Advances in Autism Spectrum Disorders: Volume I.* Online: InTech (2013). http://www.intechopen.com/books/recent-advances-in-autism-spectrum-disorders-volume-i.

Myers, Gary, and Jennifer McIlwee Myers. *Lovecraft's Syndrome: An Asperger's Appraisal of the Writer's Life.* Seattle: CreateSpace, 2015.

Uddin, Lucina Q. "The Self in Autism: An Emerging View from Neuroimaging." *Neurocase* 17, No. 3 (2011): 201–8.

Wing, Lorna. *The Autistic Spectrum.* Rev. ed. London: Constable & Robinson, 1996.

Darwin and the Deep Ones: Anthropological Anxiety in "The Shadow over Innsmouth" and Other Stories

Jeffrey Shanks
Southeast Archeological Center

In the early twentieth century, misunderstanding and misappropriation of the relatively new theory of evolution by means of natural selection was pervasive, not only in popular contexts but also within the scientific and academic establishment of the time. Evolutionary theory became intertwined with then current ideas on racialist anthropology and colonialist narratives so as to create and justify a stratified social hierarchy based primarily on the concept of race.[1] The idea that members of certain races were more "evolved" than others was used to justify Western imperialism, the eugenics movement, and the political and social marginalization of vast numbers of non-white individuals. At the same time the popular culture of the late nineteenth and early twentieth centuries began to express anxieties related to these ideas. After all, if humans are susceptible to and a product of evolution, then they can likewise be susceptible to devolution—or so the thinking went—and this idea began to find its way into Victorian and even Modernist fiction—particularly in speculative fiction. H. P. Lovecraft's work is no exception in this regard and this paper will explore several of his stories in which these evolutionary anxieties are expressed.

That Lovecraft had an avid interest in evolution and anthropology and that these concepts would often feature prominently in his fiction should not come as a surprise. S. T. Joshi has noted that Lovecraft's chief philo-

---

1. On this very broad topic see Gould (62-104) and Stocking, *Race* (56-66) and *Victorian* (186-273) for further discussion.

sophical influences are Charles Darwin,[2] Ernst Haeckel, and Thomas Henry Huxley (*IAP* 318). And Lovecraft was far from unique in this among his contemporaries. Robert E. Howard and Clark Ashton Smith often incorporated evolution and devolution into their fiction as expressions of horror and the uncanny, but so too do many other lesser-known weird fiction writers of the time. Jonas Prida has identified what he calls "Weird Darwinism" as one of four major subgenres of *Weird Tales* during its first decade (22–23). This idea of evolutionary horror no doubt resonated with Lovecraft's early twentieth-century audience, which was still coming to grips with Darwinian theory and its implications for humanity's place in the cosmos. Mankind had only recently enjoyed a solitary perch atop the taxonomic hierarchy. Man, after all, was supposed to be created in the image of God and set apart from the lowly beasts of the earth. But that privileged position had been called into to question by the new scientific establishment that declared that humans were just another animal—perhaps more intelligent, perhaps dominant for the time being, but still just another animal. As Western society wrestled with these new ideas, the fiction of the time, especially speculative fiction, began to embrace and explore them as well.

Several scholars have written about Lovecraft's use of evolutionary themes, most notably Bennett Lovett-Graff, who focuses on Lovecraft's use of evolutionary materialism and biological determinism as a framework for his stories of degeneration. For Lovett-Graff, it is the threat of reproduction itself at the heart of these stories that expresses itself in evolutionary and degenerative horror—what he refers to as Darwinian sexuality ("Reproduction" 335, "Life" 375, "Shadows" 192). While this is no doubt true, it is perhaps something of an oversimplification. Reproduction—or more specifically, the *wrong kind* of reproduction—is simply the means, the act through which the *real* horror is mediated; that real horror being the elimination of the illusion of human exceptionalism through evolutionary processes and the potential for devolution into a more bestial condition. This idea, a popular one in late nineteenth- and early twentieth-century fiction, was hardly exclusive to Lovecraft and so cannot simply be explained as a peculiar expression of his well-documented sexual anxieties.[3]

---

2. Joshi also notes, however, that HPL probably did not read Darwin's works, but was influenced by his ideas indirectly through Haeckel and Huxley (*IAP* 322).

3. HPL's sexuality and sexual anxieties have been discussed at length by many scholars.

It would perhaps be more appropriate to say to that Lovecraft's own anxieties and fears shaped the way he used already-common tropes related to evolution and sexuality.

Anthropological Anxiety

Much of the evolutionary tension in Lovecraft's work falls under the rubric of what literary theorist Virginia Richter calls "anthropological anxiety" (6-8). Richter's research focuses primarily on Darwinism and evolutionary theory and their influence and impact on Victorian and Modernist literature. In her 2011 book *Literature After Darwin*, she presents aspects of her research in this area and, in contrast with many other scholars, she includes popular fiction in her study. She applies her model to the works of H. Rider Haggard, Rudyard Kipling, Arthur Conan Doyle, Edgar Allan Poe, H. G. Wells, Edgar Rice Burroughs, and other authors who would have been among Lovecraft's influences.

I would suggest that Richter's model of anthropological anxiety is a useful tool for understanding and discussing Lovecraft's use of evolutionary themes and even his approach to dealing issues of race and colonialism.[4] With that in mind, I will give a brief introduction to Richter's model and then apply it, albeit superficially, to several stories, particularly "The Shadow over Innsmouth."

Darwin's publication of *On the Origin of Species* in 1859, followed by *The Descent of Man* in 1871, was a watershed moment not only for natural history and the biological sciences, but also for philosophy as well. At the heart of evolutionary theory is the ultimate question of human nature—as Huxley phrased it, "the ascertainment of the place which Man occupies in nature and of his relations to the universe of things" (57). For Richter, it is the 'cultural consequences' of the answers to that question and their mediation through fiction that is the core of Literary Darwinism.

In Richter's 'anthropological anxiety' model, those cultural consequences often manifest themselves in art and literature in forms and

---

For an excellent recent survey of the subject, see Derie, particularly Chapters 1 and 2.

4. I have previously used Richter's model in a discussion of the works of Robert E. Howard (see Shanks "Evolutionary" and "What the Thak?"), and I believe it can be useful in analyses of many of the other *Weird Tales* authors who explore evolutionary themes in their work.

tropes that expose the underlying tension between mankind's former role as a divine being separate from and ascendant over the animal world and its new position as just another bestial species among many (8-15). In popular Victorian and Modernist fiction, these tropes include:

1. *Regression/degeneration:* the fear of biological or cultural devolution in the form of atavistic individuals or behavior.
2. *Plasticity of the body:* the consequence of the physical body (human and animal) no longer being fixed and immutable.
3. *Simianation:* the blurring of the boundaries between human and ape (or human and beast) as one becomes more like the other.
4. *Assimilation:* the threat of cultural and biological "pollution" through contact with the Other in the form of encounters with native "savages," lost races, or missing links. It is often expressed in the form of regression, miscegenation, and even cannibalism.

These tropes identified by Richter[5] appear in differing degrees in a number of Lovecraft's stories, but in a few works they are the major concepts that create the narrative tension.

Arthur Jermyn and the White Apes

One of the earliest[6] of Lovecraft's stories to make overt use of some of these aspects of anthropological anxiety was "Facts concerning the Late Arthur Jermyn and His Family." Written in 1920, it was published in an amateur journal, the *Wolverine*, in 1921, and reprinted in *Weird Tales* in April 1924 under the title "The White Ape." The story is primarily a genealogical history of British aristocrat Arthur Jermyn and his curious

---

5. Examples of regression/degeneration include Doyle's "The Adventure of the Creeping Man" or the apelike witch Gagool in Haggard's *King Solomon's Mines*; for plasticity of the body, Robert Louis Stevenson's *The Strange Case of Dr. Jekyll and Mr. Hyde* or Wells's *The Island of Dr. Moreau*; for simianation, Burroughs's *Tarzan of the Apes* or Kipling's "Bertran and Bimi"; and for assimilation, the Oparians in Burroughs's *The Return of Tarzan* or the ape-men in Doyle's *The Lost World*.

6. An earlier story by HPL to make use of evolutionary horror is "The Beast in the Cave" (CF 1.17-25), written in 1905 and first published in 1918. The story makes use of simianation, plasticity of the body, and regression/degeneration with an apelike creature in Mammoth Cave that turns out to be a devolved human being.

family. His eighteenth-century ancestor, Sir Wade Jermyn, was a noted explorer who claimed to have discovered a lost city in the Congo populated by race of white ape-men. Beginning with the child of Sir Wade and a mysterious foreign bride he brought back from his travels, Arthur's ancestors were plagued by physical and mental abnormalities, being brutish in appearance and behavior, and having a tendency toward madness. Arthur himself was even more apish than his forebears had been:

> Most of the Jermyns had possessed a subtly odd and repellent cast, but Arthur's case was very striking. It is hard to say just what he resembled, but his expression, his facial angle, and the length of his arms gave a thrill of repulsion to those who met him for the first time. (CF 1.177)

Arthur begins researching his family history, even traveling to the Congo to search for the lost city discovered by his ancestor, Sir Wade. Ultimately, Arthur learns the truth of his ancestry when a colleague sends him the mummified remains of one of the white apes, a female worshipped as a goddess by the natives. The presence of a locket on the mummy bearing the Jermyn family crest as well as her unmistakably familiar features reveal the ape goddess to be none other than Sir Wade's strange foreign wife—Arthur's great-great-great-grandmother. Arthur reacts in horror to this revelation and he commits suicide by setting himself on fire.

In this story we have most of Richter's primary categories of anthropological anxiety on display. The Jermyn family is an example of regression and Arthur in particular is a throwback, an atavist—he is *more* simian than his forebears, not less. The Jermyn line is devolving further over time. Plasticity of the body is not a significant factor in the story other than the fact the Jermyns' physical appearance is more apelike. Simianation appears in the form of the tribe of ape-human hybrids and also in the attempt of Sir Wade to make his wife more human, bringing her home to England and fathering a child with her—the line between human and beast is being blurred and then crossed.

But it is the danger of assimilation that is primary focus of the story and the true horror that Lovecraft is trying to reveal. The regression and devolution of the Jermyn family is a direct result of Sir Wade's falling into that dreaded colonialist trap of "going native"—or in this case, "going ape." Miscegenation leads to regression and ultimately destruction for Sir Wade's descendants, but it also potentially threatens the entire human race with devolution if this taint were to spread over the generations and beyond the Jermyn family. This is the real horror for Lovecraft, and presumably for many of his early readers as well.

The Lurking Fear of Degeneration

The theme of regression and degeneration is explored more deeply in "The Lurking Fear," written in 1922 and published in *Home Brew* in 1923. The story revolves around the Martense clan, a family of Dutch ancestry that settled on Tempest Mountain in the Catskills in the seventeenth century. Generations of isolation, inbreeding, and mixing with the "menial class" and "mongrels" of the countryside turned the Martenses into a horde of subhuman, apelike cannibals living in the numerous tunnels that honeycomb Tempest Mountain:

> I saw that they were dwarfed, deformed hairy devils or apes—monstrous and diabolic caricatures of the monkey tribe. They were so hideously silent; there was hardly a squeal when one of the last stragglers turned with the skill of long practice to make a meal in accustomed fashion on a weaker companion. Others snapped up what it left and ate with slavering relish. (CF 1.372)

Simianation is the result of the regression/degeneration in the Martense clan—they have quite literally devolved into apelike creatures, even resorting to the ultimate expression of dehumanization in colonialist fiction: cannibalism.

In "The Lurking Fear" the miscegenation theme is less overt than in "Arthur Jermyn," but it is still part of problem. It doesn't require breeding with the Other in a colonialist context to trigger devolution—for a well-to-do family, just mixing with the "low-born" contributes to regression. This is the nightmare of Lovecraft's evolution: our supposed position at the top of a teleological evolutionary ladder is precarious at best. If it is allowed to spread, all humanity is at risk of sliding down a rung a two.

The narrator of the story, a sort of occult detective who discovers the horrible truth of the Martenses,[7] does the only thing a good, well-bred

---

7. As Lovett-Graff astutely notes, HPL often uses the narrative structure of detective fiction in his stories of evolutionary horror ("Reproduction" 328, "Life" 373). The protagonist slowly pieces together clues that lead to a big reveal, often the discovery of one or more of Richter's anthropological anxiety tropes—sometimes in the protagonist's own hereditary background.

Anglo-Saxon protagonist can do under the circumstances: he has the top of Tempest Mountain blown to smithereens with dynamite! As Richter notes, the death and eradication of the source of the anthropological anxiety is the typical outcome in much of the literature she discusses (65).

The Horror of Assimilation at Red Hook

In "The Horror at Red Hook," written in 1925 and published in *Weird Tales* in 1927, the anthropological anxieties are related more to racism and colonialism—or rather reverse colonization—than they are to evolution, but the basic themes are still present. Assimilation through contact with the Other and the cultural degeneration that could result is the real danger.

The protagonist Malone is a police detective investigating the disappearance of a number of children in the immigrant-filled Brooklyn neighborhood of Red Hook. His suspicion falls on a local occultist of Dutch extraction, Robert Suydam, who has been practicing foul rituals learned from the "degenerate" foreigners. By describing the foreign practitioners of these rites as less-evolved races Lovecraft makes a clear link between *cultural* degeneration and *physical* regression:

> [Malone] was conscious, as one who united imagination with scientific knowledge, that modern people under lawless conditions tend uncannily to repeat the darkest instinctive patterns of primitive half-ape savagery in their daily life and ritual observances; and he had often viewed with an anthropologist's shudder the chanting, cursing processions of blear-eyed and pockmarked young men which wound their way along in the dark small hours of morning. (CF 1.485)

The rituals themselves not only represent a more primitive and degenerate form of religion, but the practitioners themselves are "half-ape savages." And Lovecraft cites the racialist and eugenicist "science" of the time as the authority on the subject.

Miscegenation and sexual deviancy among the multi-ethnic hordes of Red Hook is implied in the mention of orgies and deformed infants. Strange cults and odd languages are part this foreign "pollution" as well. As with "The Lurking Fear" this degeneration is apparent on the surface in the form of decaying architecture, but the true horror is mostly subterranean, hiding beneath the surface. There, in underground passages, Munroe discovers that the foreign cultists sacrifice victims to a monstrous demonic creature. The final victim is Suydam himself, paying the ultimate price for his assimilation and contamination.

Once again, the real horror at Red Hook is the possibility that this contamination will spread:

> ... one might fancy that here lay the root of a contagion destined to sicken and swallow cities, and engulf nations in the foetor of hybrid pestilence. Here cosmic sin had entered, and festered by unhallowed rites had commenced the grinning march of death that was to rot us all to fungous abnormalities too hideous for the grave's holding. (CF 1.499)

This is the perceived danger of assimilation: that contact with more degenerate, lesser-evolved "races" and individuals will cause their degeneracy to spread. Typically, fictional assimilation anxiety occurs in the context of a colonizing enterprise, as with Sir Wade Jermyn's encounter with the lost race of ape-men in Africa. In "Red Hook" the threat of assimilation is greatly magnified as it occurs in the form of reverse colonization—the "degenerate" Other has invaded the land of the colonizer. The threat is ultimately dealt with in the only way it can be in fiction of this type—through death and destruction.

The Shadow of Darwin over Innsmouth

These three early works, "Arthur Jermyn," "Lurking Fear," and "Red Hook," are not generally considered to be among Lovecraft's best work. But in 1931, when he had matured as a writer and was at his creative peak, he took many of the themes of these stories and repurposed them to great effect in one of his most celebrated works, "The Shadow over Innsmouth." Here we see weird evolution, miscegenation, reverse colonization, revealed ancestry, subterranean passages, exotic cults, and all Richter's anthropological anxiety tropes fully exploited.

In this classic story, the narrator, Robert Olmstead, visits Innsmouth, an isolated New England fishing village whose inhabitants are said to suffer from unusual deformities and religious practices. A ticket agent gives Olmstead his first clue that something about the people of Innsmouth is not quite right:

> "Some of 'em have queer narrow heads with flat noses and bulgy, starry eyes that never seem to shut, and their skin ain't quite right. Rough and scabby, and the sides of the necks are all shriveled or creased up. Get bald, too, very young." (CF 3.163)

His first encounter with an Innsmouth resident, a bus driver, confirms this description:

> His age was perhaps thirty-five, but the odd, deep creases in the sides of his neck made him seem older when one did not study his dull, expressionless face. He had a narrow head, bulging, watery-blue eyes that seemed never to wink, a flat nose, a receding forehead and chin, and singularly undeveloped ears. His long thick lip and coarse-pored, greyish cheeks seemed almost beardless except for some sparse yellow hairs that straggled and curled in irregular patches; and in places the surface seemed queerly irregular, as if peeling from some cutaneous disease. His hands were large and heavily veined, and had a very unusual greyish-blue tinge. The fingers were strikingly short in proportion to the rest of the structure, and seemed to have a tendency to curl closely into the huge palm. As he walked toward the bus I observed his peculiarly shambling gait and saw that his feet were inordinately immense. . . . He was evidently given to working or lounging around the fish docks, and carried with him much of their characteristic smell. Just what foreign blood was in him I could not even guess. . . . I myself would have thought of biological degeneration rather than alienage. (CF 3.170)

This last observation and speculation by Olmstead reveals the anthropological anxieties present as he weighs regression/degeneration or miscegenation as the cause of the bus driver's curious appearance.

After exploring the rundown, partially abandoned town and talking with an elderly local drunk, Zadok Allen, Olmstead learns that the villagers have been interbreeding with a race of amphibious fish-people, known as the Deep Ones, for several generations. The people of Innsmouth therefore are hybrids, explaining their curious features like scaly skin and large, unblinking eyes. In return for the Innsmouthers' supplication and sexual submission, the Deep Ones provide them with exotic gold jewelry and plentiful fish. As Robert M. Price has noted, there are a number of similarities in the interactions between the Deep Ones and their human worshippers and the so-called "cargo cults" of the Pacific islanders (viii-ix).

As the hybrid Innsmouthers grow older, they become less and less human and more like the Deep Ones, until eventually they are able to swim off into the ocean to join their submarine cousins in the undersea city of Y'ha-nthlei. Even more remarkably, those who fully undergo this transformation will never die of old age (though they can still be killed or die by accident).

Olmstead is accosted by a group of the villagers in his hotel room and has to make a harrowing escape from the town. He is pursued by several groups of villagers who try to block his escape from the town. Some of the more inhuman individuals come out of the sea to join in the pursuit. During his escape, Olmstead witnesses a party of the more fully-transformed Innsmouthers searching for him:

> ... I saw them in a limitless stream—flopping, hopping, croaking, bleating—urging inhumanly through the spectral moonlight in a grotesque, malignant saraband of fantastic nightmare. And some of them had tall tiaras of that nameless whitish-gold metal ... and some were strangely robed ... and one, who led the way, was clad in a ghoulishly humped black coat and striped trousers, and had a man's felt hat perched on the shapeless thing that answered for a head.
>
> I think their predominant colour was a greyish-green, though they had white bellies. They were mostly shiny and slippery, but the ridges of their backs were scaly. Their forms vaguely suggested the anthropoid, while their heads were the heads of fish, with prodigious bulging eyes that never closed. At the sides of their necks were palpitating gills, and their long paws were webbed. They hopped irregularly, sometimes on two legs and sometimes on four. (CF 3.222-23)

Upon his escape from Innsmouth, Olmstead reports his experiences to government officials, which leads to a raid on the town and a result that we've seen before: the removal of the anthropological threat through the destruction of much of the town and the removal of many of the inhabitants.

But after this, Olmstead, like Arthur Jermyn, begins doing some genealogical research and discovers that he is descended from an Innsmouth villager and that he himself is one of these hybrids. Olmstead's initial horror turns to fascination as he begins to dream about life under the sea with the Deep Ones and begins to long for his future transformation so that he can join them in their undersea city.

So in this story we have assimilation as one of the primary themes. The Deep Ones are actually in the role of the colonizer, but the contact between the two species leads to miscegenation. The villagers regress, devolving not into apemen, but further back on the evolutionary scale to amphibians and fish. There is also a cultural "degeneration," as the traditional religion of the Innsmouthers is replaced by the worship of the Deep Ones. Like the Martense family, they have isolated themselves from the rest of civilization.

Rather than simianation, we have *ichthynation* as the lines between human and Deep Ones are blurred. This is seen, not just in the Innsmouthers' physical forms, but also in their dress and behavior. Some continue to wear human clothes despite being nearly fully transformed. As the transformation progresses during a villager's lifetime, they begin to spend more and more time in the sea.

Plasticity of the body is also fully exploited in this story. The Innsmouthers don't just evolve slowly over generations, but completely transform within a lifetime from human to an amphibian/fishlike creature. There is nothing supernatural about this transformation—it is explained as a function of evolution. As Zadok tells Olmstead: "Seems that human folks has got a kind a' relation to sech water-beasts—that everything alive come aout o' the water onct an' only needs a little change to go back agin" (CF 3.189).

Conclusion

In "The Shadow over Innsmouth," Lovecraft is exploring the anxieties of anthropology and evolution and the ramifications of human origins far more deeply than in his previous works, though he makes use of many of the elements that have appeared in the earlier stories discussed here. In "Shadow," however, they are combined and utilized in a more complex and effective way. In all these works Lovecraft is expressing the fears of his early twentieth-century audience, still struggling with the implications of Darwinian theory and about what it means to be human. Like the creatures under Tempest Mountain, or below the ramshackle buildings of Red Hook, or beneath the surface in Innsmouth harbor, the real horror lurks unseen. It is the fear of the animal inside us all—the beast that threatens to break through its human veneer.[8]

---

8. Lovett-Graff also sees in the story HPL's more personal anxieties of his own genealogy and heredity: "The strong resemblance between the narrator's genealogy and HPL's, the same Lovecraft who feared the Celtic taint of a great-great-great-great grandmother and her daughter and granddaughter, cannot be ignored. . . . In 'Shadow,' . . . the seething fear of Darwinian sexuality, epitomized by the alien immigrant class whose racial stock threatened the Nordic purity of Lovecraft's America, shortly gives way the allure of the matrilineal curse of the Deep Ones" ("Shadows" 192-93). Again, this would be an example of HPL's own personal anxieties shaping the way in

But unlike the earlier stories, the actions of Olmstead at the end of "Shadow" represent a more complex response to the anthropological horror he has uncovered, both externally in Innsmouth, and internally in his own genealogical background.

An early passage in "Arthur Jermyn" expresses the primal anxiety of evolution:

> Science, already oppressive with its shocking revelations, will perhaps be the ultimate exterminator of our human species—if separate species we be—for its reserve of unguessed horrors could never be borne by mortal brains if loosed upon the world. If we knew what we are, we should do as Sir Arthur Jermyn did... (CF 1.171)

Only Olmstead *doesn't* kill himself like Arthur Jermyn, though he does consider it as an option:

> So far I have not shot myself... I bought an automatic and almost took the step, but certain dreams deterred me.... No, I shall not shoot myself—I cannot be made to shoot myself! (CF 3.230)

Rather he plans to embrace his heritage and his nature:

> We shall swim out to that brooding reef in the sea and dive down through black abysses to Cyclopean and many-columned Y'ha-nthlei, and in that lair of the Deep Ones we shall dwell amidst wonder and glory for ever. (CF 3.230)

And that is exactly what makes "Shadow over Innsmouth" a more mature and ultimately more interesting story. For Olmstead, the discovery of his lineage and his pending transformation is not a tragic revelation, but is rather a liberation from the prison of humanity.

This is an exceptional example of what Istvan Csicsery-Ronay calls the *science fictional grotesque*: the distortion and deformation of the familiar—the human body—not simply to evoke feelings of horror, but to evoke a sense of wonder (71). With "Shadow," Lovecraft moves beyond the simple fears and anxieties of humanity's now more precarious evolutionary position that we saw evoked in his earlier works. Olmstead experiences those anxieties but ultimately succumbs to them, accepting his assimilation into

---

which he uses the common tropes of anthropological anxiety, and in "Shadow" it gives the effect more authenticity than some of his earlier efforts.

the world of the Deep Ones. Thus the apparent evolutionary horror becomes instead the transcendence of the human experience. And this more complex and powerful use of evolutionary and anthropological anxiety makes "The Shadow over Innsmouth" one of Lovecraft's most effective and compelling stories.

Works Cited

Csicsery-Ronay, Istvan, Jr. "On the Grotesque in Science Fiction." *Science Fiction Studies* 29, No. 1 (March 2002): 71-99.

Derie, Bobby. *Sex and the Cthulhu Mythos*. New York: Hippocampus Press, 2014.

Gould, Stephen Jay. *The Mismeasure of Man*. Rev. ed. New York: W. W. Norton, 2006.

Huxley, Thomas Henry. *Evidence as to Man's Place in Nature*. London: Williams & Norgate, 1863.

Lovett-Graff, Bennett. "'Life Is a Hideous Thing': Primate-Geniture in H. P. Lovecraft's 'Arthur Jermyn.'" *Journal of the Fantastic in the Arts* 8, No. 3 (1997): 370-88.

———. "Lovecraft: Reproduction and Its Discontents." *Paradoxa* 1, No. 3 (1995): 325-41.

———. "Shadows over Lovecraft: Reactionary Fantasy and Immigrant Eugenics." *Extrapolation* 38, No. 3 (1997): 175-93.

Price, Robert M. "Introduction: Ontogeny Recapitulates Phylogeny." In *The Innsmouth Cycle: The Taint of the Deep Ones in 13 Tales*. Hayward, CA: Chaosium, 1998. vii-xiv.

Prida, Jonas. "Weird Modernism: Literary Modernism in the First Decade of *Weird Tales*." In *The Unique Legacy of Weird Tales: The Evolution of Modern Fantasy and Horror*, ed., Justin Everett and Jeffrey Shanks. Lanham, MD: Rowman & Littlefield. 2015. 15-28.

Richter, Virginia. *Literature After Darwin: Human Beasts in Western Fiction, 1859-1939*. New York: Palgrave MacMillan, 2011.

Shanks, Jeffrey. "Evolutionary Otherness: Anthropological Anxiety in Robert E. Howard's 'Worms of the Earth.'" In *The Unique Legacy of Weird Tales: The Evolution of Modern Fantasy and Horror*, ed., Justin Everett and Jeffrey Shanks. Lanham, MD: Rowman & Littlefield. 2015. 119-30.

———. "What the Thak? Anthropological Oddities in Howard's Work." *REH: Two-Gun Raconteur* No. 17 (2014): 17–26.

Stocking, George W., Jr. *Race, Culture, and Evolution: Essays in the History of Anthropology.* Chicago: University of Chicago Press, 1982.

———. *Victorian Anthropology.* New York: Macmillan, 1987.

The "Inside" of H. P. Lovecraft's Supernatural Horror in the Visual Arts

Nathaniel R. Wallace
Independent Scholar

H. P. Lovecraft often used first-person point of view, or the "inside," as a means of creating a symmetrical relationship between narrator and audience.[1] In his short story "The Outsider," Lovecraft uses this literary perspective at the climax, to great effect, revealing what the narrator could not formerly see: its own image represented in a mirror. In a visual text, the construction of such internal framing, or embodiment, functions differently than in literature, as representation cannot merely suggest a point of view but must portray it through imagery. In fostering identification between protagonist and audience, there is tension between representing an "inside" point of view versus a detached third-person point of view, depicting the protagonist at a distance. In artistic terms the two are very distinct. First-person perspective is abstract, as the body is only seen in fragments, forcing the audience to infer perspective. Third-person perspective offers figural representation that is easier to classify. This analysis demonstrates the subtleties of employing symmetry within different modes of visual representation of Lovecraft's story, primarily through an examination of Dutch artist Erik Kriek's comic adaptation, "El Introso" (Der Außenseiter), revealing contradictions in constructing a visual receptacle for audience identification.

---

1. HPL used first-person perspective in a large portion of his fictional work, with the exception of "Facts concerning the Late Arthur Jermyn and His Family" (1920), "The Terrible Old Man" (1920), "The Tree" (1920), "Celephaïs" (1920), "Quest of Iranon" (1921), "The Horror at Red Hook" (1925), "The Silver Key" (1926), "The Strange High House in the Mist" (1926), *The Dream-Quest of Unknown Kadath* (1926-27), *The Case of Charles Dexter Ward* (1927), "The Dunwich Horror" (1928), "The Dreams in the Witch House" (1932), and "The Haunter of the Dark" (1935).

"The Outsider" Rendered in Images

Written in 1921 and published in April 1926 in the pulp horror magazine *Weird Tales*, "The Outsider" is considered by many, according to Lovecraft scholar S. T. Joshi, to be "Lovecraft's signature tale" (141). Despite Lovecraft's denigration of the story—he found it too close to the work of Edgar Allan Poe—it serves as the primary example of first-person point of view in this discussion, since much of the plot twist depends on the protagonist's limited perspective. Indeed, Lovecraft found the perspective in "The Outsider" to be the only redeeming quality of the work, remarking, "I'll concede that the tale has the single merit of an original point of view" (SL 3.379). This perspective is established through the protagonist repeatedly describing its actions as it traverses the spatial geography of the narrative, stating "I looked," "I observed," "I saw," and "I beheld," coupled with its movements such as "I now stepped," and "I stood."[2] The narrator's body is repeatedly expressed through reference to its act of looking, or specific physical actions of its body. Essentially, it is a literary representation of the self that the audience can identify, as it too experiences the fictional world in a similar way, creating a connection between the character and audience.

In his comic adaptation of "The Outsider," Erik Kriek replicates Lovecraft's first-person frame though the utilization of sequenced images that, up until the end of the narrative, maintain the protagonist's point of view as though the audience is looking at this fictional world through its own eyes.[3] Essentially, the audience is shown an approximation of what the character might see as it encounters various objects and architecture throughout the sequence of the comic. Through partial reference to the human body, such as arms and feet, this sequence of images exemplifies the illusion, assuming "the position of a subject in order to show us what the subject sees" (Branigan 103).[4] For example, Kriek represents the protagonist's field

---

2. I will use the neuter singular pronoun in referring to the protagonist. All HPL's stories refer to a male protagonist, with the exception of "The Outsider," which does not mention the gender of this character. Indeed, Ben Indick finds that "none of his narrator-protagonists is feminine" (63).

3. Horacio Lalia, an Argentinian comic book illustrator, also utilized this perspective in his own graphic novel adaptation of "The Outsider."

4. Edward Branigan is referencing the subjective shot in film; however, this POV is

of view (Figure 1) with its hands raised up toward the high walls of a blackened tower, much as readers would see if they were conducting such an action.

Modified to fit within an individual panel in a larger sequence of the comic's narrative, the frame approximates a human point of view. Such perspective creates audience identification, as it shares this mode of sight when interacting with and viewing the external world. Kriek's composition manifests the "embodied image" as it represents the "inside," possessing all limitations related to that perspective, and not permitting a detached representation of the protagonist. As Kriek has commented on his adaptation, "The whole plot is based on the final twist ... so if I hadn't used a first-person perspective I would have spoiled the punchline in the first panel" (Kriek 2015). Thus, as a means of creating tension, he saves the "punchline" third-person point of view for the very last panel of the sequence.

Figure 1. Erik Kriek, "El Introso." 12.

Concerning Kriek's utilization of this technique, Lovecraft himself advocated the representation of the "immediate visible world" anchored by "the individual" person. In a letter to August Derleth the author discussed this approach to his friend and colleague, explaining:

> I recognise the impossibility of any correlation of the individual & the universal without the immediate visible world as a background-or starting-place for a system of outward-extending points of reference. I cannot think of any individual as existing except as part of a pattern-and the pattern's most visible and tangible areas are of course the individual's immediate environment; the soil and culture-stream from which he springs, and the

---

applicable to two-dimensional art, without the temporal component.

milieu of ideas, impressions, traditions, landscapes, and architecture through which he must necessarily peer in order to reach the "outside" . . . . I begin with the individual and the soil and think outward-appreciating the sensation of spatial and temporal liberation only when I can scale it against the known terrestrial scene. (*Essential Solitude* 288)

Here, Lovecraft comments on the entry point that the audience requires in order to invest itself within the story. Essentially, the protagonist, or narrator, is embodied within the text, relaying its experiences to the audience and giving the narrative an "inside" account of events from its own point of view. Kriek's adaptation makes a direct correlation between the point of view of the protagonist, implied to be that of a human, and the audience.

To fully understand some of the decisions Kriek made in representing his own adaptation, his approach to "The Outsider" must be placed within a larger iconography of the story's visual representation. For instance, his reluctance to give away the "punch line" was not shared by the very first artist to adapt the narrative, B. Goldschlagel. In adapting "The Outsider" for *Weird Tales* in April 1926, through third-person perspective, Goldschlagel featured the protagonist looking into the mirror at the beginning of the story. Bhob Stewart and Steve Harper's comic version in the October 1989 issue of *Monsters Attack!* utilizes a hybrid approach: the perspective is mostly rendered in first person, but occasionally third-person representation is included. On the other end of the spectrum, Devon Devereaux and Tom Pomplun's version, published in Eureka Productions' *Graphic Classics: H. P. Lovecraft* anthology, maintains third-person perspective throughout its sequence of images. In a similar vein, Alec Preston Stevens's 1987 comic adaptation published in *Prime Cuts* depicts a third-person perspective, though it obscures the actual form of the protagonist using stark black-and-white silhouettes.

An adaptation of "The Outsider" that uses a rather unusual approach, is Hernan Rodríguez's 2008 comic version, which inventively includes depictions of the character's entire body throughout the story but adds a slight twist on the proceedings. Though the audience is granted an overly idealized version of what the character might look like, once the mirror reveals its actual features, the image changes into something far more monstrous in appearance. Stuart Gordon's 1995 film adaptation of the story, *Castle Freak*, also largely maintains third-person perspective, though it never directly shows the audience a view of the character's face until later in the narrative, an approach that is much in line with Stewart and Harper's comic version. Though containing a few key first-person segments, which will be discussed later in this analysis, it uses them quite sparingly.[5]

Out of the many adaptations of this story, Kriek's use of first-person perspective bears the closest resemblance to Argentinian illustrator Horacio Lalia's version published in his *Lovecraft: El Grimorio Maldito* (1998). Lalia's earlier adaptation largely adheres to first-person perspective and similarly includes a third-person reveal for the mirror sequence toward the end of the narrative. What distinguishes the earlier adaptation is that the protagonist is depicted running back to the subterranean passage it emerged from, whereas Kriek's version abruptly stops with the protagonist looking in the mirror, allowing it to leave a final impression on the audience.

Kriek and Lalia's use of first-person perspective in their respective adaptations of "The Outsider" are not just visual reinterpretations of Lovecraft's text but also variations of iconography related to third-person perspective that can be traced within a greater history of textual embodiment. Often embodiment within the visual arts is assumed: a work of art's subject matter is thought to be the product of an artist depicting his or her point of view, or speculatively, in the case of fantasy, what it might be. Nevertheless, examples of explicit embodiment, such as representing extensions of the artist's body in conjunction with a point of view, are often de-emphasized compared to those works that evoke an aesthetic distance. This approach is also uncommon in film, something Linda Hutcheon acknowledges, stating: "Attempts to use the camera for first-person narration-to let the spectator see only what the protagonist sees-are infrequent" (54). This marginalization of first-person perspective is hard to reconcile, considering that explicit embodiment existed in the earliest known images, such as the cave paintings at Pech Merle. Remarkably, the embodiment represented on these walls communicates much the same thing as the protagonists in Lovecraft's stories, as well as in Kriek's "The Outsider" in connecting the body with a point of view expressed through an image.

Within pictorial two-dimensional art, visual signifiers, like those fea-

---

5. Stuart Gordon's *Castle Freak* uses the first-person perspective of the character only in three distinct moments: when the protagonist, here named Giorgio, is abused by an unnamed woman who turns out to be his mother; Giorgio's discovery of a mirror that echoes the scene from the short story; and during a highly sexual scene between the character John Reilly and a local prostitute.

tured in Kriek's work, are utilized to represent a "portion of a character's body" inside a compositional frame (Duncan and Smith 113). Throughout the course of the story, Kriek visually refers to the body, utilizing arms, legs, feet, or indirect signifiers such as shadows. However, in conjunction with eye-level perspective, it may be used to reinforce "identification with the characters and [a] sense of involvement in the action" (143). Within the horror genre, the use of first-person point of view is especially effective, as the film theorist Thomas Sipos contends that "A victim's POV [point of view] can heighten tension and fear by increasing audience identification with that victim. Horror is more horrifying when it strikes someone we care about—or when it strikes us" (83). This identification between the protagonist and audience is crucial in understanding how Kriek's visual adaptation of "The Outsider" functions.

Additionally, Lovecraft's "inside" aesthetic is essential to understanding how Kriek's adaptation functions for the audience. In 1928, this concept was outlined in a letter to his friend, Zealia Bishop:

> My theory of aesthetics is a compound one. To me beauty as we know it, consists of two elements; one absolute and objective, and based on rhythm and symmetry: and one relative and subjective, based on traditional associations with the hereditary culture-stream of the beholder. (SL 2.229)

Symmetry, when deployed within this current analysis, can either mean a similar way of seeing, which is represented through first-person perspective, as Kriek has done, or though the visualization of figural representation, seen from an exterior view. Does symmetry arise from an abstract sharing of a similar manner of sight or from seeing the face and body of another person? The representation of "The Outsider," viewed through its many adaptations, does not produce a definitive answer to this question, as both approaches have been attempted to varying degrees of effectiveness.

Considering Lovecraft's notion of rhythm, it is significant to note that sequential art, such as comic books, rely on regularized juxtaposition of images to tell its narrative, and Kriek's "The Outsider" is no different. The rhythm in representation comes from continually depicting the protagonist's point of view, allowing no alternative to the audience other than interpreting the situation in a similar manner. Concerning Lovecraft's second component of beauty, subjectivity, Kriek stacks multiple views upon each other, forcing the audience to understand the nature of the protagonist's ascent from the subterranean passages it formerly inhabited.

Nathaniel R. Wallace 151

As Lovecraft's original text compels the audience to identify with the protagonist, so does Kriek's comic adaptation, especially in reference to the body. Of the five panels that adapt the ascension of the protagonist, four of them feature the protagonist's hand. Kriek's first depiction of the protagonist's hands (Figure 2) alludes to the original text's mentioning that it "clung perilously to small footholds" (CF 1.267). In the composition, Kriek portrays the protagonist's arms tight with strain, the very tendons of its muscles tense from attempting to hold onto the shallow crevasses in the wall of the tower. Just as a viewer would have difficulty seeing below from this position, Kriek limits the frame, including only what the protagonist sees directly in front of it. In each of the subsequent panels, hands are featured reaching up to climb the great heights of the tower. These elements come together in succession to form a representation of the "inside" that the audience can identify with, even if the setting and circumstances are not overly familiar.

Outside Images in "The Outsider"

Within "The Outsider," there are essentially four types of visual frames. The

Figure 2. Erik Kriek, "El Introso" depicting the protagonist's ascension up the dark tower.

first, as previously discussed, is the protagonist's point of view, labeled in this analysis as the "inside." The subsequent three types of frames consist of illustrations in "the coloured pictures of living beings ... found in many of the mouldy books" (CF 1.266), the open windows at the castle, and the mirror. Erik Kriek has chosen to highlight the latter three in direct relationship with the initially constructed point of view. In other words, within the narrative's sequential development, the external frames transform the reality of the environment to become the focus of the protagonist's vision.

The first example of external framing from Kriek's adaptation involves the depiction of the protagonist looking at pictures in numerous books it has found in its underground lair (Figure 3). Here one can see the narrator using its hands to examine one of the books referenced in the story, giving the audience a modified "inside" point of view. However, the composition's frame is narrow and deviates from human biocular vision, indicating the

Figure 3. Erik Kriek. Panels from "El Introso." 12.

protagonist's hands holding a candle while paging through the book. While leafing through the pages, the protagonist stops on an image of two people warmly lying with each other. In the next sequence, the protagonist's hands and sense of space is represented as the library transitions into a representation of two characters dancing in a meadow under the sun. The result of this transition is to provide equal consideration of the image and protagonist's reality. Indeed, in the text above, it translates into "I saw myself among a lively crowd, dancing in the sun", which is a distant vantage point (12). In this sequence, figural representation, via third-person perspective, is directly juxtaposed with first-person perspective. Does the audience identify with the viewer or the viewed? In a darkly lit underground passage, these idealized portraits of humans become "outside" images for the protagonist.

Later in Kriek's adaptation the protagonist discovers a castle, encountering a window that frames a large group of revelers enjoying themselves at a party (Figure 4). Here, the frame serves as a boundary between the inside and outside, mediating the events taking place inside the castle. In many regards, this sequence is very similar to what Alexander Galloway describes as a subjective shot within film, which can signify "an evil vision, or an inhuman one" (50). Indeed, within *Castle Freak*, Stuart Gordon uses a subjective shot during a sequence where the protagonist is watching a sex act take place between the main character, John Reilly, and a local prostitute. Unlike *Castle Freak*, where the subterranean figure causes violence, Kriek adheres closely to Lovecraft's original text and merely depicts the protagonist passively watching.

Within the next panel, like the earlier illustrated book sequence, the frame of the window and audience's sense of embodiment gives way to displacement. Here the text reads, "Some faces had features that made me recall the distant past," almost as though the protagonist has a connection with these strangers and is situated among them inside the castle (15). In this moment, the protagonist fundamentally changes from viewer to participant. However, the festivities are interrupted as the protagonist pierces the frame and enters their reality while the partygoers' reaction changes to fright and panic. Unlike the violence committed by the character in *Castle Freak*, the transgression represented here is merely a trespass of the inhuman into the human domain.

Figure 4. Erik Kriek. Sequence of panels from "El Introso." 15.

The last sequence in Kriek's adaptation of "The Outsider" finally reveals that which is suggested in the previous portion of the narrative: the protagonist discovers an inhuman figure within the castle, turning out to be a mirror image of itself. This moment echoes within visual culture through works such as *The Strange Case of Dr. Jekyll and Mr. Hyde* (1931), *Twin Peaks* (1990), and The Prodigy's music video *Smack My Bitch Up* (1997).[6] Where these texts strongly differ in their climax is Kriek's use of first-person perspective, which is later discarded for a disembodied third-person perspective, revealing the protagonist looking at itself in the mirror (Figure 5). However, this twist in viewpoint is certainly not an anomaly, as

---

6. One of the first visual depictions of a person looking into a mirror from a first-person viewpoint is Parmigianino's *Self-Portrait in a Convex Mirror*, made in 1524 (Kunsthistorisches Museum 2014).

the first illustration associated with the story, created by B. Goldschlagel, represents a similar third-person perspective, a spoiler for anyone viewing the image before reading the text.[7] Additionally, after maintaining first-person perspective through much of his adaptation, including the protagonist's encounter with the mirror, Argentinian comic artist Horatio Lalia gradually changes the sequence into third-person perspective.

Figure 5. Erik Kriek. Final two Panels from "El Introso." 15, 16.

The real question of Kriek's approach is what effect it has on the audience. Why would the artist spend the entire sequence building up this construction of "inside," only to abandon it during the climax of the story? I would contend that we are seeing an attempt to ground the impact of

---

7. In *Castle Freak*, the protagonist is not shown in its entirety until the latter portion of the film. As noted above, there is a mirror scene similar to the one in HPL's story, but the mirror is obscured by a fog or grime that prevents the audience from getting a clear look at it.

the revelation, almost as a cinematic reaction shot, to meet viewers halfway in allowing them to indulge in a voyeuristic moment, untethered by the illusion of embodiment. Indeed, the truly terrible becomes more tolerable when it happens to someone else rather than ourselves, something Edmund Burke remarked on, stating "I am convinced we have a degree of delight, and that no small one, in the real misfortunes and pains of others" (118). Kriek's representation of this moment as both central and distant is reinforced through his excision of the original tale's conclusion whereby the protagonist celebrates its difference from humanity. Instead the sequence of the tale is cleaved at this moment, reinforcing the revelation of difference as something abject by the protagonist's reaction. The "inside" in this instance is neglected for spectacle, reducing its philosophical and aesthetic impact on the viewer. Additionally, the sequence is a modified version of the previous frames in that it introduces the mirror as an external image and then, rather than placing the mirror as a lived image through first-person perspective, Kriek places the monstrous image into a frame. This frame, unlike the previous ones, encases an image of horror and dread, existing as an inversion of the audience's notion of beauty and acceptable subject matter.

As the mirror within "The Outsider" reveals the narrator's misguided assumptions about its identity, the image is disruptive of time and space once it finds its appearance abject.[8] This disruption also occurs within the audience as it realizes the narrator is shaken by its unrecognized reflection. Again, there is an asymmetrical relationship between reality and expectations that the image divulges, creating new identity and, more importantly, a way of seeing that assumes the protagonist's new set of values. In adapting the scene, Erik Kriek chose to break first-person point of view; while the protagonist sees a representation of third-person perspective, so does the audience (Figure 5).

In revealing third-person perspective, Kriek acknowledges the audience's difficulty with emotionally investing in an "inside" that lacks a distant or removed viewpoint of the central figure. With an absence of facial expression, as demonstrated in the previous panels of the comic, the view-

---

8. "The Shadow out of Time" similarly uses mirrors in displacing identity. The narrator Nathaniel Wingate Peaslee finds that his mind and that of an alien representative of the Great Race of Yith have been transposed, resulting in a fear of mirrors.

er has little to interpret the emotional status of the protagonist. Instead, Kriek opts to indicate the protagonist's anxiety and transformation of subjectivity by changing perspective, allowing the audience to see the character's reaction when viewing its own face in the mirror just as the character does. In his own words, the artist says of his choice of perspective, "We see what the person in the story sees and we witness his horror as he finally realizes what he actually is" (Kriek). This point of departure from first-person point of view arises in the panel sequence during a moment of self-realization when the protagonist understands that this final image reflects his true state and retroactively rewrites all the proceeding events that led to its reveal.

Here, Kriek breaks into third-person point of view demonstrating the totality of this discovery, as well as the subject's abrupt awareness of its identity, showing both the protagonist and its reflective image. Formerly invested in this human perspective, the audience is then distanced from the proceedings once this revelation occurs. In Kriek's composition the audience is shown a creature looking at itself, revealing an asymmetrical relationship of what the narrator identifies with as opposed to who the creature appears to be. Through the introduction of this newly defined relationship, the narrative is disrupted with transformative effects to the underlying premise. Exposing the limitations of first-person perspective, this moment captures the viewer's inability to comprehend reality and communicate subjective feelings to the audience, something that requires distance.

Lovecraftian First-Person Perspective in New Media

The potential dilemmas and choices a visual artist will face in adapting Lovecraft's stories are many, especially in regard to perspective. If an image is to evoke a certain mood of horror, the original intention of the author, we must ask, which visual perspective is ideal? Should the protagonist have more presence and function as horror's mediator through third-person perspective or simply serve as a passive vehicle for the audience via first-person perspective? Lovecraft himself was a proponent of using human protagonists as a point of comparison for the cosmic and weird, an approach that called for looking from the human vantage point. Through his adaptation, Erik Kriek echoes Lovecraft in representing an unemotional protagonist who is traversing the subterranean and ground-level cemetery, allowing the landscape and architecture to establish the sequence's mood. What distinguishes Kriek's version is his willingness to drop the visual trappings of first-person perspective to amplify certain effects and dissolve the line between "I" and "they."

Kriek's approach is significantly relevant as an increasing number of Lovecraft adaptations are created within the visual arts, many utilizing first-person perspective. The way in which this perspective is modified further indicates how Lovecraft's supernatural codes are shifting to accommodate changing tastes and movements. In contemporary cinema, for instance, the found-footage horror genre utilizes a modified version of the "inside" with the camera serving as an extension of the body, an approach that Alexander Galloway refers to as "camcorder subjectivity" in such films as *The Blair Witch Project* (1999), *Cloverfield* (2008), *The Tunnel Movie* (2011), *V/H/S* (2012), and *V/H/S 2* (2013) (49). In a similar development, as video games come to occupy a prominent position within contemporary visual culture, there is an acknowledgment among artists, as well as the audience, that the use of such perspective is effective in generating the kind of "awe," "fear," and "wonder" Lovecraft coveted. In recent first-person-centric horror video games, such as *Call of Cthulhu: Dark Corners of the Earth* (2005), *Amnesia: The Dark Descent* (2010), *Alien: Isolation* (2014), and *The Vanishing of Ethan Carter* (2014), this perspective continues to have relevance, reinforcing the effectiveness of Lovecraft's approach. While Kriek's adaptation of "The Outsider" indicates certain limitations of the form that will undoubtedly be taken up by subsequent artists in the genre, the continued relevance of the "inside" speaks to the creation of further works through such an approach, as Lovecraftian horror increases its presence in contemporary visual culture.

Works Cited

Branigan, Edward. *Point of View in the Cinema: A Theory of Narration and Subjectivity in Classical Film*. Berlin: Mouton, 1984.

Burke, Edmund. *A Philosophical Inquiry into the Origin of Our Ideas of the Sublime and Beautiful*. 1767. Google Books.

Devereaux, Devon, and Tom Pomplun. "The Outsider." In *Graphic Classics: H. P. Lovecraft*. Mount Horeb, WI: Eureka Productions, 2002.

Duncan, Randy, and Matthew Smith. *The Power of Comics: History, Form, and Culture*. New York: Continuum, 2009.

Goldschlagel, B. "The Outsider." April 1926. In *A Lovecraft Retrospective: Artists Inspired by H. P. Lovecraft.* Lakewood, CO: Centipede Press, 2008.

Galloway, Alexander R. "Origins of the First-Person Shooter." In *Gaming: Essays on Algorithmic Culture.* Electronic Mediations, Volume 18. Minneapolis: University of Minnesota Press, 2006.

Gordon, Stuart. *Castle Freak.* Full Moon Entertainment, 1995.

Hutcheon, Linda. *A Theory of Adaptation.* New York: Routledge, 2006.

Indick, Ben. "Lovecraft's Ladies." 1975. In *Discovering H. P. Lovecraft*, ed., Darrell Schweitzer. Rev. ed. Holicong, PA: Wildside Press, 2001.

Joshi, S. T. *A Dreamer and a Visionary : H. P. Lovecraft in His Time.* Liverpool: Liverpool University Press, 2001.

Kriek, Erik. *H. P. Lovecraft: Desde el más allá y otras historias.* Barcelona: La Cupula, 2012.

———. Email interview. 12 May 2002.

Lalia, Horacio. "El extraño." In *Lovecraft: El grimorio maldito.* Buenos Aires: Thalos, 1998.

Lovecraft, H. P., and August Derleth. *Essential Solitude: The Letters of H. P. Lovecraft and August Derleth.* Ed. David E. Schultz and S. T. Joshi. New York: Hippocampus Press, 2008.

Rodríguez, Hernán. "L'Étranger." In *Le Temple.* Paris: Atmospheres/Emmanuel Proust Editions, 2008.

Sipos, Thomas M. *Horror Film Aesthetics: Creating the Visual Language of Fear.* Jefferson, NC: McFarland, 2010.

Stevens, Alec Preson. "The Outsider." *Prime Cuts* No. 1 (January 1987): 3–8.

Stewart, Bhob, and Steve Harper. "The Outsider." *Monsters Attack!* No. 2 (October 1989): 31–36.

H. P. Lovecraft's Optimism

Matthew Beach
Ph.D., Brown University

Optimism may seem like a strange concept through which to read the weird tales of H. P. Lovecraft, who is more commonly remembered as a weaver of dark, pessimistic stories of what he termed "cosmic outsideness": the belief that man is an insignificant entity in a vast universe inhabited by cosmic beings indifferent if not hostile to his existence. Lovecraft explained the "outsideness" or "externality" of his work in a letter to Farnsworth Wright, the editor of *Weird Tales*, dated 5 July 1927:

> Now all my tales are based on the fundamental premise that common human laws and interests and emotions have no validity or significance in the vast cosmos-at-large.... To achieve the essence of real externality, whether of time or space or dimension, one must forget that such things as organic life, good and evil, love and hate, and all such local attributes of a negligible and temporary race called mankind, have any existence at all. (SL 2.150)

The apparent pessimism of Lovecraft's style is his (re)contextualizing of all human affairs within a vast if not infinite framework of cosmic space and time. This context repositions human "interests and emotions" as the "local" concerns of a transient race which have no "significance" in the "cosmos-at-large." Most readers are more familiar with the bleak opening of Lovecraft's "The Call of Cthulhu" (1926), which is often cited as a concise literary expression of the author's brand of cosmic horror as well as his "pessimism." The narrator Francis Wayland Thurston asserts that "The most merciful thing in the world . . . is the inability of the human mind to correlate all its contents" (CF 2.21). Thurston notes that only a few researchers into the esoteric have "guessed at the awesome grandeur of the cosmic cycle" and "hinted at strange survivals in terms which would freeze the blood if not masked by a bland optimism" (CF 2.22). For the narrator of this tale, optimism as a response to the "grandeur of the cosmic cycle" is little more than a defense against the stark reality of time's infinite expanse, and a "bland" one at that. The "pessimism" of this story, then, as well as much of Lovecraft's other tales, is not the belief that humanity has no future or that all human values are mere illusions. Rather, it is a bracketing of humanity's future and values as "local" so that Lovecraft may focus on his real concern: the space and time beyond the human.

Critics of the modern horror genre (and the Gothic tradition from which it emerged) often identify a strand of pessimism as foundational to the genre's form and function.[1] Most recently, Eugene Thacker's *In the Dust of This Planet* (2011) defines the pessimism of the horror genre as arising from an effort to think through what he terms the "world-without-us" or the "subtraction of the human from the world" (5). For Thacker, "*'horror' is a non-philosophical attempt to think about the world-without-us philosophically*" (9; emphasis in original). He traces the philosophical roots of the horror genre to Arthur Schopenhauer's and Friedrich Nietzsche's interrogation of the place of human values and existence within a universe devoid of ultimate meaning or teleology. Thacker positions the horror genre within this philosophical tradition of what he calls "Cosmic Pessimism," since it likewise poses "the difficult thought of the world as absolutely unhuman, and indifferent to the hopes, desires, and struggles of human individuals and groups" (17). According to Thacker, "Schopenhauer's pessimism is less about a human pessimism (e.g., the all-too-human despair of an identity crisis or a lapse in faith), and more about the way in which thought in itself always devolves upon its own limits, the hinge through which positive knowledge turns into negative knowledge" (19). He notes that in order to locate "an equal to Schopenhauer" or Nietzsche "one would have to look not to philosophy but to writers of supernatural

---

1. The Gothic is often understood as focusing on the irrational side of human nature and society left out of the more optimistic and rational portrayal of man in Enlightenment philosophy, and as such is often tentatively aligned with a form of pessimism. However, in drawing attention to what is excluded from "optimistic" philosophies, the Gothic genre also operates as a form of social critique. For more on the social and critical function of the Gothic novel, see Cathy Davidson and Julia Stern. Many critics see a line of continuation between Gothic pessimism and HPL's weird tales. For instance, Dirk W. Mosig argues that "Lovecraft was pessimistic with respect to man's ability to cope with the realization of his own meaninglessness and insignificance in an indifferent universe" (105). He then quotes the opening of "Cthulhu" to illustrate this point.

horror such as H. P. Lovecraft, whose stories evoke a sense of what he termed 'cosmic outsideness'" (19). Thacker then quotes the beginning of "Cthulhu" to demonstrate how closely Schopenhauer's bleak philosophy of cosmic pessimism is echoed in the grim opening words of the narrator Thurston.[2]

While Thacker's argument that Lovecraft's stories focus on the cosmic or the "world-without-us" rather than the local or human is difficult to deny, his reading of Lovecraft's philosophy as a form of pessimism is ultimately reductive in scope. For there is more to Lovecraft's fiction and his theory of time than his apparent cosmic pessimism or at best indifference toward the future of human affairs would suggest. It is through the "external" terrain of cosmological time, the terrain his tales work so elegantly to construct, that the question of Lovecraft's optimism should be addressed. In philosophical usage, optimism represents the theory that the universe operates according to "optimal" conditions (from the Latin *optimus*, meaning "best" [OED]), while in colloquial terms optimism defines a personal perspective characterized by "hopefulness and confidence about the future or the successful outcome of something" (OED). I take optimism to mean an orientation toward time that interprets it as full rather than empty of possibilities. A theory of or orientation toward time as devoid of potential would therefore be the meaning of pessimism in this context. What Lovecraft's work insists on in this register is the *impersonality* of these possibilities as well as the infinite expanse and complexity of time. I argue that Lovecraft's refusal to foreclose time's potentiality despite what it may bring to the fragile human ego is a form of optimism. I suggest that although Lovecraft's tales often enact a conflict with time that culminates in the narrator's (and reader's) experience of cosmic terror, these conflicts are not reducible to pessimism alone. Alongside this pessimism of the local, there is also a subtler form of cosmic optimism: a "weird" optimism we can read if we shift focus from the perspective of the narrators to the theories of cosmic temporality developed conceptually in his narratives.

---

2. HPL was familiar with the work of both Schopenhauer and Nietzsche. See "Nietzscheism and Realism" (CE 5.69–72). As S. T. Joshi notes, the title is misleading, since HPL's comments are chiefly derived from the work of Schopenhauer. However, his correspondence and other essays clearly demonstrate his familiarity with the work of Nietzsche.

Lovecraft's stories, especially his late fiction, are predominantly concerned with the conflicts brought about by time itself. In a letter to E. Hoffmann Price dated 15 August 1934, Lovecraft explains that the only conflict that has any significance to him is "that of *the principle of freedom or irregularity or adventurous opportunity against the eternal and maddening rigidity of cosmic law . . . especially the laws of time*" (SL 5.19; emphasis in original). Here we already begin to register a facet of Lovecraft's fiction that complicates (or qualifies) both his "local" as well as his apparent cosmic pessimism. The power of his stories resides in their imaginative defiance of the seeming rigidity of time in order to explore what it would mean to be free of this most "maddening" of laws. Through a dramatic conflict with time, his tales formulate a theory of temporality that represents a "weird" form of cosmic optimism rather than pessimism. Against Thacker's reading of Lovecraft's cosmic pessimism, my argument is that his cosmic philosophy represents a "local" pessimism bounded by a cosmic optimism easily mistaken for pessimism when evaluated from the limited perspective of local human values. What Lovecraft's fiction in general and late stories such as "The Shadow out of Time" (1934-35) in particular demonstrate is a weird form of cosmic optimism that relates more to the complex nature of time itself than to individual human aspirations. His correspondence, however, reveals that Lovecraft understood his cosmic philosophy as offering consolation if not a strange form of hope to those struggling with the "local" problems of human existence.

In recent literary criticism, optimism as a philosophical and aesthetic concept has emerged as a productive topic of investigation.[3] Michael Snediker's *Queer Optimism* (2009) is invested in reconsidering the "blandness" of optimism. Against what he calls a "utopic optimism,"[4] Snediker posits a "queer optimism" that "is not promissory. It doesn't ask that some

---

3. In addition to the texts discussed here, other notable recent investigations of optimism include Lauren Berlant's *Cruel Optimism* (2011) and José Esteban Muñoz's *Cruising Utopia* (2009).

4. Snediker traces the philosophical history of optimism to the work of Gottfried Wilhelm Leibniz, since his writing "underpins many of the ways in which optimism has been thought (or more to the point, not thought) about" (26). He argues that Leibniz's optimism is not at all "futurally oriented" since in Leibniz's system faith "posits optimism not as a practice but as a given" (27).

future time make good on its own hopes" (2). Instead, Snediker's work "asks that optimism . . . might be *interesting*. Queer optimism's interest . . . depends on its emphatic responsiveness to and solicitation of rigorous thinking" (2–3). The force of his argument consists of a re-evaluation of seemingly "bland" philosophical concepts as objects of critical interest. The goal of *Queer Optimism* is to make optimism as interesting and complex of a theoretical concept as pessimism has been by treating optimism as philosophically rigorous rather than trite or naïve. Snediker's case for an informed (or interesting) optimism is an important one, since it argues powerfully against the idea that optimism is by definition directed toward naïve potentialities that will be disproved by a future actuality. *Queer Optimism* argues instead that optimism represents a complex concept with critical possibilities for literary study.

Aligned with Snediker's effort to reevaluate optimism, Sara Ahmed's *The Promise of Happiness* (2010) explores the concrete possibilities of a form of happiness or optimism grounded in the unknowable potentiality of the future. Ahmed argues for a form of happiness that embraces the future as a site or horizon of potential rather than assurance. She points out that the etymology of the word "happiness," from the Middle English *hap*, means "chance" or "fortune" (22). Ahmed argues that the "history of happiness could be described as the history of the removal of the hap from happiness" (207). To correct this erasure, Ahmed argues for a happiness or politics of the "hap," that is, for the future as a horizon of potentialities or chance happenings. She suggests that this form of happiness "would be alive to chance, to chance arrivals, to the perhaps of a happening. . . . We might remind ourselves that the 'perhaps' shares its 'hap' with 'happiness.' The happy future is the future of the perhaps" (198). To embrace this version of happiness requires a (re)orientation to time that interprets it as full of potentiality or chance. Her attention to the potentialities of time is helpful for reinterpreting optimism as we normally understand it, as the future realization of a desire, to a theory of time itself that acknowledges rather than forecloses possibilities.

Lovecraft's late fiction is particularly interested in exploring the unknown possibilities of time and space. While his earlier tales are also driven by a "dramatic conflict with time," his later stories are distinct for framing these conflicts in a realistic rather than a fantasy setting. Much of his work before the 1930s depended upon or at least incorporated an element of the supernatural. While composing *At the Mountains of Madness* (1931), however, Lovecraft articulated the need for a new direction to his art:

> The time has come when the normal revolt against time, space & matter must assume a form not overtly incompatible with what is known of reality—when it must be gratified by images forming *supplements* rather than *contradictions* of the visible & mensurable universe. And what, if not a form of *non-supernatural cosmic art*, is to pacify this sense of revolt? (SL 3.295-96)

For Lovecraft, the weird tale is defined by its orientation toward the cosmic rather than the human. Up until the composition of *Mountains*, this cosmic orientation often uncovered a frightening violation of natural law from beyond the known universe.[5] Here, however, Lovecraft redefines the function of the weird tale from the violation of the "visible & mensurable universe" to elaborating a possible *supplement* to it. In short, rather than contradicting actualities, Lovecraft's late art offers a vista of weird *potentialities* that expand or revise the complexity or fullness of the known universe.

It is precisely this orientation toward strange possibilities that makes Lovecraft so critical of "bland" optimism, for his aversion to this form of optimism hinges on its uncritical faith in the known universe as well as an assured future. In "Supernatural Horror in Literature" (1927),[6] he defends the weird tale against the charge that fiction must adhere to the conditions of the known universe—that is, to actuality rather than possibility: "Against it are discharged all the shafts of a materialistic sophistication which clings

---

5. It is of course possible to classify a handful of HPL's earlier tales as examples of "non-supernatural cosmic art," such as "The Whisperer in Darkness," written between February and September 1930 (though having its genesis in HPL's 1928 visit to Vermont), and "The Mound," one of HPL's revision tales composed in December 1929-January 1930. These stories, written shortly before *Mountains*, reveal HPL beginning to explore the possibility of a non-supernatural cosmic art. Other tales that anticipate HPL's late style include "The Call of Cthulhu" and "The Colour out of Space."

6. *Supernatural Horror* was written before *Mountains*, and as such still adheres to HPL's earlier model of the weird tale as primarily supernatural. Even here, however, HPL is heavily reliant upon the "natural" as a necessary counterpoint or foil for the supernatural: "Serious weird stories are either made realistically intense by close consistency and perfect fidelity to Nature except in the one supernatural direction which the author allows himself, or else cast altogether in the realm of phantasy . . ." (87).

to frequently felt emotions and external events, and of a naively inspired idealism which deprecates the aesthetic motive and calls for a didactic literature to 'uplift' the reader toward a suitable degree of smirking optimism" (CE 2.82). It is this bland and "smirking" optimism that Lovecraft's late tales contest, for the "revolt" in his new approach to cosmic art rests precisely in its argument that the natural universe contains a vast arena of possibilities that are impossible to predict. Against the smirking assurance of a bland optimism, Lovecraft's late tales assert that finite human beings cannot imagine the vast possibilities the universe may contain until confronted with them. The non-supernatural style of these tales functions in service of this revolt against the assurance in actuality, since it frames the strange possibilities of the tales within a natural rather than fantastical framework—as a previously unknown component rather than a contradiction of nature. As S. T. Joshi puts it in *The Weird Tale* (1990), Lovecraft's later tales are a form of *"quasi science fiction"* in which "the 'supernatural' is not *ontological* but *epistemological*: it is only our ignorance of certain 'natural laws' that creates the illusion of supernaturalism" (7; emphasis in original). In short, in revolt against the stasis of the actual, the weird tale confronts the reader with the unknown. Lovecraft identifies the "one test of the really weird" as "whether or not there be excited in the reader a profound sense of dread, and of contact with unknown spheres and powers" (CE 2.84). For Lovecraft, however, the unknown possibilities represented by the weird tale inspire not only dread but also "curiosity"; the ultimate "test" of the weird tale its ability to inspire "a subtle attitude of awed listening" (CE 2.84). The reader of the weird tale listens in awe for what potentially lurks in the shadows of the infinite expanse of the cosmos.

To illustrate the weird cosmic optimism of Lovecraft's theory of time, I turn first to one of his late tales, "The Shadow out of Time." As one of Lovecraft's most "cosmic" tales in scope,[7] "The Shadow out of Time" seeks to elicit a sense of awe at man's place in the "seething vortex of time" (CF

---

7. S. T. Joshi calls "The Shadow out of Time" the "most cosmic of HPL's tales aside from *At the Mountains of Madness*" (Lovecraft, *Complete Fiction* 948). While Joshi points out the temporal *span* of *Mountains* is more expansive than that of "Shadow," I have chosen to read "The Shadow out of Time" as the most mature of HPL's tales concerning the potentiality of cosmic time because the temporal *complexity* of this tale far exceeds that of *At the Mountains of Madness*.

3.363) while remaining firmly grounded in the natural world. The scope of these cosmic potentialities is represented most concretely in "Shadow" by the Great Race's central archive. The narrator Peaslee describes the experience of reading the "closed chapters of inconceivable pasts and dizzy vortices of future time" as forming "despite the abysmal horrors often unveiled, the supreme experience of life" (CF 3.388). The description of the archive also registers the *impersonality* of Lovecraft's view of time. The "horrors" unveiled by the archive include a revelation of man's finite place within the infinite span of cosmic time (and space). Peaslee recalls that his "own history was assigned a specific place in the vaults of the lowest or vertebrate level" (CF 3.400). Within the archive, humanity has its place amidst all the possible life in the temporal-spatial span of the cosmos. Peaslee comes to know this place well. Lovecraft's placement of Peaslee's (and mankind's) record on the "lowest level" between those biological entities immediately preceding and following it is designed to highlight the smallness of the human species and individual ego within the cosmos. For the Great Race, however, Peaslee's record has clear value as a representative account of a specific class of organic life (vertebrate, etc.). The horror for Peaslee is that this value is both contextual and impersonal: in the archive, humanity suffers the "indignity" of being placed on the lowest shelf because of its relatively late and brief emergence into recorded time. The impersonality of the archive is the result of the decidedly non-anthropocentric value system ordering its classification. This classification is predicated upon a non-human perspective of time as infinite in expanse and duration. Within such a system, humanity is a slim set of volumes amidst infinite others across time and space. The impersonal archive in "Shadow" insists that from a cosmological perspective the human tendency to order time around the emergence of one species (*Homo sapiens*) represents a decidedly narrow or "local" view of time.

The Yithians themselves represent only a part of this vast universal archive. In "Shadow," the Great Race functions primarily as Lovecraft's avatar for imagining the possibilities inherent in cosmic time. Peaslee's research into the Great Race first hints at what may potentially be lurking within the vastness of time. The overall "assumption" of the texts he consults is that

> mankind is only one—perhaps the latest—of the highly evolved and dominant races of this planet's long and largely unknown career. Things of inconcei-

vable shape, they implied, had reared great towers to the sky and delved into every secret of Nature before the first amphibian forbear of man had crawled out of the hot sea three hundred million years ago. Some had come down from the stars; a few were as old as the cosmos itself; others had arisen swiftly from terrene germs as far behind the first germs of our life-cycle as those germs are behind ourselves. Spans of thousands of millions of years, and linkages with other galaxies and universes, were freely spoken of. Indeed, there was no such thing as time in its humanly accepted sense. (CF 3.385)

Here and throughout the tale, "Shadow" frames mankind as "only one" of the species to dominate the planet—"the latest" but not the last. More importantly, this passage is representative of the style of Lovecraft's tales, which often proceed by implying or hinting at dizzying cosmic possibilities beyond the narrator's knowledge and comprehension. For as much as his tales reveal, their weird power lies primarily in their gesturing toward strange possibilities that remain forever within the shadows. Here we have a history of beings who came "down from the stars," others "as old as the cosmos itself," and still more that arose "from terrene germs." At times, these beings will correlate with those described in Lovecraft's other weird tales. Just as frequently, though, these terse descriptions function only as vague hints of the possible life forms that may inhabit the cosmos.

For Lovecraft, the purpose of the weird tale is to bring the reader into "contact with unknown spheres and powers"; it is not to reveal or explain (away) the secrets of these unknown spheres and powers.[8] In order to evoke "a subtle attitude of awed listening," "Shadow" simultaneously imagines new truths about nature and time *and* implies that a vast realm of possibility remains unrevealed beyond this. As detailed or in-depth as "Shadow" may be about the history of the Great Race, Lovecraft (or his narrators) always present their tales as only scratching the surface. It is precisely for this reason that critics such as Graham Harman misread Lovecraft's late (non-supernatural) tales as revealing "too much." In *Weird Realism* (2012), Harman faults tales such as "Shadow" and *Mountains* for destroying the weird tale's atmosphere by providing extensive details about

---

8. In "Notes on Writing Weird Fiction," HPL clarifies that "prime emphasis should be given to *subtle suggestion*—imperceptible hints and touches of selective associative detail which express shadings of moods and build up a vague illusion of the strange reality of the unreal" (CE 2.177-78; emphasis in original).

the Great Race. For Harman, the Great Race "ought to remain basically unknown; just palpable enough to seem physically present, but not grasped down to the minutest details" (223). Harman's verdict on these two tales is surprising, for he is otherwise an adept reader of Lovecraft's style. He astutely identifies the "allusive aspect of Lovecraft's style" that resides in "the gap he produces between an ungraspable thing and the vaguely relevant descriptions that the narrator is able to attempt" (24). What Harman appears to miss in the later tales is how Lovecraft's shift to a "non-supernatural cosmic art" required a revision of this "allusive style": in order to supplement rather than contradict the natural world, Lovecraft must first ground his tales in descriptive and realistic detail of the "visible & mensurable universe" before alluding to what still resides beyond the narrator's knowledge (i.e., the gap Harman refers to). Harman therefore overlooks the double-movement of Lovecraft's late style, where each new revelation serves also (if not primarily) to clarify what remains concealed.[9] Hence while Peaslee gains an intimate knowledge of (some of) the history of the Great Race, his research into the Yithians also yields intimations of even stranger possibilities that remain forever beyond his reach. In Lovecraft's tales, an advance in knowledge always *expands* rather than reduces the terrain of the unknown; every discovery Peaslee makes only displaces or relocates the "gap" in (his) knowledge rather than eliminating it. It could hardly be otherwise, since for Lovecraft the infinite possibilities of the cosmos are not capable of being fully grasped by the finite mind of man. These possibilities remain forever on the edge of his consciousness, to continually frighten, intrigue, and awe him.

In addition to the myriad beings only hinted at in the above passage, there is also the implication of a cosmic temporality beyond the local human system of ordering time. Cosmic time confounds human temporality

---

9. Another way of understanding the style of "Shadow" and *Mountains* is through Fritz Leiber's argument about HPL's use of the "device of *confirmation*" (56). Leiber argues that in HPL's tales "the story-ending does not come as a surprise, but as a final, long-anticipated 'convincer.' The reader knows, and is supposed to know, what is coming, but this only prepares and adds to his shivers when the narrator supplies the last and incontrovertible piece of evidence" (56). In other words, the relation between what is revealed and concealed in these two tales (and the rest of HPL's fiction) is more complex than Harman allows for, and simply because the reader knows "too much" does not necessarily lessen the overall weird or "shivering" atmosphere of the tales.

not only due to its infinite duration but also because of its non-linear structure. As in his other weird tales, "time" in this passage and throughout "Shadow" represents a complex of embedded temporalities rather than a unitary (i.e., linear) vector. Peaslee mentions "linkages" with other "galaxies and universes" that traverse not only the expanse of space but also forge connections across the distance of time. Peaslee's previous intuition into the "vertiginous cycles of time" is represented in this passage by an overlaying of multiple temporalities: the length of thousands of millions of years and a temporality outside any "human sense" are both operative temporal markers in this passage. These two temporal modes represent supplemental rather than contradictory forms of temporality in "Shadow": an immense if not infinite span of time is woven together with a form of time beyond human measurement. In the Lovecraftian universe, time is irreducibly multiple.

Another example of this temporal overlay or embedding in "Shadow" is Peaslee's discovery of the ancient city beneath modern-day Australia. Buried or embedded within "normal" modern human time is a timeless city once inhabited by beings who themselves traversed time. Doubting his experience at the end of his narrative, Peaslee remarks: "If that abyss and what it held were real, there is no hope. Then, all too truly, there lies upon this world of man a mocking and incredible shadow out of time" (*CF* 3.449). Peaslee concludes that if the Great Race is real then there is "no hope" for the future; however, Lovecraft's choice of the image of the shadow tells a slightly different story. This shadow that emerges "out of time" does not destroy or elide "the world of man." Instead, the shadow "mocks" man and his (local) perspective of time by overlaying it with its own form. The shadow casts the world of man in a different (dimmer) light, complicating man's linear version of time by making its boundaries less distinct. In this twilight, the "humanly accepted sense" of time becomes hazier, but it does not disappear. Instead, this sense of time, previously believed to be Time itself, is re-contextualized as one form of temporality among other operative forms. Peaslee's own retrospective narrative demonstrates that he is still capable of working within linear temporal forms if he so chooses. As the narrative of "Shadow" shows, the only difference is that this temporal form is now intertwined with multiple others into a complex cycle of overlapping temporalities. The shadow cast over the world does not darken Peaslee's vision of time but rather forces him to adjust his perception to the "shadowy" or subtler operation(s) of temporality.

It is at the conclusion of "Shadow" that Peaslee has his most significant encounter with the vertiginous depths of this shadow (out) of time. While fleeing from the "polypous" being awakened by his exploration (the ancient antagonists of the Great Race), Peaslee tumbles into a vast chasm of "materially tangible darkness":

> There was a hideous fall through incalculable leagues of viscous, sentient darkness, and a babel of noises utterly alien to all that we know of the earth and its organic life. Dormant, rudimentary senses seemed to start into vitality within me, telling of pits and voids peopled by floating horrors and leading to sunless crags and oceans and teeming cities of windowless basalt towers upon which no light ever shone. (CF 3.447)

In spite of the "floating horrors" revealed by this new perception of (or through) time, Peaslee describes the experience as awakening a "vitality" in him. Like Peaslee's browsing of the archive, this encounter with the viscous, sentient shadow of time represents a "supreme experience" despite the horror it reveals. As he continues to fall, Peaslee "senses" even more of the possibilities concealed within the cosmos: "Secrets of the primal planet ... flashed through my brain without the aid of sight or sound, and there were known to me things which not even the wildest of my former dreams had ever suggested" (CF 3.447). In proper Lovecraftian fashion, Peaslee only hints at the existence of the "secrets of the primal planet" that transcend the "wildest" of his dreams. Beyond even what he has seen in his own research and experience among the Great Race, Peaslee's final fall into the inky abyss offers his most significant glimpse into the shadowy potentials of the cosmos through a strange experience of the multiplicity and expanse of time. Though the tale concludes with Peaslee doubting the veracity of these visions, his narrative reveals how deeply he has been affected by his experience of these "reachings and seizures in the cosmos-wide vortex of time" (CF 3.449).

While Lovecraft's optimism may appear to reside out of reach in the "cosmos-wide vortex of time," it is also possible this weird optimism may "come down from the stars" to cast its shadow over the "local" concerns of the human race. In his correspondence, Lovecraft often spoke of cosmic time to those struggling with the very human problems of distress, illness, and loss. It seems odd at first that Lovecraft would reference the very cosmic time he believes renders human suffering "insignificant" in these moments, but it is clear from his letters that he understands his cosmic philosophy as offering real consolation. Lovecraft's weird optimism is therefore also notable in his letters, particularly in those he wrote to console others experiencing pain or bereavement. For instance, from March to September 1935 Lovecraft wrote a series of letters to Helen V. Sully intended to cheer her up during a period of despondency. Because Sully had expressed a debilitating concern with how others perceive her, Lovecraft attempts to provide a consoling perspective by framing the life of human beings within the context of cosmic space and time: "The people on Mars will never know that any human race exists—the people on Neptune can never know that the Earth exists—the people on the planets of Alpha Centauri can never know that the solar planets exist—the people of transgalactic systems can never know that the sun exists" (SL 5.114). Lovecraft reframes Sully's concern for the opinions of those in her social circle in the larger context of the cosmos in order to stress both the futility and absurdity of harping on the opinions of others. He finishes by expanding the temporal frame from Sully's (and his) own life span to the infinite time of the cosmos: "A few trillion years hence there will be no consciousness in existence that can know of the former existence of such a thing as a human race. The universe will be just as it would have been had no Earth existed" (SL 5.114). This is certainly a weird form of consolation, but one that is deeply informed by Lovecraft's cosmic optimism about the infinite and vast potentials of time and space. Lest Sully believe he is encouraging a form of cynicism when it comes to dealing with others, he assures her, "It is certainly not necessary to be a misanthrope" (SL 5.113). Lovecraft counsels Sully "not to expect too much" and "to enjoy each [person] for his own specialty & expect no more" while supplementing her life with "non-human objects of beauty" and "significance" (SL 5.114). Though this sounds like a form of philosophical resignation, his consoling advice to Sully is best understood as a form of his weird cosmic optimism since it positions human life within a cosmic context while allowing for the possibility of enjoyment, surprise, and even (cautious) hope.

Lovecraft directly addresses the place of hope within his cosmic philosophy in his letters to Sully. He specifically positions his consoling advice to her as distinct from traditional forms of optimism and pessimism, which as we have seen are colloquially understood as different perspectives on what the future holds—i.e., on hope. In a letter dated 15 August 1935, he tells Sully that his advice to her is *"not irresponsible and platitudinous optimism."*[10] Like the "bland" optimism pilloried in "Cthulhu," Lovecraft distinguishes his weird optimism from "irresponsible" forms because his does not seek to hide the harsh truths of cosmic space and time. In a letter dated 23 September 1935, Lovecraft likewise differentiates his cosmic philosophy from traditional forms of pessimism: "I hope that my preceding epistle did not sound too unrelievedly pessimistic. I am not a *pessimist*, but merely a realistic *indifferentist*" (*SL* 5.195; emphasis in original). Lovecraft's identification of himself as an "indifferentist" does not mean he does not value human life in the cosmos, but rather that he believes the cosmos is indifferent to human life and values. He tells Sully, "It is just as childishly romantic to postulate an actively hostile & malignant cosmos . . . as to postulate a friendly, 'just', & beneficent one. The truth is that the cosmos is blind & unconscious—not giving a hang about any of its denizens, nor even knowing that they exist" (*SL* 5.195). Although the cosmos is indifferent to its "denizens," it does not follow for Lovecraft that all of human existence is for naught: "It [the cosmos] doesn't try to pain them any more than it tries to help or please them—& if any of them can manage to have a good time somehow, in spite of the chaotic jumble of conditions & emotions around & within them, that's quite all right with the universal powers that be" (*SL* 5.195). Nor does it rule out the possibility of an informed hope or guarded optimism: "It would seem to be the part of good sense to harbour great hopes in a sort of light, indefinite way—extracting from them whatever bracing power their imaginative associations may possess, but keeping also in mind the ineluctable natural laws & probabilities which actually prevail" (*SL* 5.196). The only danger Lovecraft foresees is allowing this hope or optimism to become illogical, so he cautions Sully to avoid its "extremes": "Naturally such a course is for many difficult, but almost anyone can probably—with suitable effort & the exercise of coherent logic—approach it in a degree sufficient to remove at least some of the pains & shocks of unrestrained romanticism" (*SL* 5.195). Lovecraft's correspondence offers an insightful supplement to the theories of cosmic time developed within his fiction. His letters help clarify that his philosophy does not represent a form of cosmic pessimism, nor does it necessitate a more "local" (human) stance of pessimism or resignation. Rather, Love-

---

10. Ms., John Hay Library, Brown University.

craft's cosmic philosophy, grounded in the unpredictable potentials of time, is best understood as a form of weird optimism operating on both the level of the "local" and the cosmic.

In the context of his fiction, "The Shadow out of Time" represents Lovecraft's most sustained attempt to think through the complexity and possibilities of time. As S. T. Joshi and David E. Schultz note in their edition of the tale, the story is a fitting "capstone to a twenty-year attempt to capture the sense of wonder and awe [Lovecraft] felt at the boundless reaches of space and time" (25). For Lovecraft, this sense of awe and wonder is always mixed with horror or fear; or rather, wonder and horror represent intimately related responses to the unknown possibilities of space and time. As Lovecraft succinctly expresses it in the opening sentence of "Supernatural Horror in Literature": "The oldest and strongest emotion of mankind is fear, and the oldest and strongest kind of fear is fear of the unknown" (CE 2.82). There will therefore always be a need for "a literature of cosmic fear" because "children will always be afraid of the dark, and men . . . will always tremble at the thought of the hidden and fathomless worlds of strange life which may pulsate in the gulfs beyond the stars" (CE 2.84). Yet the unknown, as we have seen in "Shadow," not only frightens but also evokes an "inevitable fascination of wonder and curiosity" (CE 2.83); Peaslee "trembles" in horror *and* wonder at what "may pulsate in the gulfs" beyond man's small (local) place in the cosmos. It is out of the depth or fullness of these shadowy possibilities that Lovecraft's tale(s) and his weird optimism are formed.

Works Cited

Ahmed, Sara. *The Promise of Happiness*. Durham, NC: Duke University Press, 2010.

Berlant, Lauren. *Cruel Optimism*. Durham, NC: Duke University Press, 2011.

Davidson, Cathy N. *Revolution and the Word: The Rise of the Novel in America*. New York: Oxford University Press, 1986.

Harman, Graham. *Weird Realism: Lovecraft and Philosophy*. Winchester, UK: Zero Books, 2012.

Joshi, S. T. *The Weird Tale*. Austin: University of Texas Press, 1990.

Leiber, Fritz. "A Literary Copernicus." 1949. In *H. P. Lovecraft: Four Decades of Criticism*, ed S. T. Joshi. Athens: Ohio University Press, 1980. 50-62.

Lovecraft, H. P. *The Complete Fiction.* [Ed. S. T. Joshi.] New York: Barnes & Noble, 2008.

———. *The Shadow out of Time.* Ed. S. T. Joshi and David E. Schultz. New York: Hippocampus Press, 2001.

Mosig, Dirk W. "H. P. Lovecraft: Myth Maker." 1976. In *H. P. Lovecraft: Four Decades of Criticism*, ed., S. T. Joshi. Athens: Ohio University Press, 1980. 104–12.

Muñoz, José Esteban. *Cruising Utopia: The Then and There of Queer Futurity.* New York: New York University Press, 2009.

Snediker, Michael D. *Queer Optimism: Lyric Personhood and Other Felicitous Persuasions.* Minneapolis: University of Minnesota Press, 2008.

Stern, Julia A. *The Plight of Feeling: Sympathy and Dissent in the Early American Novel.* Chicago: University of Chicago Press, 1997.

Thacker, Eugene. *In the Dust of This Planet: Horror of Philosophy, Volume 1.* Winchester, UK: Zero Books, 2011.

Insider, Outsider: From the Commonplace to the Uncanny in H. P. Lovecraft's Narration and Descriptions

Daphnée Tasia Bourdages-Athanassiou
Student, Université Laval

The "Cthulhu Mythos," a mythology of the "unnamable" often singled out for its uniqueness, originality, and "cosmic horror," is a core element of H. P. Lovecraft's works. It is more than just a fictional mythology, however; it is a general feeling of uneasiness infused in a bleak world. This feeling is constructed in a very complex way in Lovecraft's works. There are, of course, external elements that contribute to build the works' unique atmosphere; the contributions of other authors, for example, who repeat his themes, creating an impression of reality, but in Lovecraft's works themselves there is an entirely alien dimension that brings this horror effect to life. Various techniques are used by Lovecraft to render "the idea of a mythology based on gods that came from space or other dimensions" (Allard, 12-13; all translations by the author).

One of Lovecraft's favored themes is that the universe's logic is entirely alien. The "known universe" is but a tiny part of reality, and reality is unforgiving. It is alien to the characters and, more generally, to humankind. Considering how these themes are weaved into Lovecraft's narratives, one can find, of course, that the characters and events are strange, *fantastique* as in French *fantastique* literature, but that potential, if not well exploited, would produce only a moderate effect. Amidst the tools Lovecraft uses to set his fictional world and offer a sense of otherness to his readers, we will study more closely his narrative and descriptive techniques. We will first consider the narrators and then the descriptions, and conclude by analyzing the interactions the narrative and descriptive passages have.

Definitions

The effects produced by Lovecraft's narrative and descriptive techniques vary in intensity, but they are all are used together in order to create the strangely alien effect and menacing atmosphere typical of Lovecraft's works. "Strangely alien" is a phrase that needs to be clarified in this essay's context. It will be used to define everything that can be unsettling to the readers. If compared to the concept of the "uncanny" developed by Freud, a "concept ... close to the concepts of dread, fear, anxiety, and it is clear that the term is not always used in a precise sense, and therefore often coincides with 'what creates anguish'" (Freud 6), it seems similar but more inclusive, underlying a menace instead of a general sense of worry. Many of Freud's views on the uncanny in literature are common motifs of *fantastique* literature; for example, the idea of the "double," which can be found in Gautier's *Le Chevalier double* and, in a more subtle mode, in Lovecraft's "The Outsider." The parts of Freud's view on the uncanny that are particularly interesting to us, however, are that the uncanny appears when "what we had taken for fantasy offers itself as real, where a symbol takes the importance and the strength of what was symbolized" (Freud 26) or when the commonplace suddenly becomes alien, much like in *fantastique* literature.

The phrase "remoteness effect" will refer to everything that makes readers lose their bearings by showing them a world that bears very little resemblance to theirs. "Otherness effect" will be used to describe a remoteness effect so complete that it shows something entirely alien to humankind or, more generally, to how we apprehend our world. This otherness effect also has as a result to remind the readers of humankind's place in the universe, which is another theme Lovecraft often weaves in his stories; for example, when he writes that "We live on a placid island of ignorance in the midst of black seas of infinity, and it was not meant that we should voyage far" (CF 2.21).

Methodology

Narrative and descriptive passages were studied in parallel. In both cases, an initial analysis of the texts was conducted to find clues about the narrators, mostly their identity and personal impressions about what is happening to them. Narrators were then classified based on whether they are a part of the world of the story (intradiegetic or extradiegetic narrators) and whether they are recounting their own story or someone else's (homodiegetic or heterodiegetic narrators), and, in the case of intradiegetic narrators, their specific traits as characters were laid out.

First-person narrators—who are both intradiegetic and homodiegetic—are especially interesting to us as they are often used to build and maintain a remoteness effect and a sense of worry in the narrative by their personal experience, their characterization, or their nature. The way the remoteness effect, the otherness effect, and the strangely alien effect are created by the narrative style was analyzed, as well as the means of using the narration to create them. Descriptive passages were also studied, especially descriptions of locations. The study of these passages revealed various techniques used to create the same remoteness, otherness, and strangely alien effects. The way the descriptive and narrative techniques work together to create a truly alien and frightening atmosphere was finally studied.

Not all Lovecraft's short stories present a horror based on the concept of otherness, and to better concentrate on this aspect of his works, the short stories that present these techniques were chosen to be studied. Novellas were excluded; preference was given to short stories that present a first-person narrator, and especially an unreliable narrator, although a short story with an extradiegetic narrator, "The Doom That Came to Sarnath," was included in the corpus. "Dagon," "The Temple," "The Festival," "The Outsider," and "Polaris" all present a narrator whom the readers cannot fully trust, whether because he himself advises them not to do so ("The Temple," "Dagon," and "The Festival"), because of the reactions of the character or of the other characters toward him ("Polaris"), or because of the very nature of the narrator ("The Outsider"). These short stories also present physically or conceptually remote or alien locations, a remoteness and otherness that are built by the narration and descriptive techniques used. "The Nameless City" has a more conventional first-person narrator but presents description techniques that build dread in a masterful way. It completes, with "The Doom That Came to Sarnath," a corpus that has many examples to offer.

Remoteness: Through Space and Time

Descriptions in Lovecraft's works are not only used to set the narrative, but also to transform the reality at the right moment by the implications they have. In "The Outsider," for example, the narrator, "after an infinity of awesome, sightless crawling up that concave and desperate precipice," thinks that he is at the top of the highest tower of his castle, but, looking out, realizes that "there stretched around [him] on the level through the grating nothing less than *the solid ground*" (CF 1.269; emphasis in original). This revelation brings a surprise to the narrator—and, most probably, the readers—because it changes everything that was considered true up to this point in the narrative about the environment in which the narrator lives, thus creating a remoteness effect by pulling it away from them. Revelations, sudden or gradual, are indeed one of Lovecraft's favored techniques, and a typical trait of *fantastique* literature.

In "Dagon," the narrator's tale of his stay on the island starts as he finds himself "half sucked into a slimy expanse of hellish black mire which extended about [him] in monotonous undulations as far as [he] could see, and in which [his] boat lay grounded some distance away." The narrator indicates the conditions of his environment, saying: "There was in the air and in the rotting soil a sinister quality which chilled me to the very core. The region was putrid with the carcasses of decaying fish," and uses them as so many clues that eventually bring him to realize that "Through some unprecedented volcanic upheaval, a portion of the ocean floor must have been thrown to the surface, exposing regions which for innumerable millions of years had lain hidden under unfathomable watery depths" (CF 1.54). Small revelation if we compare it to what is coming, but nonetheless a revelation that defines the location of the analepsis as totally remote from both the narrator and the readers: a part of the ocean floor, suddenly accessible because it was ripped from its natural state by immense telluric forces. The building of the remoteness does not stop there: the narrator finds traces of an ancient civilization on the island despite the fact that it has been submerged for millions of years:

> That it was merely a gigantic piece of stone, I soon assured myself; but I was conscious of a distinct impression that its contour and position were not altogether the work of Nature. A closer scrutiny filled me with sensations I cannot express; for despite its enormous magnitude, and its position in an abyss which had yawned at the bottom of the sea since the world was young, I perceived beyond a doubt that the strange object was a well-shaped monolith whose massive bulk had known the workmanship and perhaps the worship of living and thinking creatures. (CF 1.55-56)

This further revelation sheds light on an inexplicable situation because a work of art seems very unlikely to be found in such a location and hints at a completely new aspect of history. Lovecraft further implements here the alien parameters of his fictional setting, which is not only physically remote, but also temporally, and opens the door not only to an effect of remoteness from the readers but to an otherness effect, a sensation that one touches something entirely new to human knowledge, and thus entirely non-human. In "The Temple," the situation of the characters is even more removed from the readers. The narrative starts "in the Atlantic Ocean at a point to me unknown but probably about N. Latitude 20°, W. Longitude 35°, where my ship lies disabled on the ocean floor" (CF 1.156). The very setting of the short story shows a high level of remoteness: the characters are trapped in an extremely hostile environment, since getting out of the submarine means death by drowning. Furthermore, the author makes a point of telling the readers that the exact location is unknown, and that adds a dose of uncertainty to the setting of the action right from the beginning of the story.

Lovecraft often sets a distance between his readers and the world he creates by insisting on the antiquity of the places he describes. In numerous short stories, the settings are timeworn, often predating humanity—in "The Nameless City," for example. In other short stories, the age of the setting is alluded to in soft touches, as in "Dagon": "Several characters obviously represented marine things which are unknown to the modern world, but whose decomposing forms I had observed on the ocean-risen plain" (CF 1.56). Alternatively, in "The Festival": "I saw from the diamond window-panes that it must have been kept very close to its antique state. [I was beckoned to] a low, candle-lit room with massive exposed rafters and dark, stiff, sparse furniture of the seventeenth century. The past was vivid there, for not an attribute was missing" (CF 1.408-9). The ancient aspect of the setting makes it already remote to the minds of the readers, even before their understanding of the actual age of the place. The same is true for "The Temple," where the antiquity of the buildings is implied:

> The art is of the most phenomenal perfection, largely Hellenic in idea, yet strangely individual. It imparts an impression of terrible antiquity, as though it were the remotest rather than the immediate ancestor of Greek art. Nor can I doubt that every detail of this massive product was fashioned from the virgin hillside rock of our planet. (CF 1.165)

The implication of antiquity is achieved here by the comparison to ancient Greek art: since that period is already quite remote from the readers, presenting the temple as predating it by far makes their minds jump backward multiple times. It is interesting to note that this antiquity is characterized as "terrible" instead of interesting or wondrous: if the setting is so old, it must predate humanity, and as such, be non-human and therefore alien and terrible. Fear of the Other is indeed a preferred theme in Lovecraft.

Otherness: Fear of the Unknown

Otherness is brought into Lovecraft's works by the use of strange and frightening—or at least unsettling—situations. His taste for "cosmic horror" results in phenomena that disturb reality and often affect the laws of physics. He uses his descriptive passages to suggest realities that contradict physical laws. In "The Festival," for example, the narrator realizes that no one in the procession seems to be leaving any footprints in the snow: "For though the wind had not left much snow, a few patches did remain on the path near the door; and in that fleeting backward look it seemed to my troubled eyes that they bore no mark of passing feet, not even mine" (CF 1.412). This strange detail contradicts the way we have learned to apprehend our world. Contradicting such certainties lets Lovecraft move away from a previously realistic setting in order to prepare it to become unsettling and uncanny.

In the same way, "The Temple" narrator notes anomalies in his environment, taking the time to specify that his observations seem to be in contradiction with the laws of nature: "I [...] was quick to notice two things: that the U-29 was standing the deep-sea pressure splendidly, and that the peculiar dolphins were still about us, even at a depth where the existence of high organisms is considered impossible by most naturalists" (CF 1.162). In this particular story, the abundant vocabulary linked to darkness ("vastness, darkness, remoteness, antiquity, and mystery of the oceanic abysses," "the dolphins were massed thickly and obscuringly," "the endless night and silence of an ocean-chasm," "The rays were now perceptibly dimmer," "deprivation of light," "utterly black," "waning searchlight," "aqueous abysses," "blind and mounting terror," "in the dark," "total darkness," "without a light," "the darkness of dead batteries") puts the narrator at the mercy of his searchlight and batteries. The use of this vocabulary also makes the gradual return of the light seem strange and abnormal when it happens: "Next there came to me the impression of *light* amidst the darkness of dead batteries, and I seemed to see a sort of phosphorescent glow in the water through the porthole which opened toward the temple. This aroused my curiosity, for I knew of no deep-sea organism capable of emitting such luminosity" (CF 1.168; emphasis in original). This abnormal quality of the light becomes more immediate when the light seems to have an impossible phenomenon as a source: "*For the door and windows of the undersea temple hewn from the rocky hill were vividly aglow with a flickering radiance, as from a mighty altar-flame far within*" (CF 1.169; emphasis in original).

In "The Doom That Came to Sarnath," it is mentioned that the throne of the city's king is "wrought of one piece of ivory, though no man lives who knows whence so vast a piece could have come" (CF 1.126). This implies the existence of an animal of an enormous size, since its tusks must have been big enough to carve a majestic throne out of one of them. The same theme can be found in Dunsany's "Idle days on the Yann," where the size of the tusk used to carve a city gate is immediately perceived as menacing; the danger the size of the tusk represents is heavily underlined and used as a plot device, whereas in "Sarnath" it is described as a wonder among other wonders, one of the touches that paint an otherworldly setting. There is, however, a common point: the sudden remoteness effect created by the revelation of the size of the tusk. Such a sudden change in the setting switches the impressive into the alien, and is a common theme in *fantastique* literature. It is also mentioned that "There is in the land of Mnar a vast still lake that is fed by no stream, and out of which no stream flows" (CF 1.122). These two elements contradict what we know of biology, physics, or chemistry.

Without breaking any natural law, the descriptive passages in "The Nameless City" unveil, little by little, an entirely alien reality. The narrator sets the location of the city and the city itself as extremely ancient and gives his impressions about his findings, admitting from the beginning the possibility of a non-human reality: "The antiquity of the spot was unwholesome, and I longed to encounter some sign or device to prove that the city was indeed fashioned by mankind. There were certain *proportions* and *dimensions* in the ruins which I did not like" (CF 1.233). Lovecraft then goes on with a descriptive passage that carries in itself the implication of the extent of the setting's otherness:

> Primitive altars, pillars, and niches, all curiously low, were not absent; and though I saw no sculptures or frescoes, there were many singular stones

clearly shaped into symbols by artificial means. The lowness of the chiselled chamber was very strange, for I could hardly kneel upright; but the area was so great that my torch showed only part of it at a time. (CF 1.234)

Here again, the antiquity is perceived as menacing, just as in "The Temple," and for the same reasons: it is the otherness of the spot and, by extension, of the inhabitants of the nameless city that is implied here. This otherness is built step by step, with clues slipped here and there in the descriptions.

In order to set "The Festival" in an alien location, Lovecraft starts by describing the village of Kingsport in a very precise and detailed way:

Then beyond the hill's crest I saw Kingsport outspread frostily in the gloaming; snowy Kingsport with its ancient vanes and steeples, ridgepoles and chimney-pots, wharves and small bridges, willow-trees and graveyards; endless labyrinths of steep, narrow, crooked streets, and dizzy church-crowned central peak that time durst not touch; ceaseless mazes of colonial houses piled and scattered at all angles and levels like a child's disordered blocks ... (CF 1.407)

The narrator strolls through Kingsport without any trouble and easily finds his way: "I hastened through Back Street to Circle Court, and across the fresh snow on the one full flagstone pavement in the town, to where Green Lane leads off behind the Market House." The precise location of the action is given to the readers, the "seventh house on the left in Green Lane" (CF 1.408). An uncertainty slips into the narrative at one point, when the narrator starts noticing slight differences between the actual village and what he had been told about it: "The old maps still held good, and I had no trouble; though at Arkham they must have lied when they said the trolleys ran to this place, since I saw not a wire overhead. Snow would have hid the rails in any case" (CF 1.408). However, the rest of the description of the village is so convincing and precise that it is only at the end of the story, when the narrator is found alone and freezing in the snow and brought to the real Kingsport, that the readers find themselves suddenly removed from the location where they thought the narrative was set, a location that in retrospect becomes strangely alien: "At the hospital, they told me I had been found frozen in Kingsport Harbour at dawn, clinging to the drifting spar that accident sent to save me" (CF 1.416).

Unreliable Narrators: Voices of Insanity

First-person narrators themselves are often a key element of the unique atmosphere of Lovecraft's narratives, and their impressions and reactions are used to create a sense of horror. The vast number of narrators whose word we cannot trust in Lovecraft's works is indicative of the deep psychological impact the narrated events he describes have had on them, and would normally have on human minds. The use of unreliable narrators lets the author create an ambiguity in the narration, leaving some details to the interpretation of the readers, which masterfully serves his taste for the indescribable. Some of his narrators serve to explore a mindset that is very far from the readers' own. Lovecraft's unreliable narrators' unreliability has various causes, and as such has different effects on the reader. Amidst his unreliable narrators, the majority feel "touched" or "tainted" by something, changed by the events they witnessed or they took part in. Their sanity was affected, they claim, and their credibility must therefore be questioned. This, paradoxically, brings another layer of ambiguity: if the narrator is sane enough to warn the readers of his insanity, how insane can he really be? Can the readers really dismiss his claims entirely, or might they be true? Other narrators feel entirely alien to humankind, and as such cannot be entirely relied upon to tell the truth, or what a human being would perceive as the truth. Finally, some narrators are indeed inhuman creatures and have goals entirely alien to humankind, let alone different ways to perceive the world and to describe it.

In "Polaris," it is not the narrator himself who casts a doubt on his credibility, but rather the reactions of the other characters around him. If he describes himself as a watcher serving the city of Olathoë, imprisoned in a supernatural sleep by its enemies, the people who surround him in his dreams seem convinced that he is insane: "In my shame and despair I sometimes scream frantically, begging the dream-creatures around me to waken me. [. . .] but these creatures are daemons, for they laugh at me and tell me I am not dreaming" (CF 1.69). From that moment, it becomes difficult to say whether the narrator is insane or lying or whether he truly is as he says, which would make him a being that is not entirely human.

"The Temple" offers an excellent example of a narrator who feels changed by the events he is living, since he explicitly claims to be unreliable and describes all the stages of his psychological troubles: "It is well that the reader accept nothing which follows as objective truth, for since the events transcend natural law, they are necessarily subjective and unreal creations of my overtaxed mind." He describes the influence that his discovery of an underwater temple has on him ("My impulse to visit and enter the temple has now become an inexplicable and imperious command which ultimately cannot be denied. My own German will no longer controls my acts, and volition is henceforward possible only in minor matters") and describes what he considers to be hallucinations: "The light in the temple is a sheer delusion, and I shall die calmly like a German, in the black and forgotten depths. This demoniac laughter which I hear as I write comes only from my own weakening brain" (*CF* 1.170).

The narrator of "The Festival" experiences an intense horror during his short stay in Kingsport, "a dread not of this world nor any world, but only of the mad spaces between the stars" (*CF* 1.414). Here, we find the idea of a horror entirely alien, unknowable, and inapprehensible. The narrator cannot, however, be taken seriously, because by his own admission he ends his journey in psychiatric internment: "They insisted that this was Kingsport, and I could not deny it. [. . .] They said something about a 'psychosis' and agreed I had better get any harassing obsessions off my mind" (*CF* 1.416).

The narrator of "The Outsider" is fundamentally alien. This otherness of the character is, in fact, the very object of the narrative. The narrator knows very little of himself, and his universe is very tiny at the opening of the short story: "I must have lived years in this place, but I cannot measure the time [. . .] I cannot recall any person except myself" (*CF* 1.266). His quest for the outside world sets the narrative in motion and brings him to realize his own otherness. He is fundamentally different from what he thought he was: "I know always that I am an outsider; a stranger in this century and among those who are still men" (*CF* 1.272). Lovecraft uses here what Genette calls "a very light friction effect . . . between the slight time shift of the tale ('here is what happened to me today') and the absolute simultaneity of the exposition of thoughts and feelings ('here is what I think about it now')"[1] caused by the narrator's point of view changing between the moment he lives his story and the moment he retells it. The fact

---

1. "un effet très subtil de frottement . . . entre le léger décalage temporel du récit d'événements ("voici ce qui m'est arrivé aujourd'hui") et la simultanéité absolue dans l'exposé des pensées et des sentiments ("voici ce que j'en pense ce soir")" Gérard Genette, *Figures III*, Paris : le Seuil (Poétique), 1972, p. 230

of his having changed his point of view during the narration makes what he just said even less credible, since he ultimately seems to relish his otherness. How can we trust that the longing for humanity he expressed throughout the story is genuine?

Narration and Description: Creating Weirdness

In "The Outsider," characterization stems from description. It is the description of what the narrator sees and touches that ultimately serves to characterize him properly and reveals that the monster he describes actually is his mere reflection in a mirror: "I know always that I am an outsider; a stranger in this century and among those who are still men. This I have known ever since I stretched out my fingers to the abomination within that great gilded frame; stretched out my fingers and touched *a cold and unyielding surface of polished glass*" (CF 1.272; emphasis in original). This final characterization contradicts readers' conception of natural laws, particularly as pertains to the finality of death, as there are hints that the Outsider is an undead—he lives in what seems to be a crypt, he comments on those who are "still men." The incomprehension or the misinterpretation of the narrator toward what he sees and describes is a technique often used by Lovecraft to create surprise and switch reality around, thus making it strangely alien. The narrative and descriptive passages complement each other, cooperating to transform the atmosphere in many of his narratives.

Narration and description are intertwined in "The Nameless City," where the long description of the fresco painted on the underground passage serves as narration, the fresco being a pictorial representation of the city's history. This narrative mode certainly puts a distance between the readers and the described events, which they can only apprehend in an indirect way. Indeed, the readers can only access the narrator's description of the visual representation of the events, not the events themselves. This particularity seems very clear to Lovecraft, since he writes, through his narrator's thoughts, that "Man is so used to thinking visually that I almost forgot the darkness and pictured the endless corridor of wood and glass in its low-studded monotony as though I saw it" (CF 1.239). The border between seeing and living is described here as very porous, and this is especially true when used as a narrative technique. There are in fact two narratives in "The Nameless City": the story of the inhabitants of the city is nestled in the frame narrative of the exploration of the city by the narrator.

The narrator draws the wrong conclusions from his observations, mistaking the represented creatures for allegories of the human inhabitants of the city. Looking at the fresco, he says about the city: "I saw its wars and triumphs, its troubles and defeats, and afterward its terrible fight against the desert when thousands of its people—here represented in allegory by the grotesque reptiles—were driven to chisel their way down through the rocks" (CF 1.240). When the images begin to turn grimmer, the narrator starts to doubt his first impression:

> The forms of the people—always represented by the sacred reptiles—appeared to be gradually wasting away, though their spirit as shewn hovering above the ruins by moonlight gained in proportion. Emaciated priests, displayed as reptiles in ornate robes, cursed the upper air and all who breathed it; and one terrible final scene shewed a primitive-looking man, perhaps a pioneer of ancient Irem, the City of Pillars, torn to pieces by members of the elder race. I remembered how the Arabs fear the nameless city, and was glad that beyond this place the grey walls and ceiling were bare. (CF 1.242)

What seemed to be a symbol becomes here the literal truth, revealing a grim reality. Furthermore, the bare gray ceiling and walls convey much more horror than any description could have, leaving more space to the readers' imagination. The narrator's incomprehension brings a clue of what is coming: the utter otherness of the inhabitants of the city.

The same thing happens in "Dagon," where the narrator finds vestiges of civilization where there should be none. He discovers an alphabet, "a system of hieroglyphics unknown to [him], and unlike anything [he] had ever seen in books, consisting for the most part of conventionalised aquatic symbols such as fishes, eels, octopi, crustaceans, molluscs, whales, and the like" (CF 1.56). This discovery hints to the idea of an alien form of intelligence linked to the aquatic world. The narrator, here again, misinterprets what he sees, but the readers start to understand that something strange is going on. The narrator goes on to describe what he sees, and it is his very misinterpretation of his discovery that gradually sets a great distance between what he found and what should normally exist: "I think that these things were supposed to depict men—at least, a certain sort of men; though the creatures were shown disporting like fishes in the waters of some marine grotto, or paying homage at some monolithic shrine which appeared to be under the waves as well" (CF 1.56); "Curiously enough, they seemed to have been chiselled badly out of proportion with their scenic background; for one of the creatures was shewn in the act of killing a whale represented as but little larger than himself" (CF 1.57). When the narrator finally understands his mistake because he sees one of the depicted creatures, he loses his mind: "I think I went mad then" (CF 1.57). In "Dagon," just as in "The Nameless City," what the narrator took as symbols transform themselves into a realistic depiction and a newly unveiled terrifying reality is put into light, in a Freudian blurring of the boundaries between real and unreal as the signifier suddenly becomes the signified. This is only possible because of the narrator's misunderstanding.

Conclusion

Lovecraft's masterful use of the fear of the unknown has been widely discussed. By creating remote or alien settings for his narratives, he can hint that this otherness hides dangers unknown and inapprehensible to humankind. However, before creating weirdness, he has to create this unknown, and he manages to do so, among other methods, by making the best use of his narrators and his descriptive passages. With the descriptions, he creates settings entirely alien either because of their remoteness or their strangeness, or at first very familiar, all to better twist them into alien settings, in a typical *fantastique* way. He also manages, with his descriptions, to give clues to his readers about the horrors and the dangers in his universe. These clues do not give the solution to the mysteries he sets, but rather bring the readers to suspect the reality of a universe that is hostile—or at best indifferent—to humankind. His narrators serve to bring life to these descriptions by interpreting (or misinterpreting) what they see and experience, and their incomprehension and horror add to the readers' horror while contributing to making the narrative more alien to them. By setting this remoteness, and by creating a blur around the circumstances and the settings of his narratives, Lovecraft manages to create a universe that is truly strangely alien, a universe ready to be tinged with a stain of menace to create the uncanny effect of horror.

Works Cited

Allard, Patrice. *Guide du mythe de Cthulhu*. Paris: Encrage, 1999.

Freud, Sigmund. *L'Inquiétante étrangeté*. Traduit de l'Allemand par Marie Bonaparte et Mme E. Marty. 1933. Paris: Gallimard, 1971.
   https://www.psychaanalyse.com/pdf/inquietante_etrangete.pdf

Genette, Gérard. *Figures III*. Paris: Le Seuil, 1972.

H. P. Lovecraft, Georges Bataille, and the Fascination of the Formless: One Crawling Chaos Seen Emerging from Opposite Shores

Christian Roy
Independent Scholar

It is my contention that H. P. Lovecraft's significance in cultural history becomes clearer, and indeed greater, if we see him as a close counterpart of his contemporary, the increasingly influential French theorist and (largely pornographic) writer Georges Bataille (1897-1962). For despite their extreme dissimilarity in most respects, both men managed to vividly express key features of an emerging *Zeitgeist* in their respective attempts to carry to their ultimate conclusions in thought, life and literature certain Nietzschean insights about the place of man in the universe as described by modern science. More specifically, they shared an uncanny ability to channel and dramatize the forces within man and without that undermine any attempt to impose a normative framework as objectively binding on unbridled desire or free-ranging fancy. Consummating modernity's sovereign (self-)destructive movement in the ruin of all attempts to stabilize it in manageable forms and formulas, over the last few decades, Bataille has emerged in academic, art, and cultural circles as one thinker whose authority tends to overtake that of other French gurus of once-dominant modernist and post-modernist trends, since he rejected outright the humanist reference points they still started from even in the act of subverting them under his influence. Read in light of Bataille, Lovecraft can thus help articulate the imaginative template for an era in which horror fiction, feeding on the specter of mankind's obsolescence, takes on the proportions and some of the roles of myth, albeit about the casual origins and impending demise of the human world, rather than about its sacred foundations and ultimate destiny.

Admittedly, though Lovecraft and Bataille belonged to the same generation, the science-minded aesthete of horror and the depraved mystic of evil knew nothing of each other and were poles apart in temper, lifestyle, and sensibility. Scratching the surface of the radical atheism they both professed, it is easy to detect the contrasting religious cultures in which it was rooted in each one's case. Lovecraft admired his Yankee forebears' "Puritan inhibitions" as "attempts to make life a work of art . . . out of that divine hatred of life which marks the deepest and most sensitive soul" (*SL* 1.315), and "the most healthy and practical way of securing happiness and tranquillity" (*SL* 1.275–76). His supreme goal as an Epicurean (*SL* 1.242) was to seek "solid bourgeois contentment" (*SL* 1.111), looking down on anyone—even Clark Ashton Smith—"who does not live abstemiously and purely" (*SL* 1.315). For opposite reasons, despising all self-control, whether ascetic or bourgeois, Bataille had a similarly ambivalent attitude toward his colleague Simone Weil as a "dirty, thin-blooded virgin" (Roy 2003, 582). This lapsed seminarian's Nietzschean cult of passion in mingled agony and ecstasy, conflating erotic and religious meanings in the embrace of death-in-life, was steeped in the sensuous morbidity of Baroque (e.g., Spanish) Catholicism. If Bataille perverted it as sexual depravity, it was not out of any special attachment to what Lovecraft called "the trivial pleasures of existence" (*SL* 1.156), but as degrading mortification in the pursuit of an "inner experience" of desire's dark object: the Impossible as the traumatic "divine" Real of impenetrable otherness, which his friend Jacques Lacan (who even married his ex-wife) would take up in his psychoanalytic theory.

From these divergent standpoints, Lovecraft and Bataille were both obsessed with those obscene, obscure "gods" of elusive material reality. The psychoanalytic point could be made that a similar childhood trauma of seeing their respective syphilitic fathers becoming insane and paralyzed (as well as blind in Bataille's case) not only ruined for them any sense of a providential or natural cosmic harmony, or of even a paternal master signifier anchoring all others in a meaningful symbolic order, but perversely twisted such a "solar" keystone of balanced mental development into its very opposite: the parodic divine "Nobodaddy" William Blake talked about,[1] or as Lovecraft put it, the "blind, idiot god" at the non-existent core of the "mindless vortex" (*SL* 1.56) of reality's "crawling chaos." While

---

1. The name provides a chapter heading in Surya's biography of Bataille.

"the negation of the sun, or its transformation into a 'blind spot,' is a significant trope in Bataille's general economy" (Parkinson, 136), he was, by his own admission, driven by the fundamentally religious desire to partake of what he called this "accursed share" of the sacred, understood atheistically as the breaking points of social order, rational control, and bounded individuality in the blasphemous, intertwined ecstasies of madness, tears, laughter, sex, and death. Bataille thus actively promotes everything a Lovecraftian protagonist recoils from, yet remains fascinated by. Indeed, Bataille plunges with convulsive glee into the very abysses Lovecraft is usually content to teeter over in dizzy, conflicted contemplation. Once we realize they are both drawn to the same abysses, parallels and contrasts begin to stand out in their respective approaches to them.

Lovecraft's patrician ethos demands strict self-control over lower drives; this is just what provides him with an elaborate perch of detached contemplation from which to peer into the abyss of a disenchanted universe, even as he remains enamored of its civilized railings. In his way, while denying their ontological basis, he remains beholden to the higher forms of the sacred, as embodied in established religion, the state, and cultural capital, as opposed to the lower or "evil" forms—like swearing and a range of excremental substances—that Bataille favored in his sociology of the sacred. Bataille only tolerates the trappings of culture as a diving board into the sacrificial ravishment of universal ruin, true to his nihilistic agenda of unleashing the mindless raving brute in man against the very idea of civilization. In its stead, as he writes in the final, March 1931 issue of *Documents*, he hopes to realize modernity's repressed "possibility of a humanity entirely suffocated by horror, *of no matter what derivation*" (cited in Ades and Baker 242-43), as adumbrated in the most barbaric, archaic rites of forgotten or exotic societies.

Like many a Lovecraftian hero drawn to such arcane, impious lore, Bataille was in fact a paleographer by training, dealing with old manuscripts, coins, and medals as part of his day job as a librarian at the Bibliothèque Nationale in Paris. His colleagues, however, looked askance at Bataille for appearing for work in terrible shape after nights of extreme, deliberate debauchery as a counter-spiritual path. It is in the context of this double life he led that, aside from his outlandishly violent and perverse secret pornographic writings, Bataille began to make a name for himself by launching in 1929 the short-lived but seminal review *Documents*. He used it to connect his ethnographic and archaeological interests to the arts, mass culture, and natural science, so as to spell out in deliberately unsystematic, illustrative fashion an epistemological program that betrays some uncanny connections to Lovecraft's literary universe, even in its early Dreamland expressions of a decade before (see Roy). It seems to be contained in a nutshell in two sentences of Bataille's fanciful dictionary entry on the category of "space" (and its illustrations in the February 1930 issue; e.g., p. 64—reproduced in Figure 1), where he mocks the attempts of philosophers and scientists alike to follow in the footsteps of theologians by forcing the wild heterogeneity of actual extension into the steady, uniform framework of an empty abstraction.

> In reality, the dignity of space is so well established and associated with that of the stars, that it is incongruous to assert that space might become a fish swallowing another. Space will be still more frightfully disappointing when it is said that it takes the form of an ignoble initiation rite practiced by some Negroes, desperately absurd, etc. . . .
>
> Space would of course be far better off *doing its duty* and fabricating the philosophical idea in professors' apartments! (Bataille, cited in Brotchie 75-77)

Bataille in 1930 suggests locking professors up "*to teach them what space is*" (Brotchie 77). This is precisely what the mad scientist Crawford Tillinghast does in Lovecraft's story "From Beyond" (1920), ushering his more conventional academic colleague into his house for an experimental demonstration that there are no such things as "time and magnitude," "form [and] matter," "beyond the bounds of infinity" where he has overcome the limited economy of human perceptions and successfully "drawn down daemons from the stars" (CF 1.200); among these "were inky, jellyfish monstrosities [. . .] in loathsome profusion" as "they *overlapped*" and "were never still, but seemed ever floating about with some malignant purpose. Sometimes they appeared to devour one another" (CF 1.199), just like the fish in Bataille's unscientific definition of space. The latter is illustrated by photographs of one fish eating another and a kind of "ignoble" Negro ritual that could have come straight out of Lovecraft's horror stories and racist ravings (see Figure 1, where it is attributed to the Nandi people of central Tanganyika).

In Tillinghast's laboratory, "there seemed to be pouring a seething column of unrecognizable shapes or clouds," a "luminous and shadowy chaos" in which "indescribable shapes both alive and otherwise were mixed in disgusting array," (CF 1.199) amongst themselves as well as with all known things.

Christian Roy 193

Photo Wide World
... un rite ignoble d'initiation pratiqué par quelques nègres (p. 41).
(Peuplade Nandi; plaines du Tanganika. — Expédition Colorado, 1929).

Photo Wide World
... l'espace peut devenir un poisson qui en mange un autre (p. 41).

Figure 1
Used with permission from Bibliothèque nationale de France.

This sounds a lot like what Bataille was trying to give some sense of with *Documents*'s jarring juxtapositions of often disturbing photographic materials (from animal parts in industrial slaughterhouses to shrunken severed heads in primitive tribes), something that mocked definition and nonetheless had its own entry in the review's provocative "Dictionary" section under the heading of the "formless" ("*informe*"), a concept which has generated a cottage industry of new theorizations since its belated reception in postmodernist art-historical discourse two decades ago, such as seen in Bois and Kraus, Didi-Huberman, Fédida, and Violi

Aimed against the philosophical attempt to fit all that exists into a "mathematical frock-coat," Bataille's insistence that, in itself, beyond the petty provincialism of human prejudice, "the universe resembles nothing at all and is only *formless* amounts to saying that the universe is something akin to a spider or a gob of spittle" (Bataille, in Brotchie 52). This is what Lovecraft could have had in mind when conjuring up Yog-Sothoth as a "congeries of iridescent globes"—like spittle, yet "stupendous in its malign suggestiveness"—like a spider (CF 4.388), as the "Beyond-One" the Mi-Go worship, glimpsed by a splintered, transdimensional facet of Randolph Carter, "Through the Gates of the Silver Key" (1932), in the "pits of a horror still more profound" than this fragmentation: "the horror of destroyed individuality."

> It was an All-in-One and One-in-All of limitless being and self—not merely a thing of one Space-Time continuum, but allied to the ultimate animating essence of existence's whole unbounded sweep—the last, utter sweep which has no confines and which outreaches fancy and mathematics alike. (CF 2.300)

We are here deep in the territory of Bataille's "inner experience" as he tried to evoke it in his so-called *Somme athéologique* during World War II. According to Gavin Parkinson, the pioneering specialist of Surrealism's ties to modern science, "Bataille believed that heterogeneity—the irrecuperable excess beyond human limits that cannot find form in language, knowledge or thought—could be experienced through, and therefore represented as, 'horror, violence, hatred, sobs, crime, disgust, laughter and human love'" (136). Except for his scant interest in "amorous phenomena," and allowing for his understated dark humor, this list covers much of Lovecraft's own literary territory, with two major provisos: his love of architecture and his poetic quest for dreamlands.

At one point, Lovecraft confided to Frank Belknap Long that he had "practically abandoned literary for architectural interests. I find poetry only in breathing wood, brick, stone, and marble" (SL 1.313) more than in anything connected to living, breathing humans, in whom he chiefly valued architectonic qualities such as "the cut of one's hair and regularity of one's features," so that "the greatest historical tragedy of modern times was the fall of the periwig." In a letter to James F. Morton, Lovecraft put on the same level "manners, accomplishments, and choice of cravats," above "character" and all that "utter damn nonsense and rubbish human ethics, aspirations, beliefs, and kindred illusions are. Nothing matters in a universe devoid of values or significance; and that art is the truest, which is *least connected with ideas or purpose or sentiments*," but "most frankly impersonal, decorative, and whimsical," since "uselessness and triviality are the basic essentials of real art" (SL 1.207). If Bataille might have echoed much of that antiutilitarian, antihumanist sentiment, it would only be by connecting impersonal whimsy, "uselessness and triviality" to vulgar "pop" or "street" art that desecrated all the stately, dignified forms Lovecraft held up. In *Documents*, he therefore celebrated newspaper comics, childish doodling, and mocking graffiti, e.g., the crude blasphemous scrawls found on the outer walls of ancient Ethiopian churches, as the profane, parodic "shoggothic art" of inarticulate subalterns. A famous Bataille anthology is therefore aptly titled *Against Architecture* (1989), to sum up that author's basic stance against everything that would stand erect in formal stability, impervious to time and passion, rather than be given over to the excitement of reckless self-expenditure. One might even go so far as to say that architecture is to Lovecraft what sex is to Bataille, though this provocative statement is meant to suggest more than mere incommensurability, as it implies a real parallel at several levels.

For one thing, architecture for Lovecraft, like sex for Bataille, possibly more even than "whatever satisfaction is derivable from the exercise of the mind in the pursuit of truth" (SL 1.87), seems to come closest to an excuse for otherwise pathetic and degrading human existence, making it somewhat bearable. In the broader sense of building anything up for cool aesthetic contemplation, as Nietzsche already showed in *The Birth of Tragedy*, architecture affords Apollonian enjoyment of the artificial staging of life's chaotic physical and cultural forces, and thus provides a template for "the adoption of an imaginative and detached life which may enable us to appreciate the world as a beautiful object (as Schopenhauer tells us it is) without feeling too keenly the pain which inevitably results from reflecting on its relation to ourselves" (SL 1.215). "And it is best not to make oneself absurd by getting excited, violent, freakish, and anti-social about illusory trifles," for "nothing matters, but it's perhaps more comfortable to keep calm and not interfere with other people" (SL 1.256). However, embracing absurd passion and rejecting calm comfort, it is precisely the pain of taking personally the injury that life is which Bataille seeks to heighten, to the point of deliberately adding to its insult to our sense of propriety. By actively participating in the Dionysian unleashing of the centrifugal cosmic forces that tear the self apart, he wants to dramatize their outpouring against all attempts to contain them, in order to lose himself in the explosion's burst. It all comes down to sexual erection against architectural erection, seen as tantamount to political repression as castration.

But the contrast is not as clear-cut as this might suggest. If Bataille is drawn to perverse forms of sex in life as in art, Lovecraft fantasizes about perverted forms of architecture that make a cruel mockery of the neatly classical or quaintly vernacular forms he never tires of seeking out and celebrating in real life. He may love the rational order and endearing familiarity they impress on the human habitat, but he can never forget that these are fond illusions tied to local scale and historical setting, desperately vulnerable to the vast chaos of contrary natural, social, and instinctual forces gnawing at it just beyond and beneath their hoary civilized veneer. He cannot help following the cracks and crevices in the fabric of space-time through which the dark objects of his visceral fears spread their tendrils to blow apart that cherished framework, as though drawn by the *jouissance* of this very trauma, which he manages to transpose in the archest of prose, describing poetic dreamlands and majestic architecture in the throes of subversion by the formless.

This creative tension takes the form of contradiction when Lovecraft attempts to theorize it, as when he maintains that "in art there is no use in heeding the chaos of the universe; for so complete is this chaos, that no piece writ in words cou'd even so much as hint at it"—as his best works somehow manage to do by alluding to just such an Unnamable beyond abundant written description, at the outer limits of his comfort zones. Denying any "line betwixt reality and illusion," "since the entire plan of creation is pure chaos, and wholly devoid of values" save as "mere effects of perspective," this most disturbing of writers fancies "that is best which more comfortably lulls us into acceptance of what we have" (SL 1.261). Claiming to "hate man, literature, pretence, scholarship, aspiration, sophistication, humour, and all the rest of the sickly show!" (SL 1.314), he yet seeks such "contentment or tranquil pleasure" as "can be gained only by the worship and creation of beauty" (SL 1.215), under the "true godlike inspiration" of "the lofty freedom that puts a great imagination outside mankind, outside the world, outside the universe" (SL 1.305). For "to the impersonal dreamer belongs all infinity—he is lord of the universe and taster of all the beauties of the stars," free to "roam through all history and all legend with imagination as a guide; enjoying the pleasant things of life without experiencing the anguish of participation" (SL 1.112).

Craving only anguished participation in the appalling interplay of life and death in their seductively ugly truth, Bataille had little patience for the poetic quest for perfect form or sublime imaginary spheres beyond its reach, dismissing this literary affectation as a cowardly, escapist, hypocritical diversion from human desire's unspeakable drive toward ultimately suicidal formless ecstasy in transgression of all separative individuation. Fully formulated in 1947 in *The Hatred of Poetry* (reissued as *The Impossible* after his death in 1962), this was his criticism of the Surrealists as hopeless Romantics, though he was otherwise closest to them. He could of course only share their impulse not to be ruled by the utilitarian dictates of reason and morals, but not by somehow rising "above" them in a heavenly realm of free-ranging imagination, untainted by the rawness of the real, as the "sur-" prefix suggested. He opposed his own "base materialism" of the erotic death-drive to André Breton's idealistic "Icarian naiveté," the refusal to recognize that the urge to rise above the world toward the sun subconsciously implied the secret wish to be burnt by it and fall down—not so much to the ground as in the bottomless cosmic pit lit by the "'the filthy parody of the torrid and blinding sun', a black excremental hole like the 'dark, repulsive nucleus' [. . .] he posits at the core of every body on every scale" (Parkinson 139, citing Bataille, "The Solar Anus"). "Bataille felt that only through loss, a loss adjacent to death, could human beings know the black light of divinity, 'regain the free movement of the universe . . . dance and swirl in the full rapture of those great swarms of stars'" (Parkinson 140, citing Bataille, "Celestial Bodies").

Is this not what Yog-Sothoth, enthroned in his galactic vortex, stands for and induces his followers to emulate? It is as though, when writing fiction, Lovecraft starts echoing Bataille in putting a hot Dionysian spin on his own coldly Apollonian take on the universe's meaningless chaos. Arguably, "realising that where there are no real patterns, one is as good as another" (SL 1.256), Lovecraft may here have more in common with Gilles Deleuze and the Spinozist vision in A Thousand Plateaus of a universal tangle of transitive lines of becoming that run unpredictably in all directions. As he writes to Frank Belknap Long on 8 November 1923:

> I can conceive of no true image of the pattern of life and cosmic force, unless it be a jumble of mean dots arrang'd in directionless spirals. And so far are real dots and actual curves from depicting the utter formlessness and emptiness of life and force, that they stand confest as artificial as Mr. Pope's couplets when view'd against the bland and nebulous reality they struggle to depict. (SL 1.261)

Lovecraft would thus seem to share Bataille's skepticism of the claims of detached scientific observation of the cosmos to offer a reliable picture of its actual nature, other than as but one, deceptively neat perspectival effect among many others generated by the accident of human consciousness.

> The cosmos, child, is simply a perpetual rearrangement of electrons which is constantly seething as it always has been and always will be. Our tiny globe and puny thoughts are but one momentary incident in its eternal mutation; so that the life, aims, and thoughts of mankind are of the utmost triviality and ridiculousness. (SL 1.260)

Likewise, "conscripting [Arthur Eddington's May 1930 Halley Lecture] *The Rotation of the Galaxy* and modern science in general into an attack upon anthropocentrism, Bataille notes that the immensity of the universe they describe allots barely any significance to human beings. [. . .] The behaviour of the galaxy suggests to Bataille 'the swirling suns of our light shows'," its spiraling nebulae of scattering dots no more than a slow-motion version of any fleeting fireworks display, "like the mesmeric, luminous, terminatory feats [sic; or feasts?] of the Potlatch ceremony, Aztec sacrifice and myth of Icarus" (Parkinson 138, citing Bataille, "Celestial Bodies," *October* No. 36 [Spring 1986]: 76). Such Native rituals and archaic myths were celebrated by Bataille for the wild abandon to cosmic motion and (in)human emotion they enacted: a loss of control and self that made any festival fascinatingly abominable and inherently "blasphemous" to the Puritan sensibility Lovecraft was steeped in—however selectively. All this provided raw material for the hidden cults he fantasized as alternate forms of passionate, enthusiastic participation in the truth of ultimate chaos. He otherwise claimed to apprehend the latter through the filter of self-contained, detached contemplation as vital to his identity, though it be a figment of civilization as he knew it, i.e., an arbitrary local prejudice to which he happened to be partial. This meant all that he held dear was highly vulnerable to the very realizations he embraced, as the atheistic, antihumanist nihilism they fostered could just as well take evil religious forms if a would-be cultist like Bataille had his way. Stories like "Nyarlathotep" and "The Call of Cthulhu" draw their power from this nagging suspicion that is probably widespread at this stage of our culture, accounting for Lovecraft's appeal. The mad Dionysian gods of Lovecraft's fiction thus appear as the inescapable Bataillean shadow of his professed Apollonian Epicureanism, itself a secularized form of his proud Puritan heritage.

Even before these dark gods gained prominence in Lovecraft's Mythos, the cosmic threat such deities came to personify had constantly hovered on the edges of the Dreamlands he first roamed, as "that shocking final peril which gibbers unmentionably outside the ordered universe, where no dreams reach; that last amorphous blight of nethermost confusion which blasphemes and bubbles at the centre of all infinity—the boundless daemonsultan Azathoth" (CF 2.100) as a conglomerate of Bataillean tropes! It should come as no surprise then that Lovecraft's early tales in this vein often betray the dim awareness of endless fall that attends Icarian ascension even to the most exquisitely elaborate, timeless realms of dream, according to Bataille.

In "The Crawling Chaos," the dreamer disregarded the divine child's warning not to turn back to the earth as he was led to a celestial sphere of "peace and happiness more profound" than any found in life by an angelic "throng of half-luminous, vine-crowned youths and maidens," borne on a "fragrant breeze which blew not from the earth but from the golden nebulae." But his apotheosis was turned to global apocalypse by hearkening to "the damnable, the detestable pounding of that hideous ocean" (CF 4.35)—of coital motion as per Bataille's "Solar Anus"? With or without such a subconscious association, it would still be "a seething ocean of blind forces," as Lovecraft refers to the cosmos as "mindless vortex" around the same time in a letter to Alfred Galpin and Maurice W. Moe of 6 October 1921 (SL 1.156). As "The Crawling Chaos" the year before, its upheaval exhibited a social aspect as it overwhelmed "the tottering towers of deserted cities" like London and Paris amidst the "jungles of ruin and decadence" that had been his "native land," before being itself vaporized by chthonic fire as the earth's remains blew away in deep space (CF 4.35). Lovecraft seems as keenly aware as Bataille that the idealized, aesthetic dream of Western civilization is doomed to be blown to dust by the violent eruption of raging forces from below, indistinguishable from those of the infinite universe above, with which science has replaced the closed world of premodern cultures, to quote the title of Alexandre Koyré's famous book on the Copernican revolution.

Clearly, Lovecraft's sympathies were not, like Bataille's, on the side of the upheaval of shapeless underground powers boiling beneath the surface, but of civilization's desperate attempts either to repress or to channel them as long as possible before its own inevitable entropic downfall.—Or were they? Not wholly or consistently, one could argue, given the obvious relish with which he explored and described just what he consciously feared the most. Beyond this double-minded *frisson* of vertigo on the edge of the abyss, there is one thread in Lovecraft's body of fiction that actually leads in the other direction, that of Bataille's identification with the dark side, even as it directly connects the high points of his Dreamland period and his Mythos period. This could be called "the Innsmouth connection."

The eponymous town of Lovecraft's late masterpiece actually makes its first appearance at the end of the story "Celephaïs" (1920), when the dreamer Kuranes, after a drug-induced spell in "a part of space where form does not exist, but where glowing gases study the secrets of existence," finally found his way back to the old English village of his childhood dreams. Thence he led a cavalcade of "handsome knights" back through time to Romanticism's idealized Middle Ages, down "the lane that ends in the abyss of dreams," "a seething chaos of roseate and cerulean splendour" where "invisible voices sang exultantly as the knightly entourage plunged over the edge and floated gracefully down past glittering clouds and silvery coruscations," "endlessly down" "toward distant regions where the sea meets the sky," to "the city Celephaïs" to hold his court forevermore. And yet, "below the cliffs at Innsmouth the channel tides played mockingly with the body of a tramp who had stumbled through the half-deserted city at dawn," while "a notably fat and especially offensive millionaire brewer enjoys the purchased atmosphere of extinct nobility" (CF 1.191).

Lovecraft might as well be applying to himself Bataille's critique of the Icarian seeker of timeless poetic realms where the conflict between sea and sky, ideal heights and fluid depths, is deceptively sublimated. In "Celephaïs," the thrill of leaving the earth and floating through the air cannot ultimately conceal the dream's conceit of its transfiguration of a material downfall into a spiritual ascension, using the kinetic force of a fatal plunge into the sea to simulate magical flight into the safe haven of harmless heavens. Even the *Familienroman* of a daydreaming tramp's noble origins is impotent to prevent their vestigial trappings from being bought as a trophy for the vulgar display of capitalism's triumph over older, more refined cultural forms.

A decade after "Celephaïs," its ending is reworked in the New England setting of "The Shadow over Innsmouth" (1931), whose protagonist undergoes such a ghastly physical transformation (acquiring "the *Innsmouth look*" after a brush with a formless shoggoth in a dream) that, foregoing suicide as a way out of its horror, he comes to embrace his ignoble, non-human origins. Accepting as real the madness they entail for normal society, he frees his brother from a mental institution, consciously choosing to live in the inverted undersea reflection of a timeless celestial realm (or is it the other way around, as Bataille would have it?), as their true home and heart's desire.

> We shall swim out to that brooding reef in the sea and dive down through black abysses to Cyclopean and many-columned Y'hanthlei, and in that lair of the Deep Ones we shall dwell amidst wonder and glory for ever. (CF 3.230)

Innsmouth is the site in Lovecraft's universe where the Icarian dream-quest for "wonder and glory," always haunted by the awareness of being but a compensatory reworking of the downward spiral of base reality, ends up finding them in its most abject pit, where the reverse image of heaven becomes the inadmissible primal object of desire. This is the secret attraction of horror: unaccountable sympathy for the repellent back side of life, as a site of sovereign "glory" in mad expenditure and freedom from fixed forms in the embrace of their lowest common denominator of formlessness, with the death-drive as entropy's inexhaustible dark energy. At this point of a shocking shift of loyalties away from human form and toward its monstrous "other," Lovecraft allows himself fictionally to espouse the movement of the poetic quest and the religious impulse when followed all the way to their true end in the destruction of poetry and religion, as Bataille saw it. This still takes the rhetorical form of transposing the encounter with the horror of the real into a perverted palatial imagery of the poetic sublime and religious eternity.

To find a more direct laceration of the fabric of literature, one would have to dwell on the violence Lovecraft inflicts on language itself. Departing from his own oversophisticated voice, and as an inverted counterpart of the ambivalent oddity of the archaically genteel English he was wont to slip into, he often puts in his characters' mouths degenerate vernacular dialects and ejaculatory invocations in non-human languages mixing features of god and beast. These linguistic effects are often intertwined, conveying as they do the in-bred/cross-bred miscegenation of the beings whose voice they characterize, a transgression of civilized norms or even organic form that is integral both to their hybrid nature and to the "unspeakable cults" (as in von Junzt's *Unaussprechlichen Kulten*) they practice. A related fascination was key to Bataille's own ethnographic interests, operating like Lovecraft's within "the ancient bipolarity, annexed in the late nineteenth century to evolutionist world histories, of civilization versus barbarism," with the latter partly taking up the former's legacies in "degenerate" form; "but Bataille's 'savages', creatures of instinct on the side of horror, 'nightmares' and the unconscious, also engage the modern discourse on the primitive" (C. F. B. Miller, "Archeology," cited in Ades and Baker 46). The roles these primitive "others" were assigned depended on what side a cultural critic would take: for or against Western civilization *qua* classical humanism.

> The right-wing critic Waldemar George denounced the "Afghan gods" illustrated in René Grousset's DOCUMENTS article as pernicious sops to a "fascination" for "archaic and barbarian forms," an anti-classical, anti-humanist "pessimism based on masochism, a secret desire to humiliate the human being and to degrade him to the level of a reptile." (C. F. B. Miller, "Archeology," in Ades and Baker 48)

This possibility inherent in pessimism is literally the object of horror for Lovecraft as a classical—if skeptical—humanist of sorts. It is just his keen awareness of it that makes his fiction feel like a stage for "Bataille's (none too secret) counter-evolutionary dethronements of the human" (C. F. B. Miller, "Archeology," cited in Ades and Baker 48-49). In his contributions to *Documents*, for instance, Bataille delved in odd antiquities to which he had professional access, keen to exhume hybrid monsters from the archaeological record, while Lovecraft conjured them up from his troubled imagination, aided by his wide reading on similar topics, which was key to endowing his creations with uncanny verisimilitude. Lovecraft's own drawing of Cthulhu (Figure 2) bears some comparison with an actual Gnostic amulet from the Bibliothèque Nationale's Medal Cabinet as reproduced in *Documents* (Vol. 2, No. 1, February 1930, in Bataille's article "Le bas matérialisme et la gnose," 1-8), depicting a god with human legs, a snake's body and a rooster's head (Figure 3), next to an acephalic god and a trio of duck-headed high priests.

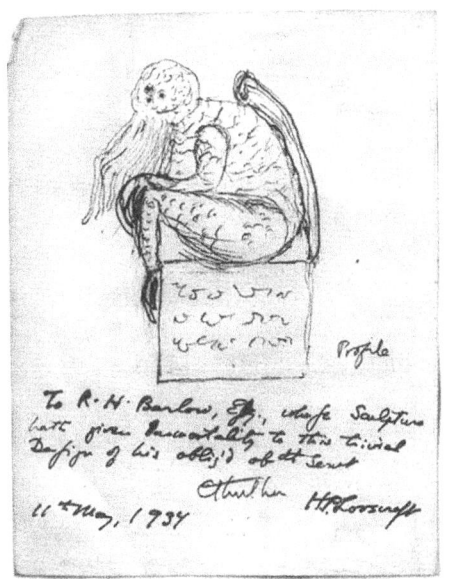

Figure 2

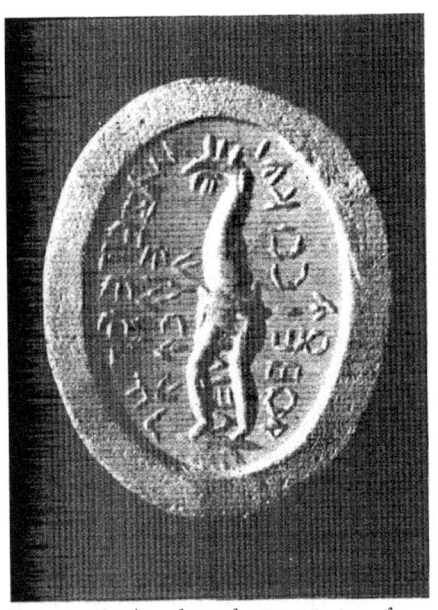

Figure 3 (used with permission from Bibliothèque nationale de France)

Then there is Bataille's fascination with old engravings of monstrous, non-viable newborns in formal poses, including an acephalic one. Like countless severed heads in *Documents* and his obsession with the guillotine, this is significant of Bataille's endeavor to disrupt the human form, taking aim at the human face and the head in general as the centralizing agencies that castrate and bottle up into finite, earthbound forms the sovereign, intemperate flow of dark energies from below into the open pit of the sky. Though headlessness was anything but programmatic for Lovecraft, he was clearly haunted by a dark fear of something like it. From the mindless, faceless Other Gods and the night-gaunts of his childhood nightmares, through the headless bodies reanimated by Herbert West or the headless alien victims in "The Mound" (1929–30) and *At the Mountains of Madness* (1931), to the "chewed and gouged head" of a man whose face was bitten off by a degenerate inbred cannibal ("the embodiment of all the snarling chaos and grinning fear that lurk behind life" [CF 1.373]) in "The Lurking Fear" (1922), Lovecraft's fiction could provide many a shocking illustration for Bataille's enduring animus against the human face as the seat of that measured, noble dignity that forever thwarts or deviates the visceral, volcanic outpouring of feral passions (not to mention Deleuze's related aversion to it in in *A Thousand Plateaus*).

Inspired by the Aztecs' death cult, Bataille was thus dead serious about the myth of the *Acéphale* he tried to foment in the late 1930s as the nucleus of a revolutionary religious movement of reckless orgiastic anarchy for a new dark age of savage revelry, through an eponymous review and secret society. There were reports the latter had seriously planned a human sacrifice, and had even found volunteer victims (apparently more eager than potential executioners) before disbanding when some members would not follow Bataille that far ... Drawing on archaic lore to consciously live out and unleash the darkest primitive impulses for their own sake beyond belief or purpose, this is a disturbing real-life echo of the kind of secret cult Lovecraft fictionally invoked precisely by drawing on uncomfortably realistic bits of contemporary "evidence" in "The Call of Cthulhu" (1926), anticipated in the apocalyptic dream that closes "Dagon" (1917) "of a day when the land shall sink, and the dark ocean floor shall ascend amidst universal pandemonium" (CF 1.58). It has been argued that Lovecraft's inaugural Mythos story owed more than he let on to theosophist Alice Bailey's New Age prophecy of the coming revival and worldwide spread of ancient mystery cults like that of Dionysus, with its mass hysteria of sexualized violence and sacrificial crime (Knowles) of just the kind Bataille was hoping to kindle on a now universal scale. And just as Lovecraft was likely inspired by actual reports of voodoo cults in the *New York Times*, *Documents*'s dictionary definition of "Cults" took the form of a report from the *New York Herald* (6 October 1929) on a police raid of the house of one of the "many cults swarming in Los Angeles," and the discovery in its basement of a hermetically sealed box containing the year-old corpse of the adoptive daughter of the order's "princess," together with the bodies of seven little dogs that were meant to facilitate its resurrection after she had died as a result of spurious medical treatments (*Documents* No. 5 [October 1929]: 274).

The sense of a disturbing transition to a universe structured by an appallingly unknowable (Lacanian) Real that defies reason, best described by ghastly images of formlessness, is perceived as likely fatal to ordered society and human sanity by both Lovecraft and Bataille, albeit as an object of imaginative dread to the former and as a prospect welcomed with evil glee by the latter. Groundlessness and headlessness are intimately related and provide intertwined, almost interchangeable images for the new "human" condition, with the underlying dynamics of "waves of destruction from ultimate space," though their default temperatures accord with these authors' contrasting tempers: the "dizzy vacua" of (not-so-)empty skies that Lovecraft's shrines of godlessness open onto bring chills of cosmic terror from interstellar abysses and pelagic depths, whereas Bataille's atheistic ecstasies communicate the searing, all-consuming energy of universal expenditure from blinding suns and telluric innards. Yet these complementary, largely overlapping sets of images and tropes point to the same world-historical experience, with uncannily prophetic relevance to further stages of that unfolding process. For mankind appears increasingly wont to suspect its own planetary contingency on the cusp of Lovecraft's "new dark age" (glimpsed at the outset of "The Call of Cthulhu"), with climate change as an echoing natural backdrop of extinction anxiety for a world in the throes of civilizational panic, as cultural backwaters act out postmodernity's telltale Bataillean fantasies of torture porn and zombie hordes, driven by all-consuming traumatic *jouissance*.

Swayed by the crawling chaos taking awful shape in reality, reminiscent of familiar nightmares that have been haunting us and spreading virally for nearly a century, it would be tempting to view Bataille as a live Lovecraft character: a self-described "sorcerer's apprentice"[2] who could very well have come across one of the known copies of the *Necronomicon* in the Bibliothèque Nationale's "inferno" of forbidden books, which he raided in the pursuit of his most transgressive interests. Such a story would have enough thought-provoking, spine-tingling verisimilitude to make a deliciously self-referential addition to the Lovecraft-inspired weird genre, loosed upon the world from some transdimensional nexus of real and imagined dark recesses of human nature and culture. This much is true: digging from opposite shores, respectively beholden to the Apollonian and Dionysian aesthetic/existential attitudes contrasted by Nietzsche, Lovecraft and Bataille were both tapping into the same underground stores of pre-human mindlessness, actually foreshadowing a coming post-human shift to formless realms of manic excess, as the apocalyptic horizon of our own belated times.

Works Cited

Ades, Dawn, and Simon Baker, ed. *Undercover Surrealism: Georges Bataille and Documents*. London: Hayward Gallery; Cambridge, MA: MIT Press, 2006.

---

2. See Bataille's eponymous manifesto in *The College of Sociology* 12-23.

Bataille, Georges. *Against Architecture. The Writings of Georges Bataille.* Ed. Denis Hollier. Trans. Betsy Wing. Cambridge, MA: MIT Press, 1989.

———. *The College of Sociology (1937-1939).* Ed., Denis Hollier. Trans. Betsy Wing. Minneapolis: University of Minnesota Press, 1988.

———. *Documents.* Ed., Denis Hollier. Paris: Jean-Michel Place, Les Cahiers de Gradhiva 19, 1991. 2 vols.

———. *Visions of Excess. Selected Writings, 1927-1939.* Trans. Allan Stoekl. Minneapolis: University of Minnesota Press, 1985.

Bois, Yve-Alain, and Rosalind E. Krauss, ed. *Formless.* New York: Zone Books; Cambridge, MA: MIT Press, 1997.

Brotchie, Alastair, ed. *Encyclopedia Acephalica: Comprising the Critical Dictionary & Related Texts, edited by Georges Bataille, and the Encyclopedia Da Costa, edited by Robert Lebel and Isabelle Waldberg.* Trans. Iain White et al. London: Atlas Press, 1995.

Deleuze, Gilles, and Félix Guattari. *A Thousand Plateaus: Capitalism and Schizophrenia.* Trans. Brian Massumi. Minneapolis: University of Minnesota Press, 1987.

Didi-Huberman, Georges. *La Ressemblance informe, ou le gai savoir selon Georges Bataille.* Paris: Macula, 1995.

Fédida, Pierre. "The Movement of the Informe." Trans. M. Stone-Richards and Ming Tiampo. *Qui parle* 10, No. 1 (Fall-Winter 1996): 49-62.

Knowles, Christopher Loring, "Lovecraft's Secret Source for the Cthulhu Mythos." *The Secret Sun* blog, 2014. (http://secretsun.blogspot.ca/2014/08/lovecrafts-secret-source-for-chthulu_9.html, last viewed Feb. 17. 2017).

Koyré, Alexandre. *From the Closed World to the Infinite Universe.* Baltimore: Johns Hopkins University Press, 1957.

Nietzsche, Friedrich. *The Birth of Tragedy.* Trans. Shaun Whiteside. London: Penguin Classics, 1994.

Parkinson, Gavin. *Surrealism, Art and Modern Science: Relativity, Quantum Mechanics, Epistemology.* New Haven, CT: Yale University Press, 2008.

Roy, Christian. "Alexander Irwin, *Saints of the Impossible: Bataille, Weil, and the Politics of the Sacred,*" book review in *H-France Review* 3, No. 131 (November 2003): 580-87. http://h-france.net/vol3reviews/vol3no131roy.pdf

Roy, Christian. "Arnaud Dandieu and the Epistemology of *Documents*", in *Papers of Surrealism*, Issue 7: "The Use-Value of *Documents*", 2007. http://www.surrealismcentre.ac.uk/papersofsurrealism/journal7/index.htm.

Surya, Michel. *Georges Bataille: An Intellectual Biography*. Trans. Krzysztof Fijalkowski and Michael Richardson. London: Verso, 2002.

Violi, Alessandra. "L'immagine informe: Bataille, Warburg, Benjamin e i fantasmi della tradizione," F@RUM (Forum avanzato di ricerca universitaria multimediale), 2004. http://www.publifarum.farum.it/violi_informe/violi_informe.pdf.

Ripples from Carcosa: H. P. Lovecraft, *True Detective*, and the Artist-Investigator

Heather Poirier
Independent Scholar

Silent, her body kneeling beneath the wide arms of the ancient oak, her hands bound, her figure seemingly in prayer but praying to a pagan god who is pleased with the antlers resting on her still, dead scalp, the spiral drawn on her lower back drawing one of the detectives to examine her closely as he draws the scene in his notebook. This scene begins *True Detective*, the HBO series famous for its use of Robert W. Chambers's *King in Yellow* (season 1 [S1], 2014). To find our way through the woods of weird fiction and detective fiction so that we find the place in *True Detective* where Dora Lange's body waits kneeling under the tree, we will look at a brief review of the history of detective fiction, then look at two writers of tales of investigation—Edgar Allan Poe, who did it consciously, and Chambers, whose characters use investigative techniques in their pursuit of love and art. Both Poe and Chambers link to H. P. Lovecraft, whose narrators function frequently as investigators even when that is not their occupation. Critical to an understanding of a new iteration of detective, the artist-investigator, is a discussion of the aesthetics of crime, investigation, and redemption. Next will come the definition of the artist-investigator, along with how Chambers, Lovecraft, and the detectives Rustin Cohle and Martin Hart in *True Detective* contribute to that definition.

The investigator as a literary figure is a contentious one. Born out of traditions established by Edgar Allan Poe and Sir Arthur Conan Doyle, the investigator changed radically in twentieth-century detective fiction—moving from amateur to professional, investigator to criminal—and continues to change within the genre. As Christopher Pittard notes in his book *Purity and Contamination in Late Victorian Detective Fiction*, the investigator operates in the social margin because he has contact with criminals, with evil, and often with the very body of the victim (20). Similarly, Lovecraft's narrators move from center to margin and from social norms to cosmic horror. Lovecraft uses the same techniques as numerous detective fiction writers, a matter that I will address later. Without the investigator, without some figure fortified by curiosity and determination, much of the work of H. P. Lovecraft would not have been possible.

Detective fiction's roots extend far back in literature, including such diverse narratives as the story of Bel and the Dragon in the biblical Book of Daniel (which is referenced by Reverend Joel Theriot in S1, episode 3 [E3] of *True Detective*, "The Locked Room," 2014) and the story of Oedipus in *Oedipus Rex* (which is referenced in S2E1, "The Western Book of the Dead," 2015). The function of detective fiction in culture has largely been to reinforce norms. For example, in the story of Bel and the Dragon, Daniel reveals the methods of the false priests and, in so doing, reinforces the cultural position of those following YHWH. Later, beloved detective Sherlock Holmes reinforces the norms and values of Victorian England in numerous stories. For example, "The Man with the Twisted Lip" is a story about an ostensibly successful businessman, Mr. Neville St. Clair, who has in fact been posing as a beggar—and earning a high income by doing so. Holmes agrees to keep St. Clair's secret so long as St. Clair discontinues his deceit. True to Victorian norms, the scandal is less that St. Clair has been deceiving his wife than it is that a beggar should earn a gentleman's income. Holmes's goal in his detective work is both to catch criminals and to shore up the values of the British Empire. He does not do it for fame or wealth, but for both the sake of the game and the good of British society.[1]

In the twentieth century, detective fiction changes in parallel with changes in philosophy and literature. Agatha Christie may have refined the parlor-game subgenre of detective fiction, but in *Curtain: Poirot's Last*

---

1. Gavin Callaghan notes in his discussion of Sherlock Holmes and HPL, "It would indeed be ironic if it was *Holmes's own theory of human insignificance* that influenced Lovecraft in his decision to eschew not only realistic or compelling characters, but also the opportunity to create a heroic, recurring Holmes-like figure in his own tales. Holmes repeatedly berates Watson that he would rather solve his mysteries in anonymity. For him, the *work* is everything—*he* is nothing. Dr. Watson may have ignored Holmes's fictional advice, but *Lovecraft*, it appears, took it to heart" (Callaghan 201; emphasis in the original).

Case, her final novel for Hercule Poirot, she makes him the murderer of a man who has committed no crimes himself—the detective becomes the criminal, though in the service of society as a whole, an action that also appears in *True Detective*. Poirot's victim, Stephen Norton, is a skilled manipulator of others, to the degree that persons kill or attempt to kill others after being in Norton's presence for what seems nothing more than awkward yet casual conversation. Norton's powers of suggestion, masked by what seems to be extreme social awkwardness, make him the perfect murderer by proxy.

Poirot recognizes Norton's technique, sets up and executes the man's murder, then four months after his own apparent heart attack and death, leaves a full, written confession as part of what is revealed to be his suicide. Poirot kills his victim to protect society, then kills himself to right the wrong he has himself committed, making both himself and his victim societal scapegoats whose deaths relieve the guilt of the society-in-miniature in which they both live, a matter discussed at length by anthropologist René Girard.[2]

During the Cold War, espionage fiction became its own genre, deriving some techniques and dynamics from detective fiction while developing its own identity. An important parallel between espionage fiction and detective fiction is the triangular dynamic at its core that drives other tropes and dynamics. The primary dynamic in espionage fiction is that of the lover, the beloved, and the interloper, corresponding to the handler, the spy, and the counterspy; in detective fiction, it is the priest, the sacrifice, and the community, corresponding to the detective, the criminal, and society.[3] This dynamic in detective fiction becomes critical for the understanding of the aesthetics of crime, investigation, and redemption, which is the triangular dynamic driving the artist-investigator.

Finally, by the end of the twentieth century, the limitations of human action and knowledge that have been a part of more serious literary fiction begin appearing in detective fiction. Following in Agatha Christie's footsteps, detectives become criminals themselves; clues become increasingly

---

2. Rene Girard's *Violence and the Sacred* is key to understanding the necessity of ritual violence in maintaining societal norms.

3. Girard devotes extensive discussion of the dynamics of ritual sacrifice and societal absolution in *Violence and the Sacred*.

difficult to distinguish from their surroundings; and culprits' motives become clouded by the general murkiness of modernity.

Even though stories of investigation have appeared throughout Western literature, the genre officially begins with Edgar Allan Poe's short story "The Murders in the Rue Morgue" (1841). It is in his subsequent story "The Mystery of Marie Rogêt" (1842), however, that Poe outlines via footnotes and editorial comments the process of creating a tale of ratiocination. The narrative is a dual one: it is a fictionalized version of an actual murder investigation, that of Mary Cecelia Rogers in New York; more importantly, it introduces the trope of the palimpsest to detective fiction, which will become one of the central tropes of the genre.

The story opens with a quotation about suspension of disbelief, in a way parallel to the manner in which some of Lovecraft's narrators begin their stories with a statement about believability. Gothic fiction and tropes are heavily influential, including Southern Gothic influences much as we see in *True Detective*,[4] and "The Mystery of Marie Rogêt" establishes some of the key tropes of detective fiction: clarity/obscurity, darkness/light, presence/absence, the discovery of the palimpsest of narratives, and the warring of narratives for dominance. Finally, though not thoroughly, Poe begins approaching an aesthetics of crime and investigation as he constructs the fictional narrative concerning Marie Rogêt that, as a palimpsest, overlays the actual narrative of Mary Rogers. The delicate sensibilities of detective C. Auguste Dupin and the aesthetics of the crime scene itself are key points in Dupin's discovery of the circumstances of Marie Rogêt's murder and the identity of the criminal.

The parallels between "The Mystery of Marie Rogêt" and H. P. Lovecraft's narratives in general are many. The mysteries are solved at a distance, using items such as newspaper accounts, diaries, cult-related texts, and other documents. This supported, validated research is critical to the investigation. Both Dupin and Lovecraft's narrators perform a close analysis of all available evidence. In contrast with these narrators, both the police in Poe and the scientific, medical, and legal communities in Lovecraft

---

4. For example, macabre events, criminal behavior, death, betrayal, and rural settings figure in both Gothic and Southern Gothic literature. A strong sense of place is present in both Southern Gothic and Southern literature in general, and presents an equally strong sense of place in his writings.

use poor thinking and judgment in their evaluation of the evidence. The narrator in "The Mystery of Marie Rogêt" is unnamed (he is, however, named in another story, as is Dyer in Lovecraft's *At the Mountains of Madness*), and Lovecraft populates his stories with a number of nameless narrators. The stories move from a hidden narrative offered by an unreliable narrator to a revealed narrative that is adequately documented or otherwise proven. In "The Mystery of Marie Rogêt," when the narrator is called on by the public to reveal his findings, he chooses to do so; in Lovecraft, the narrators' motives vary, but often they decide on their own to come forth with their findings. Both authors provide as documentation items translated from other languages, even though in both authors' narratives the documentation is as fictional as the narratives they support, and certainly in Lovecraft's case, the fictional documentation spurred other writers in his circle to use them creatively (Lauterbach 98). Finally, there is a struggle between narratives. In Poe, the struggle is between the accepted version, which has been published by newspaper reports and the police, and the narrator's version, which has been deduced by Dupin. In Lovecraft, the struggle between narratives is that of the narrator versus authorities and/or society, and aptly so: the core of detective fiction is the struggle between fictions, the layered narratives of the innocent and the guilty, the criminal and the detective. Later detectives will sort through evidence as though solving a logic problem on a grid, but Dupin uses exegesis to discover the truth about the murder. The key difference between the world in which Dupin functions and the world of Lovecraft and the *True Detective* investigators is that Dupin's world is a knowable one with no sense of cosmic horror. Dupin's solving of the murder of Marie Rogêt returns the community to a sense of safety and familiarity and normalizes the community ethos. Lovecraft's narrators, as well as Cohle and Hart in *True Detective*, can do neither.

Just as a detective pieces together clues and constructs a narrative, the narrator of "The Call of Cthulhu" pieces together clues and constructs a glimpse of the cult of worshippers surrounding the figure of Cthulhu. The narrator is the late Francis Wayland Thurston, who, by his own account, first glimpses the truth about the cult and its leader when he "fleshed out from an accidental piecing together of separated things—in this case an old newspaper item and the notes of a dead professor" (CF 2.22). This collation of a variety of information sources, including among other items dream journals, a dead sailor's monograph, interviews with a police detective from New Orleans, and a mysterious stone statuette, leads to

Thurston's understanding not only of the existence of Cthulhu and his cult, but also of Thurston's own approaching demise at the hands of a cult member. The last mystery is Thurston's own death, a mystery that must be solved by someone in the future. Although his death is assured, given the suspicious deaths of the others investigating the cult, it has not happened yet. Lovecraft constructs a palimpsest of narratives: the arrival of Cthulhu and others on our planet is overlaid by Cthulhu's entombment; the subsequent development of his cult through dream messages and the passing down of the cult through generations is overlaid by the murders in the Louisiana swamps; the sudden re-emergence of dreams and other phenomena, and the investigation by Detective Legrasse and Thurston, is overlaid by Thurston's ultimate collation of the evidence and his apprehension of cosmic horror.

The plot elements of "The Call of Cthulhu" are similar to those of standard detective fiction. The death of a relative brings the narrator into the story. As executor of the estate, the narrator examines the deceased's possessions, finds some oddities, and investigates. The investigation leads to more questions, then initial answers are gathered, and the narrator's review of the assembled evidence provides fuller explanations. What makes the difference is Lovecraft's use of cosmicism and cosmic horror.

"The Dunwich Horror" is another Lovecraft story with a central figure investigating strange events. We read of external documentation of the Whateley residence and its associated peculiarities, this time from three sources: government officers, government medical experts, and newspaper reporters. Next, Dr. Henry Armitage launches his investigation after he spends time with Wilbur Whateley and becomes suspicious. Armitage collects all possible data about Wilbur and the goings-on in Dunwich, then talks with Dr. Houghton of Aylesbury about Old Whateley's death. Armitage next visits Dunwich to see for himself the remaining evidence. After his return to Miskatonic, Armitage reads the passages in the *Necronomicon* that were of interest to Wilbur. Armitage then speaks with students of the occult in Boston and elsewhere. Finally, Armitage collates the available information and begins to understand the cosmic horror that has come to Dunwich. Once Armitage decides to take action, he enlists the aid of Professor Warren Rice and Dr. Francis Morgan. Together, they confront the cosmic horror and, after repelling it, partially restore the social norms of the tiny community. Despite using many of the tropes and dynamics of detective fiction, Lovecraft uses cosmic horror to upend the seemingly normal narrative of detection and investigation.

Through the use of these tropes, dynamics, and other devices, detective fiction is rich in its development as a genre as it parallels developments in twentieth-century Western thought. James Arthur Anderson's book *Out of the Shadows* serves as an easy introduction to a structuralist analysis of Lovecraft's works. For our purposes, Anderson's elucidation of binary relationships—one of the key methodologies of structuralism—helps us start examining tropes in detective fiction.[5] In addition to the tropes established by Poe in "The Mystery of Marie Rogêt" outlined above, another is that of the mask. Masking/unmasking is key to Chambers's work *The King in Yellow*. Characters struggle with the social masks they are required to wear in light of the desires they feel for love, sex, and freedom. Within this context, the play *The King in Yellow*—the text-within-the-text—references masking and unmasking in the chapter "The Mask":

> Camilla: You, sir, should unmask.
> Stranger: Indeed?
> Cassilda: Indeed, it's time. We all have laid aside disguise but you.
> Stranger: I wear no mask.
> Camilla: (Terrified, aside to Cassilda.) No mask? No mask! (Chambers 29)

Once the characters in Chambers's work *The King in Yellow* read the text-within-the-text, they are socially unmasked, less able to fit within society's constraints. Other characters in Chambers, such as those in the vignettes in the chapter "The Prophets' Paradise," struggle with the way our masks obstruct us in our search to understand love, death, and beauty. For Chambers's characters throughout *The King in Yellow*, love and art are interchangeable, and it is the heightened sensibilities of the artist that make fuller access to love possible and help them in their investigative pursuits. At the same time, each chapter of Chambers's book is about loss in some way, and thus absence. All these are key elements of the detective's makeup in detective fiction.

---

5. Revelation/concealment is arguably the dominant dynamic in detective fiction. Just as the detective struggles to reveal what the perpetrator or criminal wants to conceal, the author navigates between revealing enough for the sake of fair play—a critical point among devotees of detective fiction—and keeping details concealed so that the final revelation is still a surprise for the reader. From revelation and concealment come many of the other paired tropes, especially those related to vision.

Aesthetic sensibilities derived from artistic training form the basis of the characters' successes as quasi-investigators. Chambers's central characters—largely painters, but sometimes those involved in other arts, such as sculpture and theater—have aesthetic sensibilities available only to those with training in the arts. Most of the chapters of *The King in Yellow*—that is, the book that Chambers wrote—involve an encounter with beauty, such as the Sylvia in "The Street of the First Shell" or Trent's encounter with war in the same story, or the Sylvia of "The Street of the Four Winds," who is only a memory to the narrator Severn. It is through beauty that the narrators discover love. Their sense of aesthetics leads them to investigate moments of intensified beauty. Chambers's narrators would seem to be highly conventional figures, then, but for the presence of *The King in Yellow*—that is, the play that destroys lives, upends cultures, and provokes the power of authorities. The curiosity and determination possessed by Chambers's narrators both moves them toward love and, in some instances, toward madness and death when that same curiosity and determination, along with the power of the very text of the play, lures them into the realm of the King in Yellow—that is, the shadowy figure central to the play. It is these heightened artistic sensibilities that figure so strongly for both H. P. Lovecraft's narrators and the figure of Rustin Cohle in *True Detective*.

Lovecraft's narrators, who are from many walks of life (when specified, that is), possess the curiosity, courage, and determination that are key to development of artistic sensibilities. In *At the Mountains of Madness*, the narrator Dyer traces the history of the Great Old Ones through bas-reliefs and begins to understand the scope and depth of the Old Ones' civilization, as well as the formidable opponents they represent. Dyer's capabilities in understanding the significance of the bas-reliefs is central to the revelations to come; his determination to survive and warn others drives his documentation of the Antarctic expedition once he returns home.

Similarly, the narrator in "The Music of Erich Zann" is not a musician himself, but is instead someone who has an educated appreciation for it. It is this appreciation that leads him to the door of the violinist Zann and to the mind-rending discoveries therein. For Lovecraft, unlike Chambers, aesthetic sensibilities can lead beyond mere encounters with beauty to encounters with cosmic horror. Zann's apartment window does not display a cityscape or a pastoral view; instead, it reveals an opening into space, possibly into a different dimension. But for the narrator's aesthetic sensibilities, Zann might have survived the end of the narrator's story, and the narrator might have remained an innocent, though less well-informed, man. Other narrators, such as Thurber in "Pickman's Model," follow similar aesthetic instincts. Thurber himself notes that "only a real artist knows the actual anatomy of the terrible or the physiology of fear" (CF 2.57).

In Poe, we have an aesthete in the figure of Dupin. In Chambers, we have artists who follow leads, track down people, and discover the truth behind numerous sets of mysterious circumstances, sometimes going mad in the process. In Lovecraft, we have a wide variety of narrators who end up investigating circumstances and events of all kinds. Who, then is the artist-investigator?

The phrase "artist-investigator" arose in the theater world of San Francisco to describe an artist-in-residence whose purpose as a member of a troupe was to push the boundaries of current thought and practice. The artist-investigator brings the highly developed aesthetic sense of a professional artist to the works of a given troupe. To do this, an artist-investigator must have an understanding of the community for whom the troupe performs, the typical texts performed by the troupe, and the abilities and experiences of the members of the troupe. The artist-investigator must also understand his investigation as an epistemology—as an examination of how what is known has come to be known—so that he understands both where the boundaries have been laid by others and the limits of his own perceptions and experiences.

Thus, part of the work of the artist-investigator involves an epistemology of investigation. It is not enough for an artist-investigator simply to claim to know something; to know how he knows it is as important as knowing why he needs to know it. Richard Foley, in his article "An Epistemology That Matters," notes, "The two most fundamental questions for an epistemology are, what is involved in having good reasons to believe a claim, and what is involved in meeting the higher standard of knowledge that a claim is true?" (1). In a police procedural such as *True Detective*, epistemology and teleology cannot be separated. That is to say, how the detectives know something—how they claim that something is known and significant—cannot be separated from their purpose in knowing it. The teleological ends of goodness, betterness, and value—elements that affirm that something is worth knowing—cannot be separated from the deontological ends of rightness, obligation, and duty. The ends of investigation cannot be separated from the duty of the investigator. Thus, investigation is innately both epistemological and teleological.

The context for discussion of the epistemology of investigation is usually within the realm of criminal law and legal theory. However, its core questions are appropriately discussed here. The epistemology of investigation has as its basic question,

> Does the criminal investigation rise to the level of scientific investigation? That is, is it a truth-finding pursuit—if not, it is little better than a witch hunt—and is it normative, i.e., can narrative values be attached to behaviour and attribute responsibility to the persons involved in the behaviour under investigation? (Zeegers)

If so, then there is a basis for an epistemology of investigation. This is why the detective as a literary figure and the detectives in *True Detective* all wrestle with moral issues as well as criminal ones—normative values are often the same as moral ones in their world.

How, then, does the artist-investigator approach this necessity for an epistemology? Through the aesthetics of crime, investigation, and redemption as they are functions of narrative and normative systems. Perhaps the most notable investigator possessing a fine aesthetic is Sherlock Holmes, with his appreciation of music and his aptitude for disguise, and certainly his extreme intellectuality in his approach to crime solving. Another one would be Dupin, Poe's detective, who combines ratiocination with his own creative imagination. Both of these detectives use their aesthetic sensibilities in their crime solving: aesthetics becomes a tool through which the detective perceives what others are missing and by which he gains understanding of the criminal and his motivation.

Discussions of the aesthetics of criminality go back as far as Jack the Ripper. Simon Joyce in his essay "Sexual Politics and the Aesthetics of Crime" notes that readers during the late nineteenth century had available to them both works of popular fiction, such as Sir Arthur Conan Doyle's detective, and newspaper stories of Jack the Ripper, the exploits of whom became increasingly compared to Robert Louis Stevenson's novella *The Strange Case of Dr. Jekyll and Mr. Hyde* (502), as well as to familiar villains found in both legends and in Gothic fiction. These events and fictions became part of the public imagination, leading to a strong narrative understanding of crime. Thus, a criminal's activity forms a narrative, and his skill as a criminal becomes a set of aesthetic criteria, with more skilled criminals having a better reputation among the public and, perhaps, the authorities. The aesthetic of redemption for the criminal who is still on the loose is the aggregation of successful criminal acts, possibly to include trophies from victims, items that would then remind the criminal of his freedom from societal norms.

The aesthetics of investigation follows that of police procedure, where the normative function of the legal system creates a structure by which evidence can be evaluated and criminals can be charged with crimes. The narrative of a given crime becomes the background of the narrative of police activity. The aesthetics of investigation involves thorough collection of evidence, analysis of its significance, and reconstruction of the crime narrative. The investigator's special skills in perception form the basis of the investigative aesthetic. A highly developed investigative aesthetic would be indicated by a detective's knowledge of details and fine understanding of the criminal mind.

The aesthetics of redemption involves the story of the redeemed criminal, that is, how the criminal was at one time, what happened to change him, and how he is different now. These aesthetics also involve the investigator and the community. The criminal's personal narrative forms the basis of his story of redemption, and the quality, nuance, and authenticity of his narrative inform the aesthetic judgment of it. The investigators redeem the community in the biblical sense of the redemption of the people: the investigators catch the criminal to buy the freedom of the community. The freedom of the community depends on the simultaneous existence and imprisonment of the criminal. If the criminal has not been captured, the community cannot be redeemed.

All these matters, from the tropes established by Poe and others to the aesthetics of the artist-investigator, are important components of the world of Rustin Cohle and Martin Hart in *True Detective*. Cohle and Hart are different in almost every way, especially in terms of their differing aesthetics. Hart's personal aesthetic operates out of a similar sense of loss and absence to that of the conventional detective, especially the gumshoe. Hart is a womanizer who seeks to fill his growing feelings of emptiness with sexual relationships. Unable to resist advances from women, his adulterous liaisons do not offer him a way out of his core isolation. Hart has all the external evidence of a successful life: a beautiful wife, two daughters, a home, a good job as police investigator, and the usual testosterone-laced relationships with his fellow officers. When his life falls apart after his mistress tells his wife of their affair, Hart retreats even deeper into the conventional world by dropping his sexual liaisons and finding religion.

Ultimately, his efforts fail because he does not understand himself or his core aesthetic of deceit and entitlement. Even at the end, in S1E8, when his now ex-wife and daughters visit him in the hospital after the death of Errol Childress, Hart lies to them again, telling them that everything will be all right when he knows that he and Cohle cannot stop the cult of the King in Yellow. Hart's aesthetic remains one of deceit and corruption masked by conventionality.

Despite the emotional inadequacies of his life, Hart is supremely comfortable with keeping up the façade of family man and social conformist. Even his infidelity is simply another conventional item, merely kept secret; his public and his secret life mesh thoroughly with his social and cultural milieu. The hollow moral didacticism he offers his children is a poor attempt to guide his daughters on a path he cannot follow himself. Hart's lives—both of them—are empty, hollow, conformist, and conventional.

Interestingly, Hart uses this conventionality to throw the police department's internal affairs investigators, Gilbaugh and Papania, off his track. In "The Secret Fate of All Life" (S1E5, 2014), he tells the two men, "I tell it the same way that I told the shooting board and every cop bar between Houston and Biloxi. And you know why the story is always the same seventeen years gone? Because it only went down the one way." Hart knows that the investigators will likely find his version reliable because it agrees with the findings of the shooting board, a higher authority than Hart alone. During this sequence, the creators of *True Detective* employ the technique of the palimpsest—overwriting, as it were, the original narrative of the shooting at the LeDoux encampment with the narrative that Hart and Cohle gave to the shooting board—to misdirect Gilbaugh and Papania in their investigation of Cohle. The palimpsest is portrayed visually through sequences of Cohle and Hart at the LeDoux encampment shootout—which shows the audience what "really happened"—that are intercut with their calm, reasoned testimony before the shooting board, which presents a very different version of events at the encampment.

The bridge between Hart and Cohle is, ironically, *The King in Yellow*—here, the play, the forbidden text within the available text. As Lovecraft warns us in "The Call of Cthulhu," "The most merciful thing in the world, I think, is the inability of the human mind to correlate all its contents" (CF 2.21). This is what the play *The King in Yellow* does in Chambers's work. It is also what the idea of the King in Yellow ultimately does in *True Detective*: it forces Cohle and Hart to correlate the evidence and discover horrible things. The King in Yellow is never revealed in *True Detective*, yet its power drives Errol Childress and other members of the cult to torture and murder, just as it drives Cohle to continue investigating. In fact, it is the very name The Yellow King, used by Guy Leonard Francis during his own interrogation in S1E5, "The Secret Fate of All Life," that brings Cohle back into the investigation. The King in Yellow wrecks Cohle's life by driving his obsession; the King in Yellow wrecks Hart's life by bringing him local fame that ultimately wrecks his family, largely by making Hart unwilling to resist women.

In contrast with Hart, and to use a section of Lovecraft's essay "Supernatural Horror in Literature" as a palimpsest for a reading of Cohle's character (CE 2.100-101), Cohle's impartiality is what makes him a great investigator and interrogator, yet it is also what keeps him from being intimate with others. He is the vivid and detached chronicler of crimes and crime scenes. He is neither teacher nor sympathizer (although he convinces the suspects he interrogates that he is sympathetic), and the only opinions he vends are his own—and only when asked. Cohle, as the artist-investigator, sees life and thought as rightful considerations during any given investigation. His work requires that he interpret powerful feelings and happenings that attend crimes, that he see the decay, terror, adversity, and indifference of victims and criminals, that he disregard the taste and traditional outward sentiments of mankind, and that he sacrifice his own health, sanity, and normal expansive welfare for the sake of the community.

As Fritz Leiber famously named Lovecraft, Cohle is a Copernicus in *True Detective*. Leiber says of Lovecraft, "He shifted the focus of supernatural dread from man and his little world and his gods, to the stars and the black and unplumbed gulfs of intergalactic space. To do this effectively, he created a new kind of horror story and new methods for telling it" (50). Cohle does this in *True Detective* with the social and cultural iconography of south Louisiana. He re-centers the dialogue so that Marty Hart and others are forced to look at the world from a position very different from their native understanding. This ability to re-situate the narrative is also why those around him are resistant to his ideas: through his intellectual and philosophical prowess, Cohle invokes similar "black and unplumbed gulfs."

Given that human significance is so limited, one would wonder why Cohle stays with the murder cases. One reason would be because of their weird tale elements, specifically the philosophy and aesthetic of the events. The cult of the King in Yellow has adopted a set of beliefs that removes it from conventional thinking and action, that is, it has created for itself the environment of the weird tale. Cohle comes to recognize this in his own terms first as a police investigator, then as a private citizen. In a scene in "The Locked Room," Cohle tells the detectives,

> This [patting folder with photo of latest victim]. This is what I'm talking about. This is what I mean when I'm talking about time and death and futility. That there are broader ideas at work, mainly what is owed between us as a society for our mutual illusions. (S1E3, 2014)

Just as with Danforth in *At the Mountains of Madness*, Cohle possesses the vulnerabilities associated with the artistic temperament: heightened awareness, a gift for connecting things that are not obvious, and an awareness of the aesthetics of a given situation that might be related to the aesthetics of another, that is, a trans-aesthetic sensitivity.

Cohle's aesthetic is that of an artist who seeks to understand and see before he begins to work and whose ultimate act of seeing is to capture a perpetrator and gain his confession. As an example, in S1E1, "The Long Bright Dark," Cohle brings a ledger to the scene where the body of Dora Lange was left to be discovered—Cohle's nickname from another police force, as it turns out, is "Tax Man"—and in it, Cohle documents evidence, findings, leads, and numerous other items related to the investigation, including drawings of Dora Lange and the devil nets surrounding her body. For now, the investigation seems to remain within normal limits, despite the odd elements around the body of Dora Lange. Things change the more the detectives learn, however, and exposure to these new ideas soon leads to their mental disarray, just as in *At the Mountains of Madness* the oppressive polar solitude, paired with sights inducing cosmic horror, leads to the mental disarray of Dyer and ultimately to the insanity of Danforth. What keeps Cohle and Hart (and Dyer/Danforth) on the level is a mutual agreement about there being a plausible explanation involving human agency.

Later, in the episode "After You've Gone" (S1E7, 2014), Hart joins Cohle in Cohle's storage unit, which he has turned into an artist's studio of sorts, filled with drawings, maps, documents, and all the evidence that Cohle could assemble as a civilian, arranged as a collage on the surfaces of the storage unit. As Anderson notes in *Out of the Shadows*, "In a strange sort of textual code of its own, the horror story becomes a metaphor for the quest for knowledge—even though we know it may not be pleasant, so does it attract and seduce in its own perverse way" (87). Similarly, Cohle's storage-unit-as-atelier helps him to begin correlating what he knows about the cult, the murders, and the victims.

As an artist-investigator, Cohle sorts his personal beliefs by removing the human and focusing on the realm of ideas. Human insignificance in the cosmos is the basis of his philosophical beliefs, which in turn forms the basis of his aesthetic as an investigator.[6] Cohle tells Gilbaugh and Papania in S1E3, "The Locked Room,"

> I've seen the finale of thousands of lives. Each one is so sure of their realness. That their sensory experience constituted a unique individual with purpose, meaning. So certain that they were more than a biological puppet. The truth wills out, and everybody sees that once the strings are cut off, all fall down. (2014)

As S. T. Joshi notes in "Lovecraft Criticism: A Study," "This reflexion of man's ludicrously minute position in the cosmos is perpetually conveyed in [Lovecraft's] fiction, and may perhaps be Lovecraft's major contribution to literature" (20–21). This stems from the understanding of the utter meaninglessness of human agency in both Lovecraft and *True Detective*. In *True Detective*, normal, garden-variety people have no way of withstanding the actions of those in positions of power. The cult members are so highly placed in local society that they enjoy perpetual protection.[7] Despite this powerlessness, Cohle affirms the power of right action at the end of S1E8, "Form and Void" (2014), when he announces to Hart that he believes the light of the stars is winning the battle against the darkness of space.

So now that we have established Cohle as the artist-investigator, can we say that there really is such a thing as a true detective? There is substantial doubt, especially in light of the development of detective fiction since the middle of the twentieth century. Hart and Cohle are both Janus figures. Hart is duplicitous yet seen as trustworthy; Cohle has integrity and is brutally honest, but none of his fellow officers trust or even like him. Hart's strengths are in police procedure work; he is rough and unrefined, and he knows how to work a suspect over. He has tremendous skill in fer-

---

6. Thomas Ligotti's book *The Conspiracy against the Human Race*, while not appropriate for this discussion of detective fiction and the artist-investigator, is illuminating with regard to Rustin Cohle's personal philosophy.

7. The same sense of the powerlessness of normal people, those who are not wealthy and well-connected, is a driving force behind season 2 of *True Detective*.

reting out leads and details. Still, Hart is too much of a conformist to fit into the worlds that Cohle inhabits. By the end of season 1, Hart is a private investigator, a gumshoe detective, estranged from his family and on tenuous terms with his former colleagues on the police force.

Cohle, on the other hand, resembles a gumshoe detective in some ways, but he does not embrace the role. He is rejected, dismissed, an outsider to both his fellow police officers and the civilians who know him. He is brilliant and has no problem demonstrating that to his fellow officers, which they resent. He is more experienced in detective and undercover work than they are, and he also "knows some moves," as Hart puts it (S1E3, "The Locked Room," 2014). He is an interrogator supreme, the best "box man" in the state (S1E5, "The Secret Fate of All Life," 2014). In contrast with Hart, Cohle doesn't fit in among other cops and only just fits in as a police investigator. His natural milieu is the nighttime, that of the noir detective, as demonstrated by his easy burglary of Reverend Tuttle's home (S1E7, "After You've Gone," 2014). To paraphrase from Dirk W. Mosig's article "H. P. Lovecraft: Myth-Maker," *True Detective* does similar things with human relationships and society that Lovecraft does with cosmic horror (111). The world of *True Detective* is mechanistic and materialistic. It illustrates realms within normal life that exist in front of everyone yet are nevertheless unseen. We normal, everyday people are in a laughable position in the cosmos; we are powerless to affect the circumstances in which we find ourselves.

So who is the true detective? Is it possible for there to be such a person any more, given the many changes in culture, police procedure, philosophy, and the legal system that have taken place since the first of Poe's stories was published? Perhaps the answer is in a section of dialogue from "The Locked Room" (S1E3, 2014):

> "You think . . . you wonder, ever, if you're a bad man?"
> "No, I don't wonder, Marty. The world needs bad men. We keep the other bad men from the door."

Works Cited

Anderson, James Arthur. *Out of the Shadows: A Structuralist Approach to Understanding the Fiction of H. P. Lovecraft*. Hollicong, PA: Wildside Press, 2011.

Callaghan, Gavin. "Elementary, My Dear Lovecraft: H. P. Lovecraft and Sherlock Holmes." *Lovecraft Annual* No. 6 (2012): 199–229.

Chambers, Robert W. *The King in Yellow*. 1895. Ebook, 2015.

Foley, Richard. "An Epistemology That Matters." 4 December 2015. philosophy.fas.nyu.edu/docs/IO/1161/epistemologythatmatters.pdf.

Girard, René. *Violence and the Sacred*. Baltimore: Johns Hopkins University Press, 1979.

Joshi, S. T. "Lovecraft Criticism: A Study." In *H. P. Lovecraft: Four Decades of Criticism* 20–26.

———, ed. *H. P. Lovecraft: Four Decades of Criticism*. Athens: Ohio University Press, 1980.

Joyce, Simon. "Sexual Politics and the Aesthetics of Crime." *English Literary History* 69, No. 2 (2002): 501–23.

Lauterbach, Edward. "Some Notes on Cthulhian Pseudobiblia." In Joshi, *H. P. Lovecraft: Four Decades of Criticism* 96–103.

Leiber, Fritz, Jr. "A Literary Copernicus." In Joshi, *H. P. Lovecraft: Four Decades of Criticism* 50–62.

Mosig, Dirk W. "H. P. Lovecraft: Myth-Maker." In Joshi, *H. P. Lovecraft: Four Decades of Criticism* 104–12.

Pittard, Christopher. *Purity and Contamination in Late Victorian Detective Fiction*. Farnham, UK: Ashgate, 2011.

True Detective, season 1. Created and written by Nic Pizzolatto, directed by Cary Joji Fukunaga, HBO, 2014.

True Detective, season 2. Created and written by Nic Pizzolatto, HBO, 2015.

Zeegers, Nicolle. "What Epistemology Would Serve Criminal Law Best in Finding the Truth about Rape?" *Law and Method*, 4 May 2015. http://www.lawandmethod.nl/tijdschrift/lawandmethod/2012/1/ReM_2212-2508_2012_002_001_005

Lovecraft for the Little Ones: *ParaNorman,* Plushies, and More

Faye Ringel
U.S. Coast Guard Academy in New London, CT
and
Jenna Randall
Independent Scholar

When H. P. Lovecraft first conjured up his tentacled Elder Things and monsters, he could never have imagined that ninety years later a four-year-old child would be cuddling a plush Cthulhu as he drifts off to sleep. What would he make of the bookshelf in that child's room, with picture books titled *Where the Deep Ones Are* and *Cliffourd the Big Red God?* What better sign of how thoroughly Lovecraft has entered the mainstream of popular culture than the explosion of Lovecraft-inspired plush toys, games, puzzles, picture books, coloring books, and films?

    The terrors of Lovecraft's materialist cosmos are the latest instances of domesticating the monstrous, joining earlier Gothic icons as consumable objects for children. Since the mid-twentieth century, beginning with Frankenstein's Creature (*The Munsters*) and the Transylvanian vampire (Count Chocula cereal, *Sesame Street*'s Count von Count), continuing through today's zombies (*Plants vs. Zombies*), American manufacturers have repackaged the formerly monstrous into the cute and cuddly. There has been a continuous escalation in the consumption of Gothic material by American children via video games, cartoons, and lines of toys such as the Monster High dolls and Lego's Monster Fighters series. This phenomenon the authors have dubbed "KinderGoth," a term once applied to underage-and hence illegal-would-be participants in the Goth subculture, which we have applied to the Gothic-inspired toys, games, books, and movies aimed at the younger generation, rather than to the children themselves.[1] Kenneth Hite's essay in *Cthulhurotica* provides more examples of this Gothic consumerism, especially the recent "wave of ...'Cthulhu kitsch'" (283); appropriately for its venue, however, Hite's focus is on materials designed for an adult audience. Victoria Nelson's *Gothicka* traces Lovecraft's influence on American popular culture, but her survey of games, films, heavy metal bands, and magickal cults slights the KinderGoth phenomenon. She claims that Lovecraft enthusiasts prefer their gods and monsters to be monstrous, "resistant to this millennial sentimentalizing of the demonic," though she does mention "the notable exception of the 'cute Cthulhu' toy" (Nelson 61). Yet these children's films, games, and toys would seem to support her thesis that the new millennium has seen a shift toward the light side of Gothic transcendence.

Americans are not the only consumers of these materials: the *Guardian* sees a similar phenomenon in Britain. According to David Barnett's horror blogpost "Cuddly Cthulhu," "the muck-encrusted god has spawned an entire industry that seems intent on making the Great Old Ones cuddly." Other Lovecraft-derived monsters of game worlds seem designed to warp the minds of the young players, whose first plush toys might have been the Baby Shoggoth. "The plush Baby Shoggoth may not be as amorphous as its namesake, but it's certainly a squishy beany-filled plush toy of many eyes and adorable terror" ("Baby Shoggoth"). A larger-sized toy Cthulhu is advertised in this fashion: "Entertain the children or summon Yog Shoggoth with this 17″ plush hand puppet. Guaranteed you'll have a good time . . . or call up a few demons" ("Cthulhu Hand").

Print is not neglected in this KinderGoth universe. Kenneth Hite, the critic and game creator, has promulgated a Mini Mythos series based on famous picture books including *Where the Deep Ones Are*, a parody of Maurice Sendak's already monstrous work *Where the Wild Things Are*; *Cliffourd the Big Red God*, a cozy version of "The Dunwich Horror"; *Antarctic Express*,

---

1. For earlier attestations of "KinderGoth" see Nancy Kilpatrick, *The Goth Bible*, and the online Urban Dictionary. We have used the term in our sense in presentations, including one at the International Conference on the Fantastic in the Arts. While KinderGoth makes monsters cozy, a related term, "GynoGoth," transforms the cozy familial bond into gory horror, as in our conference presentation "Haunted Wombs and Demonic Mothers."

which retells *At the Mountains of Madness* in the style of Chris Van Allsburg's *Polar Express*; and *Goodnight Azathoth*, based on the ultimate bedtime story, Margaret Wise Brown's *Goodnight Moon*. Although this series is inspired by best-selling children's classics, Hite has informed us that his intended audience is adult fans and collectors. Despite his intentions, Amazon.com describes the audience for these books as "8 and up."

Other picture books aimed more directly toward the youngest fans include *C Is for Cthulhu: The Lovecraft Alphabet Book* by Jason Ciaramella and Greg Murphy. Robert M. Price wrote the foreword to the graphic novel *Baby's First Mythos*, which promises to "Blast your child's soul as they learn their letters and numbers," with text by C. J. Henderson, drawn by Erica Henderson. *Where's My Shoggoth?* by Ian Thomas, author, and Adam Bolton, illustrator, is a double parody, since the title and story-line seem inspired by Terry Pratchett, whose *Where's My Cow?* (2005) began as an imaginary kid's book in his Discworld. There are also *The Very Hungry Cthulhupillar* by Ben Mund, a parody of Eric Carle's classic picture book *The Very Hungry Caterpillar*; *Littlest Lovecraft: The Call of Cthulhu* by Tro Rex and Eyona Bella, and many more.

It is difficult to generalize about the intended audience for these toys, games, and books. While certain of these items seem designed as humorous collectibles for older worshippers, author Jenna Randall's house is full of "Lovecraft for the little ones." She and her young sons read the Kenneth Hite books and the alphabet books, play "Recall of Cthulhu," a Memory-like game whose cards feature Mythos monsters instead of hearts and spades, and nary a nightmare results. Other Lovecraft fans are buying these products for their children: The "C is for Cthulhu" Facebook page is filled with pictures of happy parents reading the book to their preschoolers. Reviewers on Amazon.com mention how much their children love the Cthulhu plushies and picture books. Praising *Goodnight Azathoth*, one reviewer writes, "I spent so many hours reading *Goodnight Moon* to my kids, I was thrilled to share this with them at Halloween now that they are older" (Mandrekar).[2] Should concerned parents eventually inform their children

---

2. Internal evidence suggests that some buyers of the Mythos plushies may not themselves be readers of Lovecraft. For example, a reviewer on January 18, 2016 posted "A tiny Counthulu! [sic] How awesome is that? I bought this for my granddaughter. I am hoping her parents will share it with her siblings" ("Toy Vault").

as to the true origins of their cute, cuddly, tentacled friends? Will the generation raised on *Littlest Lovecraft ever* be able to read "The Call of Cthulhu" un-ironically? Those children, in turn, are happily slaying Lovecraft-inspired monsters (or being slain) in their game worlds.

The toys, games, and picture books provide a more-than-adequate introduction to the Lovecraft Mythos, but what about his New England settings, his abandoned farmhouses and decaying towns, with secrets buried beneath? The hypocritical Puritans whom Lovecraft reviled are at the heart of the 2012 animated film *ParaNorman*, and their most famous "achievement," the Salem witchcraft hysteria, is the film's subject.

ParaNorman's writer-director Chris Butler also directed Neil Gaiman's *Coraline* (2009). Together with *The Nightmare Before Christmas* (1993), *Corpse Bride* (2005), *Monster House* (2006), and *Frankenweenie* (2012), *ParaNorman* exemplifies cinematic "KinderGoth." Although their target audience is children, these films often cleave more closely to the themes of traditional Gothic literature than do most contemporary horror movies. In place of blood, gore, and gratuitous sex, *ParaNorman* relies on creepy Byronic heroes, inescapable ancestral curses, and a Novanglian landscape of dilapidated houses to create its spooky mood. *ParaNorman* is more historically accurate than most adult movies that portray or mention the Salem panic: no witches are burned, and *ParaNorman*'s condemned witch Agatha is a little girl, as was Dorcas Good and several others accused of witchcraft in Salem. Dorcas, the four- or five-year-old daughter of condemned witch Sarah Good, was not hanged, but she was examined and imprisoned for seven months (Rosenthal 88–89).[3] The writers of *ParaNorman* may have based their witch's curse on the one Sarah Good laid upon Rev. Nicholas Noyes at her execution, which Hawthorne transferred to his own family in *The House of the Seven Gables*: "God will give him blood to drink!"

ParaNorman is set in Blithe Hollow, a small town whose location is apparently somewhere in New England. Like Lovecraft's Dunwich, it might have been founded by exiles from Salem, as described in "The Dunwich Horror," where "The old gentry, representing the two or three armigerous families which came from Salem in 1692, have kept somewhat

---

3. Legend has it that Dorcas Good was driven mad by her prison experience. This is the story told in Salem. Sarah Good gave birth while in prison; that baby died.

above the general level of decay" (CF 2. 419-20). Its own glories beyond recovery, Blithe Hollow exploits its witch-hunting past for the sake of tourist dollars. Similar to Lovecraft's *The Case of Charles Dexter Ward*, the film centers on communicating with and reviving the dead. Necromancy is the real secret sin of the Puritans and their descendants: literal ancestor-worship. Dread family secrets, enshrined in forbidden books, found in crumbling ancestral mansions: this is Lovecraft's Gothic vision of New England—it is equally *ParaNorman*'s vision.

In place of Lovecraft's ancestral mansions, the film substitutes the tumbledown house of Uncle Prenderghast (as in ghast-ly), who appears to be the decayed member of one of Lovecraft's inbred Yankee families. Norman's parents have forbidden him to have contact with Uncle Prenderghast, who nevertheless seeks him out, because they share the gift of necromancy—a gift that must be used to stop the curse of the vengeful child witch. When Norman visits his spooky old house in the woods, he finds his uncle dead on the floor. Instead of reviving this ancestor, Norman attempts to carry out his last command: "Read from the Book at the witch's grave."

Norman is a zombie-loving kid, alienated from the living. His own family is disturbed by his relationship with the ghost of his grandmother. He dreads going to school because the other kids either mock him or avoid him, yet he is seen happily conversing with spirits as he travels the streets of his blighted little town. For Norman, the dead are his most trusted friends: he is an Outsider. This twenty-first-century child reminds us of one of Lovecraft's most autobiographical protagonists, Jervas Dudley of "The Tomb," who like his creator once saw dryads dancing in the woods.

ParaNorman incorporates these tropes of the New England Gothic, but in a consciously postmodern way. When the Puritan court members who executed Agatha are reanimated, the contemporary residents of Blithe Hollow react to them as any early twenty-first-century American would: "The zombies are coming to eat us!" Rationalizing historians theorize that the Salem witchcraft hysteria arose because late seventeenth-century Puritan anxieties—loss of the colony's charter, Indian attacks, poor harvests, land disputes—were projected onto Satan and his human agents, witches and wizards. Today, in similar fashion, our fears of terrorists, epidemics, and illegal immigrants are expressed as the zombie apocalypse. The reaction is the same as in the 1690s, except that the present-day mob in *Para-*

Norman has access to guns in addition to pitchforks and torches.

One of the mob leaders is Norman's drama teacher, Mrs. Henscher. She also serves as the voice for the idealized but ultimately failed Puritan ancestors who troubled Lovecraft so much. Earlier in the movie, as she coaches her students in a skit that commemorates the anniversary of the witch's curse, she criticizes the children, bellowing:

> Pilgrims? The *Mayflower*? Don't any of you know anything about the history of this town? Puritans were strict and devout settlers, who came here to build a home, a place without sin.

This is the same founding myth that both Lovecraft and the writers of *ParaNorman* wish to explode. Lovecraft is merciless in his revelation of Puritan hypocrisy.[4] Here is Lovecraft's characterization of the seventeenth century in New England from "The Unnamable":

> The witchcraft terror is a horrible ray of light on what was stewing in men's crushed brains, but even that is a trifle. There was no beauty; no freedom—we can see that from the architectural and household remains, and the poisonous sermons of the cramped divines. And inside that rusted iron strait-jacket lurked gibbering hideousness, perversion, and diabolism. (CF 1.400-01)

Those same "architectural remains" feature prominently in Blithe Hollow, though in *ParaNorman* the reanimated judges eventually express their guilt that the ideas "stewing in their crushed brains" caused them to persecute little Agatha.

The explanation in the film for Agatha's persecution as a witch turns out to be that, like Norman, she is a ghost-seer who talks to the dead. Her necromantic gifts terrify the townspeople and fuel their hysteria. When Norman questions the undead judge as to how he could kill a child, he says, "I believed we were doing what was right. I was wrong.... We thought we knew our way in life, but in death we are lost." It is revealed that Agatha's curse was not on the townspeople, but on the undead court that sentenced her to death. In a clever inversion of the zombie trope, the frantic, terrified twenty-first-century residents of Blithe Hollow are the monsters and the monsters are the victims. This creates a sort of retribu-

---

4. For further information on Lovecraft's theory that New England's Puritans transplanted Europe's Gothic superstitions to the New World, see Ringel, "Diabolists and Decadents: Lovecraft's Gothic Puritans" and *New England's Gothic Literature*.

tive justice, causing the undead Puritans to experience the same fate as Agatha: being annihilated by those who ignorantly assume that they are innately evil. The Puritan judges and the modern mob exemplify Lovecraft's vision of New England's Gothic Puritans. Writing to Frank Belknap Long, he said that while he did not share Puritan theology, he (probably sarcastically) expressed admiration for their worldview: "Verily, the Puritans were the only really effective diabolists and decadents the world has known" (SL 1.275).

Norman breaks the witch's curse and resolves the plot by bravely talking to her and—in an example of reverse necromancy—allowing her to return to her happy childhood, go to sleep, and "enter the light," crossing over as the screen goes white. Norman's matter-of-fact and downright cozy relationship with the Invisible World, whose denizens are visible to the viewing audience, if not to the other living characters of the film, recalls another chapter of New England's Gothic history: the spiritualism craze of the mid-nineteenth century. After the Fox Sisters' ability to communicate with the dead via raps was revealed in upstate New York, all over New England, mediums appeared, ready to do the same (Ringel, *New England's Gothic* 18). Young girls like the accused witch Agatha were thought to be the most gifted mediums.

Nineteenth-century psychic investigators, meanwhile, theorized that the accusers as well as the accused in the Salem witchcraft panic might have been spiritualist mediums, with what we today call telekinetic and other psychic abilities. In 1880, Allen Putnam, who claimed descent from Salem's Ann Putnam, the only "bewitched girl" accuser to repent, published the popular work *Witchcraft Explained by Modern Spiritualism*. These words in his introduction make me wonder whether Chris Butler, scriptwriter of *ParaNorman*, might have read this book: "Teachings of spiritualism have luminated [sic] the places where witchcraft has been sent to slumber" (Putnam 13); and "we shall show that benighted man formerly, in good conscience, made certain events fearful curses, which, when rightly understood and used, may become gladdening and rich boons to mortals" (Putnam 21). Like these nineteenth-century spiritualists as well as today's purveyors of "crossing over," Norman's world is one where the dead surround us, harmlessly, with business to take care of and benevolent feelings toward the living; if we could only see the dead through his eyes, we would lose our fear.

The rest of Blithe Hollow's inhabitants, however, share a more traditional fear of witches and revenants, like the Puritans, but unlike Lovecraft the atheist and philosophical materialist who nevertheless shared his ancestors' gloomy outlook on the downward direction of human life. He revered New England's rise from the medieval superstition of the witch trials to what he saw as the pinnacle of civilization, the later eighteenth century. In his own life and times, however, he saw nothing but a tragic decline and fall. He watched in horror as Providence crumbled, as his New England became a stagnating backwater instead of the nation's cultural arbiter. He saw Salem become a city of manufacturing instead of the Queen of the China Trade, saw with dismay its swarming immigrant masses and the House of Seven Gables turned into a settlement house. All this he chronicled in "The Dreams in the Witch House" (1932), his only completed excursion into the New England witch belief, though he may have planned to write a novel about Salem, as he told Clark Ashton Smith in 1927 (*Dawnward Spire* 120)—an idea that apparently metamorphosed into *The Case of Charles Dexter Ward*.

"The Dreams in the Witch House" is set in Arkham, in this story at least a stand-in for Salem. The protagonist travels through fourth-dimensional time and space with Keziah Mason and her ratlike familiar Brown Jenkin, who have been stealing children for sacrifice at the seasons of the witches' sabbats, Walpurgis Night and Halloween. The protagonist's dreams in the old witch house can be compared to the time travel in *ParaNorman*, when the hero's school pageant dissolves into the seventeenth-century courtroom, a pageant during which the children sing Donovan's Sixties-vintage number "Season of the Witch." In "The Dreams in the Witch House," Arkham is fallen from its former glory—as Salem was when Lovecraft visited in the 1920s. In *ParaNorman*, Blithe Hollow's town hall is decayed, its archives desecrated, while Main Street features casinos, bars, and witch-kitsch shops that appall the reanimated Puritan judges. In Blithe Hollow, as in Lovecraft's Arkham, "strange things had happened once, and there was a faint suggestion behind the surface that everything of that monstrous past might not . . . have utterly perished" ("The Dreams in the Witch House" [*CF* 3.234]).

Lovecraft's Arkham and Salem and their inhabitants have much in common with *ParaNorman*'s Blithe Hollow, though some things have changed in the decades between the two works. The film willfully overturns some of the tropes of Lovecraft's New England Gothic. Instead of a medieval Latin translation of an Arabic grimoire, the film's version of the *Necronomicon*—the book Norman must read to keep Agatha's curse at bay for another year—is a tome of fairy tales. Still, like Lovecraft's Jervas Dudley, Norman spends a good deal of time in graveyards and among the tombs of his ancestors, whose Puritan epitaphs and headstone-carving styles are authentically rendered by Irish illustrator Ross Stewart, Concept Artist for the animated film. It is clear that Norman and Jervas, through their ability to communicate with the dead, share a "knowledge of topics almost forgotten for many generations" ("The Tomb" [CF 1.43]).

An element unlikely to be found in Lovecraft's work is a jock character, the older brother of one of Norman's friends, who comes out as gay at the end of the film. The attempt to humanize and redeem the Puritan judges who execute Agatha might have troubled Lovecraft. But he might have appreciated the way the movie presents us with the myth of the noble, stoic, resolute, and rational New England settlers while simultaneously subverting that image. And no doubt he would have nodded his head knowingly at the modern townspeople who whip themselves into a frenzy over monsters who are more terrified than terrifying. Indeed, both *ParaNorman* and Lovecraft's work seem invested in demonstrating to the reader/watcher that humans are frustratingly absurd, superstitious, and just plain stupid, no matter the century.

Of course, *ParaNorman*, an animated feature film aimed at children and their parents, must end on a bright, uplifting note: Norman cannot end his days in an asylum. Instead, his former tormentors are now his friends, Agatha is at rest, as are the zombie Puritans, and Blithe Hollow has been spared. Characters have grown and changed: alongside the gay jock, the airhead cheerleader has become a kick-ass heroine, and Norman's oblivious parents seem grateful for his macabre gifts. But—as at the end of "The Dunwich Horror" or "The Shadow over Innsmouth"—the town is in ruins, and it's unclear whether the townsfolk have truly repented of their actions. Human beings are still the real monsters.

Whether based upon Lovecraft's stories or unknowingly kin to them, cuddly Cthulhus, zombie video games, stop-animation kids' movies about terrifying curses, and other KinderGoth fare have one thing in common: they situate children in a dark landscape that conventional wisdom believes children should never traverse. Though Gothic horror themes appear to dominate today's canonical children's literature, from Maurice Sendak to Lemony Snicket and J. K. Rowling, it was not ever thus. In a collection of essays on *The Gothic in Children's Literature,* Dale Townshend sees the origin of fiction designed for children as a reaction against the excesses of the eighteenth century Gothic novel. Children were meant to be protected against fear, superstition, and the bad behavior of Gothic heroines and hero-villains. "Simply put, culturally approved forms of children's literature become everything that the Gothic is not" (Townshend 21). Today, all has changed. Witches are friends. Otherworldly creatures become relatable. Apocalypse is imminent, but that's all right. Recent criticism of the Gothic mode has read its monsters as metaphors for difference, grotesquely bodying forth cultural fears and projecting those horrors on to the Other.[5] Jeffrey Jerome Cohen's "Monster Theses" assert that we can comprehend how a culture hates, fears, and desires difference by studying its monsters. KinderGoth goes further to suggest that there really *is* no difference between monsters and humans. Cthulhu isn't here to devour your child's soul; he just wants to cuddle and teach the alphabet.

Works Cited

"Baby Shoggoth Plush." *Noble Knight Games.* www.nobleknight.com/ProductDetail.asp_Q_ProductID_E_2147343010_A_InventoryID_E_0_A_ProductLineID_E_1324338765_A_ManufacturerID_E_27_A_CategoryID_E_12_A_GenreID_E_. Accessed 11 Aug. 2016.

Barnett, David. "Cuddly Cthulhu: How HP Lovecraft's Dark Materials Turned Soft." *Guardian, Horror Book Blogs,* 7 March 2012. www.theguardian.com/books/booksblog/2012/mar/07/cuddly-cthulhu-hp-lovecraft-merchandising. Accessed 11 Aug. 2016.

Bishop, Kyle William. *American Zombie Gothic: The Rise and Fall (and Rise) of the Walking Dead in Popular Culture.* Jefferson, NC: McFarland, 2010.

"C is for Cthulhu." *Facebook.* www.facebook.com/cisforcthulhu/?fref=ts. Accessed 14 August 2016.

Ciaramella, Jason, and Greg Murphy. *C Is for Cthulhu: The Lovecraft Alphabet Book.* Newburyport, MA: ComixTribe, 2014.

---

5. In addition to many works by Jeffrey Jerome Cohen, see Bishop, *American Zombie Gothic,* and Punter, *A New Companion to the Gothic,* especially Catherine Spooner's essay on "Goth Culture."

Cohen, Jeffrey Jerome. "Monster Culture (Seven Theses)." In *Monster Theory: Reading Culture*. Minneapolis: University of Minnesota Press, 1996. 3-25.

"Cthulhu Hand Puppet." *ToyVault*. toyvault.myshopify.com/collections/cthulhu. Accessed 11 Aug. 2016.

Henderson, C. J., and Erica Henderson. *Baby's First Mythos*. New York: Z-Man Games, 2004.

Hite, Kenneth. *Antarctic Express*. Mini Mythos Series. St. Paul, MN: Atlas Games, 2009.

———. *Cliffourd, the Big Red God*. Mini Mythos Series. St. Paul, MN: Atlas Games, 2011.

———. "Cthulhu's Polymorphous Perversity." In *Cthulurotica*, ed., Carrie Cuinn. Ithaca, NY: Dagan Books, 2011. 281-93.

———. *Goodnight Azathoth*. Mini Mythos Series. St. Paul, MN: Atlas Games, 2015.

———. *Where the Deep Ones Are*. Mini Mythos Series. St. Paul, MN: Atlas Games, 2009.

Kilpatrick, Nancy. *The Goth Bible: A Compendium for the Darkly Inclined*. New York: St. Martin's Griffin, 2004.

"Kindergoth." *The Urban Dictionary*. www.urbandictionary.com/define.php?term=kindergoth. Accessed 11 August 2016.

Lovecraft, H. P., and Clark Ashton Smith. *Dawnward Spire, Lonely Hill: The Letters of H. P. Lovecraft and Clark Ashton Smith*. Ed. David E. Schultz and S. T. Joshi. New York: Hippocampus Press, 2017.

Mandrekar, P. "Customer Review of *Goodnight Azathoth*." Amazon.com. https://www.amazon.com/Goodnight-Azathoth-Kenneth-Hite/dp/1589781481/ref=sr_1_1?ie=UTF8&qid=1471303653&sr=8-1&keywords=Good+night+azathoth. Accessed 15 August 2016.

Mund, Ben. *The Very Hungry Cthulhupillar*. Signal Fire Studios, 2015.

Nelson, Victoria. *Gothicka: Vampire Heroes, Human Gods, and the New Supernatural*. Cambridge, MA: Harvard University Press, 2012.

ParaNorman. Dir. Chris Butler. Focus Features, 2012. Film.

Putnam, Allen. *Witchcraft of New England Explained by Modern Spiritualism*. Boston: Colby & Rich, 1880. archive.org/details/witchcraftofnewe00putnuoft. Accessed 11 August 2016.

Rex, Tro, and Eyona Bella *Littlest Lovecraft: The Call of Cthulhu*. Redmond, WA: Esoteric Order of Publishing, 2013.

Ringel, Faye. "Diabolists and Decadents: Lovecraft's Gothic Puritans." *LIT: Literature Interpretation Theory* 5, no. 1 (1994); 45–51.

———. "Golems Take Manhattan: Jewish-American Magical Realism." International Conference on the Fantastic in the Arts (ICFA), 21 March 2015, Marriott Orlando Airport, Orlando, FL. Conference Presentation.

———. *New England's Gothic Literature: Folklore and History of the Supernatural from the Seventeenth Through the Twentieth Centuries*. Lewiston, NY: Edwin Mellen Press, 1995.

Ringel, Faye, and Jenna Randall. "Haunted Wombs and Demonic Mothers: The Gynecological Gothic in *American Horror Story: Murder House*." Buffy to Batgirl Conference, 2 May 2014, Rutgers University-Camden. Conference Presentation.

Rosenthal, Bernard. *Salem Story: Reading the Witch Trials of 1692*. Cambridge: Cambridge University Press, 1995.

Spooner, Catherine. "Goth Culture." In *A New Companion to the Gothic*, ed., David Punter. Chichester, UK: Wiley-Blackwell, 2012. 350–68.

Stewart, Ross. "ParaNorman Conceptual Sketches." In *Art of Ross Stewart*. rossstewart.net/. Accessed 11 August 2016.

Thomas, Ian, and Alan Bolton. *Where's My Shoggoth?* Boom Entertainment, 2012.

Townshend, Dale. "The Haunted Nursery: 1764–1830." In *The Gothic in Children's Literature: Haunting the Borders*, ed., Anna Jackson, Roderick McGillis, and Karen Coats. London: Routledge, 2013. 15–29.

"Toy Vault 12004 Mini Cthulhu Plush Product Reviews." *Amazon.com*. https://www.amazon.com/Toy-Vault-12004-Cthulhu-Plush/product-reviews/B0006FUAD6/ref=cm_cr_dp_synop?ie=UTF8&showViewpoints=0&sortBy=recent#R2VA67JK10RV6H. Accessed 14 August 2016.

Contributors

Lars G. E. Backstrom has an M.Sc. in physics from Uppsala University, Sweden, an M.Sc. in geophysics from University of Alaska Fairbanks, and a M.A. in war studies from King's College, London. His papers have appeared in several learned journals including *Journal of Geophysical Research, Cold Regions Science and Technology, e-International Relations,* and the *Spectrum–The KCL Think Tank Society Journal*. He is also an award-winning author of short stories.

Matthew Beach received his Ph.D. in English from Brown University, where he was awarded the S. T. Joshi Endowed Research Fellowship for 2016. His research focuses on time and the body in American literature, particularly in popular genres such as pulp and sentimental fiction.

Daphnée Tasia Bourdages-Athanassiou is a literature undergraduate at Université Laval. In 2008 she graduated from the Conservatoire d'art dramatique de Québec, where she studied stage design. She completed a postgraduate certificate in teaching in 2010 and completed a degree in French and Québécois literature in May 2015. Her main interests are ancient and medieval literature, along with theatre and paraliterature. She has participated in two research groups, one on medieval literature and the other on nineteenth century journalism.

Sean Moreland is creator of the weird fiction–focused website *Postscripts to Darkness* (www.pstdarkness.com) and editor of a number of essay collections, including *The Lovecraftian Poe*. He teaches at the University of Ottawa.

Byron Nakamura is an associate professor of history at Southern Connecticut State University, where he has taught classes in ancient history, Greco-Roman religion, and courses in Latin and Greek. He has published on the subjects of Roman religion and the history of the Roman frontier in such journals as *Greek, Roman, and Byzantine Studies,*

Classical Philology, and the *Journal of Military History*. Recently, he has developed interests in classical reception and the supernatural.

Juan L. Pérez-de-Luque is a lecturer at the Department of English and German studies at the University of Cordoba, Spain. He has been a visitor scholar at Wheaton College, at the University of Nottingham, and at the John Hay Library at Brown University. He is the author of several articles and book chapters on Lovecraft and Poe. He is currently working on a project on secrecy in the narrative of Jeanette Winterson.

Connor Pitetti is a visiting scholar of American literature at Philipps-Universität Marburg. Supported by the S. T. Joshi Endowed Research Fellowship, he spent the summer of 2015 in Providence researching Lovecraft's architectural writings and was an ACLS dissertation completion fellow in 2015–16. His research interests include narrative theory, urban studies, science fiction, and the environmental humanities; his dissertation work focused on apocalyptic and postapocalyptic narrative strategies in modern and contemporary environmentalism.

Heather Poirier is a writer/editor living in Washington, DC. After teaching at the university level for ten years and working at a biomedical research center with a world-class researcher for five years, she moved to DC to work as a senior editor at an oncology journal. Her current project is a book on H. P. Lovecraft and detective fiction.

Dennis P. Quinn is chair of the Armitage Symposium and professor and chair of the Interdisciplinary General Education Department at Cal Poly Pomona. His publications include works on Roman influence on Lovecraft's fiction and Lovecraft's influence on modern religions, appearing in such venues as the *Lovecraft Annual* and *Lovecraftian Proceedings*. He has also published on early Christian and Greco-Roman demonology, appearing in such publications as *Studia Patristica*, and a book in Baker Academic's Holy Cross Studies in Patristic Theology series.

Jenna Randall holds a B.A. in English and women's studies from Smith College (2004). A lifelong fan of horror in all its manifestations (film, art, theatre, literature), she is drawn to all the places where feminism, pop culture, and horror intersect.

Contributors 239

Marcello Ricciardi is an associate professor of English at St. Joseph's College (Patchogue, NY). His areas of expertise include Milton, Lovecraft, and speculative fiction. He is the author of *John Milton's Incarnational Poetics: The Roles of Mary and Christ in Paradise Regained* and is currently working on his new book, *Prophets of Light and Darkness: Cosmic Horror and Sacred Terror in the Weird Worlds of Milton and Lovecraft*.

Faye Ringel, professor emerita of English, taught for twenty-five years at the U.S. Coast Guard Academy in New London, CT, where she directed the honors program. Her A.B. in comparative literature is from Brandeis University, her doctorate in comparative literature from Brown University. She is the author of *New England's Gothic Literature: History and Folklore of the Supernatural* (Edwin Mellen Press, 1995) and articles on Lovecraft in scholarly reference books and journals.

Troy Rondinone is a professor of history at Southern Connecticut State University. He received his Ph.D. in history at UCLA. He is the author of *The Great Industrial War: Framing Class Conflict in America, 1865–1950* (Rutgers University Press, 2010) and *Friday Night Fighter: Gaspar "Indio" Ortega and the Golden Age of Television Boxing* (University of Illinois Press, 2013). He has also published articles in *American Quarterly*, the *Journal of the Gilded Age and Progressive Era*, *Connecticut History*, and *Labor Studies*.

Christian Roy is an independent scholar in cultural history by vocation, a multilingual freelance translator by trade, and an art and cinema critic, who has published extensive analyses of the science-fiction films *The Abyss* and *Oblivion*. Based in Montreal, he is an associate researcher with the Centre International de Formation Européenne (Nice). He is the author of numerous articles in addition to *Traditional Festivals: A Multicultural Encyclopedia* (ABC-Clio, 2005).

Jeffrey Shanks is an archaeologist and historian specializing in early twentieth-century speculative fiction, particularly writers such as H. P. Lovecraft and Robert E. Howard. His work has appeared in numerous publications, including *Critical Insights: Pulp Fiction*, *Undead in the West II*, and *Conan Meets the Academy*. He serves as area chair of pulp studies for the Popular Culture Association and was co-editor of the Bram Stoker Award–nominated essay collection *The Unique Legacy of Weird Tales*.

Nathaniel R. Wallace is a sponsored programs manager at Ohio University and holds a bachelor's degree in political science from Ohio State University, a master's in political science from Ohio University, and a Ph.D. in interdisciplinary arts from Ohio University. His dissertation, "H. P. Lovecraft's Literary 'Supernatural Horror' in Visual Culture," is available through OhioLINK.

René J. Weise is the English language arts and literature content specialist at Hampshire Educational Collaborative Academy in Northampton, MA. In 2015, he received his M.A. in English from the University of Massachusetts Amherst. As an independent scholar, he continues to pursue his interest in the roles that occultism and religion as well as mythic structure and psychological symbolism play within horror and dark fantasy, advocating for higher academic appreciation and thoughtful scholarly analysis of overlooked genre texts.

Appendix: Abstracts of Papers Presented at the Dr. Henry Armitage Memorial Scholarship Symposium NecronomiCon Providence 20–23 August 2015

Dennis P. Quinn, Chair

The Dr. Henry Armitage Memorial Symposium aims to foster exploration of Lovecraft's elaborate cosmic mythology and how this mythology was influenced by, and has come to influence, numerous other authors and artists before and since. The Lovecraft Arts & Sciences Council (the organizer of NecronomiCon Providence) organizes this symposium of new academic work to explore all aspects of the writings and life of famed weird fiction writer H. P. Lovecraft, including the influence of history, architecture, science, and popular culture on his works, as well as the impact he has had on culture. Attendees heard the latest cutting-edge research on Lovecraft, topics related to Lovecraft, and his circle. Presentations were 15 minutes each in order to allow time for questions at the end of each panel.

Matthew Beach
Brown University
"H. P. Lovecraft's Optimism"

H. P. Lovecraft has often been regarded primarily as a weaver of pessimistic tales of "cosmic horror." My talk contests the simple reading of Lovecraft's fiction as pessimistic, not by denying instances of pessimism in his fiction but rather by arguing that various forms of pessimism and optimism may coexist in the same literary framework and interact in interesting ways. Beyond a (re)reading of his pessimism, I suggest that Lovecraft has something to contribute to the discussions of futurity and optimism currently taking place within literary studies. To make this case, I read "The

Shadow out of Time" in the context of the debates about futurity, negativity, and optimism that have taken place over the past decade in queer theory. Contrary to the majority of readings of his work as representative of literary pessimism, I argue Lovecraft's fiction also advances a form of "weird optimism" that resides in both an embodied relation to time as well as a particular theory of temporality that transcends the individual body. This optimism is enacted at the formal level of Lovecraft's narratives, which proceed toward the revelation of truth, through the gradual transformation of the narrator's embodied relation to time, and finally through their specific theorization of time as simultaneously an inexhaustible longue durée and a complex of overlapping temporalities.

While his narrators' new relation to time often drives them mad, I argue there is an underlying optimism to Lovecraft's theorization of time as enduring and multiple: a weird optimism that resides in knowing and feeling the terrors of time which is not reducible to pessimism. The weird optimism of Lovecraft's tales, however, resides less in their transformation of the narrator than in their theory of the infinite potentiality of time itself.

Lars G. Backstrom
Independent Scholar
"The Color out of Mind: Correlating the
Cthulhu Mythos Universe to the Autism Disorder Spectrum"

In this presentation I use clinical diagnostic criteria, my own experience, and the experience of others to compare the situation of an Asperger's sufferer to that of humanity in Lovecraft's universe.

Asperger's syndrome, an incurable neurological condition, belongs to the autistic spectrum disorder. It is also called high functioning autism or unofficially alien world syndrome. People with Asperger's are affectionately nicknamed Aspies. Some of the main symptoms are a restricted ability to interact socially and a pursuit of very specific interests. Both of these tend to lead to alienation and social isolation.

We Aspies are often drawn to science fiction, horror, and fantasy, partially as an escape from a world we do not really understand, but mostly because we find the sense of otherness in these genres very attractive. One author we find fascinating is H. P. Lovecraft, because he captures better than most the predicament of living with Asperger's.

The Cthulhu Mythos universe is a chaotic, unpredictable, and terrifying place in which humanity does not even belong. It is populated by disjointed and disparate beings (see Great Cthulhu himself and Brown Jenkin), whose motives are incomprehensible to us exactly in the same way the motives of non-Asperger's people are to an Aspie.

Very much like many Aspies, the typical Lovecraftian protagonist is usually either an alienated loner or someone being dominated by a more forceful companion. He is often an autodidact, collector, or dreamer and is pursuing a specific interest obsessively. He is unable to foresee the consequences of his actions until too late, and then he faces the ultimate horror of oblivion and loss of individuality alone and completely unable to communicate his plight to others.

Daphnée Tasia Bourdages-Athanassiou
Université Laval, Quebec City
"Insider, Outsider: From the Commonplace to the Uncanny
in Lovecraft's Narration and Descriptions"

Lovecraft is best known for his mythology of the "unspeakable," often singled out for its uniqueness and cosmic horror. It is therefore very interesting to determine how the idea of the alien is woven into Lovecraft's narratives. The situations Lovecraft creates are, of course, *fantastiques*, but proper literary tools are required to fully develop their potential. This research, based on a formalist approach, explores the means used by Lovecraft to establish the uncanny mood leading to horror in his works, in an analysis of his use of narration and description techniques. Indeed, detailed studies of Lovecraft's work and writing are as much needed as studies of the influences he may have followed or historical accounts of his life and ideas.

The studied corpus comprises "The Nameless City," "Dagon," "The Outsider," "The Festival," "The Temple," "Polaris," "The Doom That Came to Sarnath," and "He," which present plenty of interesting examples of both narration and description techniques, as well as unique applications of their use in order to create a strangely alien effect, such as the use of the commonplace as a tool, or the use of intradiegetic and homodiegetic unreliable voices. Lovecraft's themes point to the alien, and the narrative and descriptive techniques he uses all tend toward the creation of a sense of menacing alterity, the menace often coming from the concept of alterity itself. We can see that a great variety of narrative and descriptive techniques are used, and more importantly, that those techniques are used in conjunction, the narration and descriptions supporting each other to build a strangely menacing effect, thus creating the very unique "Lovecraftian" atmosphere.

Anthony Camara
University of Calgary
"H. P. Lovecraft and the Dimensions of Speculation"

Philosopher Graham Harman deems H. P. Lovecraft a "writer of gaps and horror." This striking phrase refers to the way in which Lovecraft's fictions dramatize and explore the weird incommensurability between human thought and the reality of objects—in other words, the gaps in our knowledge of the cosmos that open when perception, science, language, and thinking falter in their capacity to confer adequate understandings of existence. The Continental thought of Kant, Husserl, and Heidegger informs Harman's "object-oriented" readings of the gaps that populate Lovecraft's fiction; however, I question Harman's approach by proposing that mathematics affords the better understanding of the onto-epistemological gaps featured in Lovecraft's work, especially in the later tales that push weird writing ever closer to science fiction. Focusing on "The Dreams in the Witch House" (1932), I show how Lovecraft recruits concepts from the pioneering higher-dimensional geometry of late nineteenth-century mathematicians such as Arthur Cayley, W. I. Stringham, and C. H. Hinton. Accordingly, Lovecraft relates the gaps that characterize his fiction to higher-dimensional spaces beyond the perception and comprehension of ordinary human agents. What is ultimately at stake in "The Dreams in the Witch House," I argue, is Lovecraft's urgent attempt to conceive a speculative, higher-dimensional materialism capable of accounting for matter's alternating strangeness and consistency. Higher-dimensional space suffuses matter with the unknown qualities of otherworldly realms, while at the same time allowing matter to retain certain invariant properties and explanatory powers in lower dimensions. Consequently, higher-dimensional geometry opened up speculative spaces for Lovecraft wherein he could reconcile, albeit uneasily, his rigorous scientific naturalism and materialism with his ineradicable desire for the supernatural. This interpretation, I think, offers a better appreciation of the overlooked tensions that undergird Lovecraft's later fiction and, more generally speaking, his intellect.

Philip Chang
University of Colorado Boulder
"The Music of 'Erich Zann'"

Very little has been written about the actual *musical* aspects of H. P. Lovecraft's short story "The Music of Erich Zann." A number of contemporary musical artists have written pieces reflecting the tale's mood or plot, but these works are very much of the late twentieth (and now, twenty-first) centuries. What kind of music might Erich Zann have played?

Unfortunately, Lovecraft's term for Zann's instrument, "viol," is superficially confusing. Illustrations accompanying or inspired by the story reveal that "viol" has been interpreted inconsistently and, indeed, incorrectly: S. T. Joshi noted in 2001 that Lovecraft referred to Zann as a "cellist." Another ambiguous aspect of "The Music of Erich Zann" is its historical setting and location, although regarding the latter there seems to be a general consensus that it is likely Paris.

This audiovisual presentation suggests solutions hinging on Lovecraft's use of the word "viol" to describe Zann's instrument. By incorporating certain other features of the plot, appropriate musical historical contexts, and other scholars' speculations, each traditional historical period—Baroque, Classical, Romantic, and Twentieth-Century—can be proposed, with actual music from that time. In a way, we can now hear the music(s) of Erich Zann. Nevertheless, Lovecraft himself mentions a fairly definitive model for the music, an observation apparently unexamined by previous scholars.

Anthony Conrad Chieffal
University of Rhode Island
"From Crawling Chaos to Elder Things:
Mythic Evolution in Weird Fiction"

Evolution is central to H. P. Lovecraft's concept of cosmicism. Lovecraft's "cosmic horror" derives from challenging the perceived superiority of human beings as the pinnacle of terrestrial life—the zenith of evolution on this planet and in this universe. Cosmicism undermines the perception of evolution as progress, effectively condemning the development of civilization as regression or, at best, stagnation. In comparison to the enigmatic Old Ones, who exist beyond the confines of space and time, human beings are the lowest of mammalian vermin.

The correspondence between Lovecraft and fellow weird fiction author Robert E. Howard delves into the terrors of devolution. The ensuing dialogue illuminates twentieth-century anxieties regarding Western notions of purity and authority that are embedded in their fiction. This anxiety manifests itself as sources of intrigue and titillation in their respective contributions to weird fiction, insofar as tales of horror and suspense are meant to thrill their readers. The audience is provoked by sensation; the feeling that the societal obligation to which they are indebted by birthright is veritably meaningless. However, rather than a nihilistic negation of purposive existence, these tales are testaments to the resolution that the apparent obviousness of genetic supremacy is a fiction.

This essay explores the influence of Darwinism and the Modern Evolutionary Synthesis on Lovecraft and Howard while challenging the popular misconception that their works proliferate racism. Readings that merely dismiss the literary contribution by Lovecraft and Howard as racist fail to acknowledge the intrinsic quality of these works to embrace counterintuitive definitions of evolutionary superiority. Cosmicism subverts such hierarchical ordering of life forms, be they biological or societal. In cosmic horror, it is ultimately the crawling chaos that is empowered over insignificant *Homo sapiens*.

D. Allen Crowley
Baldwin-Wallace University
"The Arcane and The Rational:
Lovecraft's Development of a Unique Mythos"

This paper examines the confluence of myth and modernity and shows how H. P. Lovecraft, through stories such as "The Call of Cthulhu," *At the Mountains of Madness*, "The Shadow over Innsmouth," and others, redefined the growing literary subgenre of weird fiction. As the world became more and modernized, Lovecraft developed his own universe and mythos that was a unique mix of new and old. He created monsters that would have been at home in fairy tales or the ancient mists of folklore. These ancient, mythic evils were at odds with his twentieth-century protagonists—men of education, breeding, and science.

Literature before Lovecraft portrayed ancient religions and gods as benevolent protectors of mankind and the devout. Lovecraft subverted this paradigm and instead argued that the cosmos, and the godlike beings that reside there, are indifferent to the plight of man. Tempered by his own rationality and atheism, he created a world that was unique only in its insignificance. An avid reader, Lovecraft understood the prior works of writers such as Milton and Dante, and the concept of higher and lower worlds that bookend our own place in the universe, and where heaven, hell, and the earthly world were places of equal size and influence. Lovecraft rejected this notion and instead minimized the human realm to a sliver, sandwiched between the pitiless depths of an indifferent underworld and an infinite, cold, and remorseless cosmos.

<p style="text-align:center">Jerry C. Drake
US Department of State
"Searchers After Horror: H. P. Lovecraft <i>contra</i> M. R. James"</p>

H. P. Lovecraft was only nine years old when he began writing about scientific topics. A significant portion of his juvenilia is dedicated to serious writings on science, and his early life is very much that of a nascent late Victorian "natural philosopher." In parallel to this scholarship, he began to craft the weird fiction that would later make his name. Gradually his literary output turned almost exclusively to fictionalized tales, though heavily influenced by his grounding as an atheist, skeptic, and man of science.

At the same time Lovecraft's storytelling career was launched, that of his literary contemporary, M. R. James, was hitting its mid-career stride. In addition to being the inventor of the modern ghost story, James was a professional scholar and academic (provost of King's College, Cambridge, and Eton College) and very much a member of the Victorian intellectual establishment. Unlike Lovecraft, this conservative antiquarian began his career in flights of fancy, presenting papers to his student colleagues on topics such as alchemy and writing as late as 1931 of a willingness to believe in ghosts.

Lovecraft and James are a study in mirrored contrasts. The academic career of a stolid professor seemed to be a life craved by Lovecraft, while James was perpetually abandoning his serious professional pursuits to dabble in sensational fiction and Bohemian explorations of the macabre. Lovecraft was a man of science who, rather frustrated, wrote fantasy and James was at heart a fantasist struggling to remain a level-headed scholar. Yet their respective paths led them to a very similar literary conclusion.

This paper explores the comparisons and contrasts between these two men, their backgrounds, and the worldviews that led to the creation of their respective fictions and the modern weird tale.

Nicole Emmelhainz
Christopher Newport University
"'It Was from the Artists and Poets That the Pertinent Answers Came':
Shared Authorship in the Discourse Community of the Lovecraft Circle"

When analyzing the writings of the authors in the Lovecraft circle—Clark Ashton Smith, Robert E. Howard, August Derleth, Frank Belknap Long, and of course, Lovecraft himself—an acknowledgment of the shared authorship among these writers as they helped to shape weird fiction and horror cannot be overstated. Though Lovecraft, with "The Call of Cthulhu," certainly is the initial author figure of the fictional mythology, it was through these writer-colleagues that the mythology took on its full depth and detail. Lovecraft's own influence within and over his writing colleagues is well known, but further work can be done to show that the genre-building work needed in order to create this foundational vein of weird fiction moved across all members of this group. Using Michel Foucault's notion of author-function and James E. Porter's understanding of discourse communities, this paper treats the collaborative moves these authors made in order to establish the mythology. Short stories by Lovecraft, Smith, Howard, Derleth, and Long are discussed, as are selections from letters exchanged between Lovecraft and Howard, and Lovecraft and Smith, and Lovecraft and Derleth.

Mark Finn
Independent Scholar and Editor
"No Black Stone Unturned: A Critical Examination of
Robert E. Howard's Most Significant Cthulhu Mythos Story"

Robert E. Howard and H. P. Lovecraft's epistolary correspondence is one of the most important documented conversations in the history of contemporary weird fiction. Their ongoing and animated discussions of such topics as folklore, mythology, history, and literature, to name just a few, found their way into each other's body of work in surprising ways.

Howard was a founding member of what came to be known as "The Lovecraft Circle," a loose affiliation of writers held together largely by Lovecraft's voluminous letter writing. Regarding the then-nascent Cthulhu Mythos, Howard's greatest contribution to the shared universe was the story "The Black Stone." Widely considered to be one of Howard's best horror tales, as well as one of the best non-Lovecraft Mythos stories, "The

Black Stone" has been reprinted over two dozen times since it first appeared in the November 1931 issue of *Weird Tales*.

This essay examines the influences and underlying concepts that Howard used to draft this influential story. Some of Howard's other Cthulhu mythos stories and historical tales, are discussed in relation to "The Black Stone" as examples of common Howardian themes and tropes. Using Lovecraft's own ideas about what constitutes a "Cthulhu Mythos" story, this paper measures the efficacy of Howard's writing style and techniques in capturing the spirit of Lovecraft's self-described "Yog-Sothothery."

Joe Fritsch
Independent Scholar and Poet
"Half-Limitless in Starlit Night: H. P. Lovecraft's Vision"

"... if the mind does construct its world there is always that world immanent or imminently outside which at least as a term has become an entity."–Louis Zukofsky, 1931

This paper discusses the centrality of the glimpse—the precipitous, semantic moment, lost as suddenly as gained—in H. P. Lovecraft's formulations of horror and fantasy. The methods Lovecraft devised to belabor his reader's sight were manifold, as this paper demonstrates: veiled settings, like distant Devil Reef, barely visible from Innsmouth; a flash of clarity amidst darkness and the unknown, as that *indescribable and unmentionable monstrosity* in "The Outsider"; academic knowledge, meant to elucidate, but rendered suddenly useless to William Dyer in *At the Mountains of Madness*; the metaphysical experience poised upon the limen between sight and the void as presented in "The Colour out of Space."

A century's journey from 1937, in either direction, will encounter efforts that resonate with those of Lovecraft. Literary figures as renowned as Mary Shelley, Herman Melville, and Oscar Wilde, to those closer to Lovecraft, such as, Charlotte Perkins Gilman, Robert W. Chambers, and Clark Ashton Smith, present their own uses of the glimpse, helping to frame it as a major literary device. The paper also considers the modern filming technique known as "shaky cam"—presently enjoying widespread use in the horror genre—as an interpretation of the glimpse in another medium. Finally, a connection will be drawn between these varied, diachronic efforts and that primordial, visionary monster story, *Revelations*. Special attention will be paid to Lovecraft's poetry when appropriate.

Alex Gladwin
Independent Scholar
"Stylometry and Collaborative Authorship: Eddy, Lovecraft, and 'The Loved Dead'"

The authorship of the 1924 short story "The Loved Dead" has been contested by family members of C. M. Eddy, Jr., and S. T. Joshi, a leading scholar on H. P. Lovecraft. The authors of this study apply stylometric methods—which use statistics in order to examine literary features—to provide evidence for a claim about the authorship of the story. We focus on the nature of Eddy's collaboration with Lovecraft by examining the history of the story's contested authorship and the results of our tests. This talk does not require knowledge of statistics to understand the results.

Christian Haunton
University of Nebraska Omaha
"The Sombreness of Decay: Lovecraft in Wilbraham, Massachusetts"

In the 1928, H. P. Lovecraft visited friend and fellow writer Edith Miniter at her home in Wilbraham, Massachusetts. His experience of the Connecticut River Valley during this short stay left a lasting mark on Lovecraft's work, most notably as an inspiration for the backwoods town at the center of "The Dunwich Horror," which he would write later in 1928. Many of the geographic and cultural descriptions that Lovecraft used in that story can be traced directly to experiences he writes about having during his visit to the area. Wilbraham has changed considerably in the last century, but many of the features that Lovecraft encountered during his stay remain. This talk, through Lovecraft's letters, and particularly through his memorial of Edith Miniter, explores the aspects of the Wilbraham area that influenced Lovecraft, and what impact, if any, the author's presence has left on the community today. Particular attention is paid to sights and locations that can still be seen by modern visitors.

Daniel J. Holmes
Villanova University
"The Suffering Intellect: H. P. Lovecraft's Weird Epistemology"

Like many weird writers, the sense of horror in the works of H. P. Lovecraft tends to be highly intellectualized: the chief horrific element in many of his stories is the shattering of an unlucky intellect that "pieces together that which must never be pieced together again" in order to reveal "the horrors that lurk ceaselessly behind life in time and in space." Lovecraft's plots often follow the rational path of an individual intellect to the boundary of human categorical knowledge, climaxing with a plunge into a maddening abyss of unassimilable knowledge. Any critical work evaluating Lovecraft must therefore pay careful attention to the phenomenological and epistemological issues faced by the fictional residents of Lovecraft's horrific universe. This paper expands on the existential framework introduced in my presentation at the 2013 NecronomiCon by offering an evaluation of Lovecraftian epistemology, or the erosion of the intellect in the face of the ineffable. Of great assistance here are the philosophical and poetic writings of Raïssa Maritain (1883–1947), especially her reflections on the mystical process. Maritain outlines a definition of theological inquiry as intellectual suffering, oriented toward and founded upon the "sacred dread" (*crainte sacré*) of experiencing the ineffable. The "annihilation" of the intellect described by Maritain directly mirrors the shattered intellect of Lovecraftian horror and can aid critics in a comprehensive appraisal of Lovecraft's work. Read through the lens of Maritain, Lovecraft can be seen to turn *anagnorisis* ("recognition," the turning point of Aristotelian tragedy) into the rapid transition from the active, subjective pursuit of knowledge to passive process of intellectual objectification.

Jason Ray Carney
Christopher Newport University
"'Shapeless Congeries of Protoplasmic Bubbles':
H. P. Lovecraft and the Plasticity of Users and Tools"

A commonplace thesis is that science fiction fictionalizes technology as both a form of salvation and a harbinger of doom, a tool for engineering utopia or dystopia. Moreover, literary critics and scholars have long acknowledged this central preoccupation with technical enterprises in their genre histories, rhetorical analyses, and thematic surveys of SF. However, less attention has been paid to the "user" of fictional tools and technology; i.e., the working agent who engages *nova*, following Darko Suvin, to engineer a particular reality, be it utopian or dystopian.

My presentation contributes to the much-needed treatment of this gap by framing key works of H. P. Lovecraft's corpus of fiction as distinctively dissolving the philosophical distinction between user and tool, body and prosthesis. These works, I argue, propose an imaginary working class that is a liminal, unindividuated, homogeneous, and dangerously plastic mass that extends from and interpenetrates the site of poverty and production, a mass poignantly exemplified by Lovecraft's organic metaphor for the working classes in "The Horror of Red Hook": "a horror of houses and blocks and cities leprous and cancerous with evil dragged from elder worlds." Central works treated are "The Horror at Red Hook," "The Call of Cthulhu," and *At the Mountains of Madness*, as well as two important works by other *Weird Tales* writers: Clark Ashton Smith's "The Vaults of Yoh-Vombis" and Robert E. Howard's "The Black Stone."

Jarett Kobek
Independent Scholar and Editor
"A Closet Quetzalcoatl: Intimations of H. P. Lovecraft and Same-Sex Desire in R. H. Barlow's 'The Wind That Is in the Grass'"

For decades, speculation about H. P. Lovecraft's sexuality has proved to be an oft ill-informed byway of Lovecraftian studies. As Lovecraft left behind little evidence of his sexuality, the debate has been fueled by the apparent absence of evidence. In this paper, I offer a radical reading of R. H. Barlow's "The Wind That Is in the Grass: A Memoir of H. P. Lovecraft in Florida," theorizing that this short text, in print since 1944, offers a coded gay interpretation of Lovecraft's sexuality.

In his final paragraph, Barlow offers a series of cultural references that appear to be a surface poetic strategy invoking the loss of his mentor. In actuality, each of these references—*The Last Puritan* by George Santayana, "a cloistered Akhnaton," "a civilizer among barbarians," "a closet Quetzalcoatl"—is either an overt (in the case of the first two, with Santayana's novel revolving around same-sex desire and Akhnaton widely speculated in the first half of the twentieth century as the "first homosexual") or implicit (in the case of the latter two) reference to homosexuality. Taken together, the references supply the definitive impression that Barlow, himself a gay man, believed in Lovecraft's homosexuality. As almost all evidence of Lovecraft's heterosexuality relies on the statements of his former wife, Sonia Davis, we must give Barlow's some weight, as he was the only other person in Lovecraft's circle to cohabitate with Lovecraft for any prolonged length of time (a little more than five months). Finally, there is speculation as to Barlow's motivations in this gay coding, with an emphasis on his poor relationship with Arkham House, a situation referenced obliquely in his memoir of Lovecraft.

Fred S. Lubnow
Independent Scholar
(Illustrations by Steve Maschuck)
"The Lovecraftian Cosmos: How the Tales of H. P. Lovecraft Can Be Interpreted through the Concepts of Modern Science"

H. P. Lovecraft's love and fascination for science is well established. However, in addition to this strong scientific curiosity, he also saw the horrors associated with the absolute indifference the universe has for humanity as well as how science can be used to generate terrifying results. This mixture of curiosity and fear, fueled by his unique imagination, allowed Lovecraft to craft some remarkable stores, bringing the Gothic horror tale into the twentieth century.

This presentation discusses how many of the ideas in Lovecraft's stories can be interpreted through modern science. In his time some amazing scientific discoveries were being made and expanded upon, such as Einstein's theory of relativity, the birth of quantum mechanics, astronomical discoveries such as the identification of Pluto, the use of radioactive substances, and strides in geological and evolutionary theory. Lovecraft incorporated many of these discoveries of the early twentieth century into tales such as "The Dreams in the Witch House," "The Whisperer in Darkness," "The Colour out of Space," and *At the Mountains of Madness*.

While the scientific ideas discussed by Lovecraft were born in the twentieth century, they are not limited or only applicable to the science of that century. Instead, many current concepts such as dark matter, superstring theory, anti-matter, the origins of the universe, alternate dimensions, and genetic engineering are also explored in his stories such as "From Beyond," "The Shadow over Innsmouth," and "The Shadow out of Time." Thus, this presentation also reviews and examines these tales through the lens of the most recent scientific hypotheses that at least attempt to understand the Lovecraftian cosmos.

Rolf Maurer
Independent Scholar and Editor
"Lovecraft, Rand, and the Abyss of Opportunity"

Intrigued by the proposition of how better-suited an "Old One" or "Elder Thing" might be than any real human being as one of the socially indifferent heroes of *Atlas Shrugged* or *The Fountainhead*, I discuss the similarities and differences between the work and themes of weird fiction iconoclast H. P. Lovecraft and the controversial founder of Objectivism, Ayn Rand, as expounded collectively across their short fiction, novels, verse, plays, and commentary.

The presentation would focus on several areas:
- The writers' comparable social origins and how abrupt changes to their families' fortunes and personal expectations shaped the more reactionary aspects of their work;
- Their evolving philosophical and political trajectories in relation to class, economic equality and personal integrity (especially regarding New Deal reforms), as well as the influence of Nietzsche, Spengler, and others;
- How mythic and biblical allegory in their fiction is applied to support their atheistic and materialist worldviews;
- The differences in Lovecraft's and Rand's attitudes toward the distorted, sometimes fractious dissemination of their creative and sociological concepts by followers and how the resulting legacies would shape public perception;
- How, despite the greater commercial success of Rand, it is actually Lovecraft's genre fiction that is more convincing in presentation and genuine in exploring its thematic underpinnings.

Sean Moreland
University of Ottawa
"The Poet's Nightmare:
The Nature of Things According to Lovecraft"

This paper derives from a book I am writing that traces the vestiges of first-century BCE Roman poet Lucretius' *De Rerum Natura* in the work of Edgar Allan Poe and H. P. Lovecraft. I begin by noting some of the overarching continuities between Lucretius and Lovecraft; while Lovecraft scholars including Joshi have noted Lucretius' importance for Lovecraft, there has yet been no sustained critical engagement with this relationship. I then focus specifically on the influence Lucretius' poem (and particularly its fifth book, containing his non-teleological account of natural history) has on Lovecraft's conceptions of monstrosity, and on specific ways his most influential monsters respond to aspects of Lucretius' poem.

While because of his vituperations against the irrationality of religion, Lucretius is often characterized as atheistic, this is not entirely accurate. The pagan gods do appear to exist in Lucretius' account, but are, like the human soul itself, material beings and a part of the cosmos—as are Lovecraft's gods and monsters, whatever their superstitious followers might maintain. In Lovecraft's fictions, there is no ultimate distinction between a monster and a god; both are liminal figures, calling into question our knowledge of the natural world, and embodying in their threatening strangeness the principles of cosmic horror. Lovecraft follows Lucretius in proposing beings whose mode of existence is far removed from ours, and for whom our fates are a matter of complete indifference, but who are also able to communicate with and manipulate humanity for their own ends through methods including simulacra, oneiric apparitions, and psychic influences. Specific examples I consider include the Magna Mater (whose worship Lucretius condemns, but who also informs his representation of a fecund but dangerous nature), the macro-atomic horror of Azathoth, the primordial hybridity of Cthulhu, and the revolting shoggoths.

Byron Nakamura
Southern Connecticut State University
"Dreams of Antiquity:
H. P. Lovecraft's Great Roman Dream of 1927"

One need not look far to find references to classical antiquity in the works of H. P. Lovecraft. This is not surprising, as his education in classical literature and history is well attested, particularly in his early youth. His article "The Case for Classicism" (1919) provides a staunch defense of classical models of literary style and rhetoric. Yet there are scant examples of Lovecraft's writing that directly feature the Greco-Roman world. The best-known example is "The Tree" (1920), one of Lovecraft's Dunsanian-styled short stories, which takes place in Greece during the fourth century BCE. An often overlooked piece, however, is an account of a dream of

Lovecraft's set in the late Roman Republic and preserved in a letter to Donald Wandrei. In this account, Lovecraft the dreamer assumes the persona of a Roman official, Lucius Caelius Rufus, who encounters an ancient evil from the Spanish hills of Pamplona. Published posthumously as "The Very Old Folk" (1940), this dream text reveals Lovecraft's detailed and textured understanding of the Roman period. My paper argues that Lovecraft's dream does more than use ancient world as a backdrop to his narrative; it employs the historical canvas of Rome to project the author's own attitudes toward race, imperialism, and the role of civilization. Lovecraft's dream persona as the Roman patrician Caelius Rufus also mirrors the author's perception of himself as among the last of the Yankee patricians. This study contributes to our understanding of how the classical tradition influenced Lovecraft's thinking and how the author himself expressed key elements of his personality though the venue of ancient past.

Juan L. Pérez-de-Luque
University of Cordoba, Spain
"Unspeakable Languages: Lovecraft Editions in Spanish"

"There Are More Things," a short tale by the Argentinian writer Jorge Luis Borges (1975), was dedicated "to the memory of H. P. Lovecraft." Borges was, without question, influenced by the writer from Providence, as has been proved by some scholars. The reception of Lovecraft in the Spanish-speaking countries has been steadily increasing during the last forty years, due to the different translations and studies carried out by several academicians who rescued his texts and highlighted his relevance as a major weird fiction author.

In this paper my goal is to explore the different stages that the literary work of H. P. Lovecraft has undergone in the process of reception in Spanish-speaking countries, and how the universe created by the writer has affected, with or without explicit acknowledgment, several writers, from Julio Cortázar to Juan Perucho. At the same time, I analyze how nonfictional works by Lovecraft (mainly essays and letters) have been traditionally neglected in the Spanish-speaking publishing market, the possible reasons for that lack of interest, and what is the current situation of the Hispanic Lovecraftian studies.

Connor Pitetti
Stony Brook University
"'The Discriminating Urban Landscapist': Tradition and Innovation in the Architectural Writings of H. P. Lovecraft"

Although he was a passionate amateur student of American architectural history, Lovecraft had no official training in the field, and most of his nonfictional writing on architecture consists of descriptive accounts of buildings he visited on sightseeing trips. One of the few occasions on which he wrote publicly and prescriptively about architecture was when he tried to rally support for the preservation and restoration of the "Old Brick Row," a block of warehouses in central Providence that were scheduled to be demolished during construction of the new Providence County Courthouse. Lovecraft often spoke of himself as an anti-modern nostalgic and once wrote that "the only beautiful places left in America are those progress has passed by." But the alternative to demolition he proposed in the case of the Old Brick Row suggests a much more nuanced position, in which the transformations and upheavals attendant upon modernization are treated not just as a threat to traditional culture, but as a potentially productive force capable of enhancing the sense of historical depth and local rootedness that Lovecraft considered the "one true source of authentic cultural identity." Although he ultimately failed to save these buildings, the incident is interesting for the light it sheds on Lovecraft's relationship to his beloved hometown and, more broadly, on his understanding of tradition and innovation and the proper role of each in modern American culture.

Heather Poirier
Independent Scholar and Editor
(Formerly with Louisiana State University)
"Ripples from Carcosa:
H. P. Lovecraft, *True Detective*, and the Artist-Investigator"

The role of the investigator as a literary figure is a contentious one. Born out of traditions established by Edgar Allan Poe and Sir Arthur Conan Doyle (and tracing back to the biblical Daniel and the story of Bel and the Dragon, the first locked-room mystery), the investigator changed radically in twentieth-century detective fiction—moving from amateur to professional, investigator to criminal—and continues to change within the genre. Without the investigator, without some figure fortified by curiosity and determination, much of the work of H. P. Lovecraft would not have been possible.

In the HBO series *True Detective*, the investigator has evolved into the "artist-investigator." This term is most often used in theater—and then only by a few groups—to describe an artist, employed by a theater company, who pushes against theater's current boundaries. It is noteworthy that the term is not used to describe an epistemology of investigation or the figure employing that epistemology, nor does the extant body of detective fiction criticism address the artist-investigator as part of its canon. These are critical omissions.

In this talk, a review of selected works by Robert W. Chambers and H. P. Lovecraft through the lens of detective fiction tropes and conventions, along with a discussion of *True Detective*, shows how the investigators in *True Detective* are a new kind of character derived from atelier fiction, weird fiction, and detective fiction. This new character, based on the aesthetics of crime and redemption, pits the artistic sensibilities of the detective against those of the criminal. This talk, by closely examining the above elements, sheds new light on the little-recognized figure of the artist-investigator.

Dennis P. Quinn
Cal Poly Pomona
"'The Reference to Atys Made Me Shiver':
Romanitas in the Works of H. P. Lovecraft"

In December 1933, H. P. Lovecraft summed up his lifelong love for Roman civilization in a letter to his friend, Clark Ashton Smith: "Rome is a subject which has fascinated me uncannily since I first heard much of it around the age of six. From the moment I picked up any idea of its nature, history, and characteristics, and held in my own hands the actual Roman coins . . . of my grandfather's collection, I have had the most persistent sensation (out of which occultists would make a case of metempsychosis, and of a pseudo-scientist one of hereditary memory) of some ineluctable connection with the ancient *Respublica*" (SL 4.332).

This uncharacteristic language about handling some ancient Roman coins (the atheist embracing the empathies of occultists) punctuates the fact that Lovecraft was unapologetically obsessed with Rome. And even more so: in the same letter he declared that it "is utterly impossible . . . for me to regard Rome in a detached way." This presentation explores some examples in which Roman history, mythology, and even what he understood about Roman Republican senatorial elitism (*Romanitas*, or Roman-ness or identity), infiltrate some of his stories, particularly the work of Roman historian Livy (64? BCE–17 CE) in the "The Call of Cthulhu."

Marcello Ricciardi
St. Joseph's College
"Resisting Cthulhu: Milton and Lovecraft's Errand in the Wilderness"

In many ways, the American wilderness was the birthplace of the weird. Faye Ringel speaks of how the first Puritans, upon arriving in the New World, encountered the Native American as the Dark Other and saw in them the paradigm for all that is diabolical and mysterious. The early colonists proceeded to transgress a rugged frontier, removed and remote from the civilities of European culture, fostering the emergence of witchcraft that, if not transferred from England, at least found a healthy breeding ground in this remote, desolate corner of the world and, ultimately, imparted psychogenic life to all the werebeasts, water serpents, and ghostly entities that excited the popular imagination of the times. In this context, American literature was born, a macabre Gothic phenomenon that has its roots in American colonialism and which undergoes a rich transmogrification under the dark auspices of Hawthorne and Melville. Milton and Lovecraft clearly demonstrate all these proclivities and inherit the puritanical cosmic consciousness of the Michael Wigglesworths and Jonathan Edwards of the New World.

In this respect, of all English and American men of letters, Milton and Lovecraft best embody American Puritanism. Employing a desert hermeneutics, I argue that both authors could be considered desert poets in the ancient hermetic-monastic tradition of the desert fathers, attempting to fulfill, to appropriate the words of Perry Miller, their own errands in the wilderness. Both writers sought a sense of spiritual isolation and a removal from the quotidian concerns of secularity, and both purposely pursued an active engagement with those ominous forces which threatened to ravage the human psyche.

Milton's Hebraic consciousness as another David seeking to bring down Goliath, or as a Jacob wrestling with the Angel of the Lord, is all part of his Mosaic and Abrahamic identity, another founder and deliverer of a renegade people. In Milton's world, an Eden can be raised in the wilderness, psychologically, if not geographically. As for Lovecraft, modifying a Miltonic self-image, such an enterprise is also part of his Puritan legacy, yet doomed to defeat since defiance, although ultimately futile, is not without its own consolatory benefits in momentarily maintaining a steady interior resistance in the face of oppressive odds.

Lovecraft's occult questers encounter the very same phantasmagoria as Milton's religious heroes, replete with entities, enigmas, and malevolent presences, but the struggle to reclaim that open bit of space and sanctify it, redeem it from the abyss, as Milton does interiorly and the Puritans attempted exteriorly, bears bitter fruit and comes nothing short of total despair ridden defeatism. The darkness can momentarily be held at bay, and although it promises to return, like Milton's Satan and Lovecraft's Nyarlathotep, any immediate ascendancy leads at best to a temporary respite, a short-term psychic victory of intermittent personal and public liberation. The human boundary situation is safe for now, and the Chaos monsters have not encroached too deeply into the social order—as of yet. However, one thing remains certain: Milton and Lovecraft's Agonistes consistently wrestle with the diabolical intelligences that haunt their mental landscapes and govern their imaginative worlds as they undergo their own desert trials of self-immolation and release.

Faye Ringel and Jenna Randall
U.S. Coast Guard Academy and Hebrew College
"Lovecraft for the Little Ones: *ParaNorman*, Plushies, and More"

H. P. Lovecraft would be surprised at the extent to which his work has entered the popular culture. Most surprising of all may be the current transformation of his dark visions into entertainment for children. Plush Cthulhu has been joined by toy versions of many of the monsters of his (and his circle's) imagination. Entities derived from Lovecraft star in video games, including some designed for the youngest players. There is even a *Lovecraft Alphabet Book!*

While these examples may seem limited to the Old Ones and their cultists, a better introduction to Lovecraft's New England Gothic vision—ancestral curses, inbred families, outsider narrators with the ability to see monsters—can be found in the animated film *ParaNorman* (2012), the story of Norman, a pint-sized necromancer who resides in Blithe Hollow, a crumbling New England town based on Salem, MA. Like Salem, Blithe Hollow has a past rooted in the witch trials which it exploits for tourist dollars. Norman is called upon by an estranged uncle who shares the same necromantic gift to stop the curse of a vengeful child witch who was executed during the witch hysteria. Ironically, this "kiddie movie" more accurately represents the Puritan mindset and events of the Salem witch panic of 1692-93 than many "historical" films.

ParaNorman's writer-director Chris Butler also directed Neil Gaiman's *Coraline* (2009), both part of the thriving genre of "Kinder-Goth" in literature and—especially—animated film, following upon the success of Tim Burton's *The Nightmare Before Christmas*. These films often cleave more closely to the themes of traditional Gothic literature (including Lovecraft's work) than do most contemporary horror movies.

Our paper draws upon the definition of New England Gothic found in Dr. Ringel's *New England's Gothic Literature* (1995) and in her chapters for *A Companion to American Gothic* (2013).

Troy Rondinone
Southern Connecticut State University
"Tentacles in the Madhouse:
The Role of the Asylum in the Fiction of H. P. Lovecraft"

The asylum haunts the fiction of H. P. Lovecraft. Though in only few instances does internal action take place in mental hospitals in his stories, Lovecraft uses asylums critically to highlight key themes in his plots: namely, the false front of rational order, the limits of mind science, the brittle nature of sanity, and the racial degradation of mankind. In this essay, I explore the role of the asylum in Lovecraft's work, examining his use of mental institutions in such stories as *The Case of Charles Dexter Ward*, "Herbert West—Reanimator," "The Thing on the Doorstep," and "Beyond the Wall of Sleep," among others. I combine a textual analysis of the asylums in these tales with a broader historical exploration of the view of mental hospitals in American popular culture in the early twentieth century. I add some speculative comments about Lovecraft's own experience with the asylum as well. Ultimately, I intend to root the Lovecraftian asylum in its original cultural and historical milieu, allowing me to shed some new light on both the evolution of horror and Lovecraft's own presuppositions.

Daniel Rottenberg
Metropolitan State University of Denver, Colorado
"The Derleth Mythos: Literary Evidence of Weird Realism"

H. P. Lovecraft wrote a fantastic mythos during the beginning of the twentieth century. His stories provide a great leap in a movement from standard mythology to a slowly developing new mythology. Lovecraft had a close protégé named August Derleth. Derleth acquired Lovecraft's stories after his death and is applauded for keeping Lovecraft's work around through all these decades. However, many scholars deride Derleth for his many fallacies surrounding the Lovecraft Mythos. Derleth wrote the mythology to Lovecraft's weird realism. He was the primitive mind attempting to describe and categorize under a Catholic perspective that which science cannot yet (or ever) show, and in this sense, the allegorical Cthulhu Mythos of August Derleth is valid as a secondary view not willing to acknowledge the science and weirdness. Lovecraft provides the stupendous nature, while Derleth provides a cultural reaction and fight for reason and the mythological why. In Derleth's misunderstanding of Lovecraft's anti-mythology, he stumbled upon something very significant, revealing us as an anthropocentric culture, something often overlooked by scholars who just point out where he went wrong. He was indeed wrong about Lovecraft but right about the formation of myth and societal claims to value. And while he was wrong about Lovecraft and the mythos, he may have been standing in the way of the evolution of mythology to come.

Christian Roy
Independent Scholar and Translator
"H. P. Lovecraft and Georges Bataille: One Crawling Chaos Seen Emerging from Opposite Shores"

Lovecraft's significance in cultural history becomes clearer if we see him as a counterpart of his contemporary, the increasingly influential French theorist and pornographic writer Georges Bataille (1897-1962), in attempting to carry to their ultimate conclusions in thought, life, and literature certain Nietzschean insights about the place of man in the universe as described by modern science. To be sure, the Puritan atheist aesthete of horror and the debauched ex-Catholic mystic of evil knew nothing of each other and were unquestionably poles apart in temper, lifestyle, and sensibility. And yet, from these contrasting standpoints they were really talking about the same thing, namely: the fascinating attraction and repulsion of an obscene black hole at the core of every entity, ultimately as divine parody ruling the swirling maelstrom of celestial bodies at the bottom of the formless abyss of the universe in its general economy of excess, defying the rational mind's attempts to enfold it within its anthropocentric grasp, yet luring the lower passions to act out this "base materialism" by joining in the wild dance of the elements through orgiastic festivals and sacrificial rituals of "primitive" peoples in thrall to cruel prehuman powers, whose archaic and future hegemony they celebrate and adumbrate. This apocalyptic horizon of mindless panic and choking horror upon the coming demise of Western civilization in a new dark age of savage revelry was fantasized as fearful ancient cults in Lovecraft's literary Mythos, but Bataille actively welcomed it by fomenting similar cults and myths of his own, complete with human sacrifice, like his Acéphale secret society, following upon his paleographic research on ancient worship of hybrid or headless monsters. Life emulates fiction, since the librarian Bataille drew material and inspiration from the "inferno" of the Bibliothèque Nationale, which Lovecraft mentioned as holding a copy of the *Necronomicon*.

Jeffrey Shanks
Southeast Archeological Center, National Park Service
"Darwin and the Deep Ones: Anthropological Anxiety in
'The Shadow over Innsmouth' and Other Stories"

After the 1859 publication of Darwin's *On the Origin of Species*, Western culture was forced to confront and assimilate a new paradigm regarding humanity's position in the natural world. Racialist anthropology popularized the erroneous notion of a unilineal and teleological framework for human evolution by creating a hierarchy of higher and lower "races" based on supposed morphological differences in various populations. As a result, elements of these ideas and anxieties about what they meant for humanity began to permeate popular culture and had a significant impact on the speculative fiction of the Victorian and Modernist periods. They were often expressed by tropes such as physical devolution and cultural degeneration, atavists and ape-men, the plasticity of the human body, and cultural and racial "contamination" through miscegenation. Much of H. P. Lovecraft's fiction was heavily informed by these concepts. This paper explores their use in stories such as "The Lurking Fear," "Facts concerning the Late Arthur Jermyn and His Family," and, in particular, "The Shadow over Innsmouth," and discusses how Lovecraft exploited these themes of anthropological anxiety to create an effective sense of existential unease in the reader.

Jesús Emmanuel Navarro-Stefanón
Benemérita Universidad Autónoma de Puebla
"A Lawyer Looks at a 'Layman' Gentleman"

In the last years of his life, Lovecraft wrote about economic, political, and social topics, since he was worried about the effects of the Great Depression and supported the New Deal. His thought is more realistic, too. In spite of his lack of university studies, I consider that Lovecraft proposes an incipient analysis of Economic Law, similar to that of other jurists of his epoch, for example, the Argentinian lawyer Juan B. Siburu. I think that it is enough to compare Lovecraft's program, as exhibited in his essays and some letters in the 1930s, with the ideas put forward by specialists in Economic Law.

In his essays "Some Repetitions on the Times" (February 1933), "A Layman Looks at the Government" (November 1933), and "The *Journal* and the New Deal" (April 1934), Lovecraft analyzes the financial crisis that was affecting life in the United States and tries to explain how the government should intervene and control the economy, so that governmental intervention in the economy is equivalent to the frame of the Economic Law. Therefore Lovecraft is at the forefront in this matter. Other aspects that he considers are the nature of the right of property throughout history and the possible nationalization of several production modes. Also Lovecraft proposes his own political program that, as I consider it, is related with the Theory of the State. In his last letters, Lovecraft updated some aspects related to his previous essays, showing his advanced point of view on this matter.

Miles Tittle
University of Ottawa and Carleton University
"Rarebit Dreamers:
The Poetics of Lovecraft, Poe, and Winsor McCay"

I present a new paper, currently being revised for an upcoming collection of essays (*The Lovecraftian Poe*), which draws close parallels between the artistic dreamlands of early Lovecraft, Poe, and cartoonist Winsor McCay, and discusses influences and shared philosophies thus revealed. "The Poet's Nightmare," written in 1916 and first published in the July 1918 issue of the *Vagrant*, stands as Lovecraft's earliest published overt homage to Poe, one of the best poems of his career, and the earliest articulate expression of his nascent cosmicism. However, this ambitious weird poem hides other secrets, including clues to the origins of his Dream Cycle. This paper examines the relationship of dreams and nightmares to the industrialized wartime America of the early twentieth century, pursued through Lovecraft's compositions, Poe's Dreamland legacy, and Winsor McCay's oneiric newspaper cartoons of the period, *Dream of the Rarebit Fiend* and *Little Nemo in Slumberland*. The metamorphosis and transformation of dreamer and dreamland is the dangerous attraction of these exercises in oneiric objectivism, whether conducted by poet or cartoonist. The elastic and uncontrolled experiences of their fictional reveries are an escape not only from the highly regulated and fixed expectations of modern society, but from all laws of nature and reality itself. A close reading of the poem as a whole provides valuable insights into Lovecraft's early struggle to find a genuine approach to horror and an original use of Poe's legacy.

Ken Van Wey
George Mason University
"Lovecraft and Folkloric Methodology"

This paper examines how Lovecraft's understanding of folklore and folkloristics affects the narrative structure of "The Call of Cthulhu," "The Whisperer in Darkness," "The Shadow over Innsmouth," and other stories. Rather than focusing on the folklore that infused and inspired these stories, the purpose of this study is to examine what Lovecraft understood folklore to mean, and how this affected his storytelling. Close analysis of Lovecraft's relevant fiction, correspondence, and the folklore-related books from his library or that he is known to have consulted provide the material for this analysis.

This paper also explores contemporary developments in folkloristics and ethnography, including the changing emphasis on folklore as cultural survival, and in the tools and methods of ethnography that made their way into Lovecraft's work. These tools and methods are particularly important to "The Whisper in Darkness," whose plot hinges on the acquisition and exchange of photographs, sound recordings, and archaeological specimens gathered by an informant/correspondent, and "The Call of Cthulhu."

Stephen Walker
University of Central Missouri
"The Unspeakable Onomasticon"

For his imaginary beings, places, and books H. P. Lovecraft deployed a variety of strategies in originating their names, which are divisible into the fantastic and the mundane. The purpose of the first is to assist in constructing a weird atmosphere, and that of the second is to enable familiarity. Many better-known names—Cthulhu, the *Necronomicon*, etc.—are explored for their mechanics and how they relate to one another. Syllabic and letter patterning are shown as a way of providing a cohesive relationship between names. Linguistic approaches encompass embedded words (words found within names and their possibly subliminal significance), digraphs, consonant clusters, anagrams, letter and syllable substitutions and omissions, etymology, spelling and sound, the challenge of pronunciation, and the use of the apostrophe. There are also glances at the influence of the past, history and immigration, the importance of mental associations, name magic, and nomenclature as a mask or a representation. The symbolic presence of chaos and the influence of Lord Dunsany and that of Egypt contribute to Lovecraft's inventiveness. Names are a unifying and defining force in what is known as the Cthulhu Mythos.

Nathaniel R. Wallace
Independent Scholar
"The 'Inside' of H. P. Lovecraft's Supernatural Horror
in the Visual Arts"

This paper examines the use of the first-person point of view in Lovecraft's fictional work, specifically his story "The Outsider" (1926), and applies his theory of aesthetics regarding repetition and symmetry to the visual arts. The focus of this chapter is the occurrence of disruption within the author's texts, exemplified through an encounter with the "outside" that is relayed to the audience through the first-person narrator, or the "inside." The framework of this analysis stems from a letter Lovecraft wrote to August Derleth on 21 November 1930, in which he articulates "the impossibility of any correlation of the individual and the universal without the immediate visible world as a background-or starting-place for a system of outward-extending points of reference." Within this quotation, Lovecraft establishes a centrifugal construct of human perspective originating with the body that fosters an imagined relationship with the external world through the sense of sight. This passage introduces a form of subjectivity that finds parallels within the first-person point of view so often utilized by Lovecraft.

To transpose the first-person point of view from Lovecraft's original text of "The Outsider" to the visual arts, this study begins with an analysis of the comic adaptation of "The Outsider" by Dutch comic artist Erik Kriek; it subsequently examines the earlier first-person perspective work of the nineteenth-century German artist Adolph Menzel, Lovecraft's own sketches that reflect embodiment, and later Lovecraft-related visual works. This lecture takes the structure of the first-person perspective in literature in order to discover parallels within the visual arts through these aforementioned works, briefly presenting a historiography of embodied images within the genre of supernatural horror. The primary intention of this exercise is to demonstrate how the "inside" as represented in Lovecraft's texts and within the visual arts reflects the author's notion of subjectivity, and the manner in which works balance the unity of individual subjectivity with an ever-encroaching postmodern internalization of outsideness.

René J. Weise
Independent Scholar
"Reordering the Universe: H. P. Lovecraft's
Subversion of the Biblical Divine"

This graduate research project investigates how H. P. Lovecraft incorporated scripturally inspired imagery, characterization, and language within his works of weird fiction to deliberately conceive a paradigm shift of the Biblical Divine. Though an atheist, Lovecraft was profoundly intrigued by the vivid aesthetic sensationalism found within religious texts as well as the balances and counter-balances that theologies proposed for the cosmos. Through comparative analysis of the biblical influences found within Lovecraft's pantheon of Great Old Ones and Other Gods, this project examines his calculated parodic subversion and atheistic negation of the source scriptural material. Select passages from both canonical and apocryphal books of the Bible are examined against the works of Lovecraft.

First, the Bible itself as a monstrous text is considered with both Leviathan and the Lord God its predominant chaos monsters in correlation with Lovecraft's Cthulhu. Second, Lovecraft's parody of the Holy Trinity is argued, with his interstitial Other Gods Azathoth, Nyarlathotep, and Yog-Sothoth revealed as parallels of the Lord God, Jesus Christ, and the Holy Spirit. Lovecraft's conscious subversion questions the very notion of divinity in an inscrutable universe. Though he is commonly held as the greatest originator of the subgenre of cosmic horror, it should be recognized that even he emphasized its origins as belonging to religious texts. His qualifying of the subgenre as exuding a dread and terror in the face of the unknown identifies the literary features found in both biblical cosmology and the weird tales of the beings of chaos that Lovecraft imagined. For the genre and its current and future readers, writers, and students, this crucial correlation should be made apparent.

Justin Woodman
Goldsmiths College, University of London
"'The Undying Leaders': Ultraterrestrial Demonologies, Cthulhoid Conspiracies, and the Rise of Lovecraftian Parapolitics"

From claims that the HAARP installation is a military-funded summoning grid purposed to call forth weaponized Great Old Ones, to the allegation that the "global elite" are quite literally the spawn of Cthulhu, and even the admission by one popular online conspiracy theorist of having been contacted by Nyarlathotep (taking the form of one of the classic Men-in-Black of UFO lore), explicit references to the Cthulhu Mythos have appeared with regularity in contemporary paranormalist and parapolitical/conspiracy theory narratives. Indeed, the question has been asked within the parapolitical community as to whether Lovecraft is best understood not as a writer of horror tales but as a conspiracy historian.

Such claims raise important questions regarding Lovecraft's popcultural and paranormalist salience, which this paper explores with regard to three claims: first, that the fusion of science and the supernatural in Lovecraft's secular mythography is congruent with a wider set of epistemological transformations in paranormal pop culture; second, that Lovecraft's conflation of racial difference with monstrousness reflects equally racialized anxieties surrounding global flows of difference often evident within parapolitics; and third, that his cosmic futilitarianism is resonant with popular perceptions (especially evident in the seemingly widespread acceptance of some conspiracy theories) of the indifference and inhumanism of the modern state, of transnational corporatism, and of unregulated global, neoliberal capitalism. These three issues are explored with regard to how contemporary paranormalist and parapolitical discourse has been undergoing a major conceptual shift: away from prior dominant materialist and secularizing narratives, and toward the elaboration of a 'postsecular' and esoteric demonological metanarrative concerning the establishment of a dehumanizing 'New World Order' by interdimensional and 'ultraterrestrial' entities—sometimes of explicitly Lovecraftian provenance.

Index

"A la manera de Lovecraft" (Perucho) 115
Antarctic Express (Hite) 226-7
"Archeology" (Miller) 202
Areopagitica (Milton) 68
Arkham Asylum: A Serious House on Serious Earth (Morrison and McKean) 106
At the Mountains of Madness (Lovecraft) 111, 113, 114, 124, 165, 203, 212, 215, 221
"Atypical Sense of Self in Autism Spectrum Disorders" (Lyons and Fitzgerald) 125, 128
Autism: Explaining the Enigma (Frith) 120, 121, 122, 125, 126

Baby's First Mythos (Henderson) 227
"bas matérialisme et la gnose, Le" (Bataille) 202
"Beyond the Wall of Sleep" (Lovecraft) 94, 100, 103, 105
"Biblical Bits in Lovecraft" (Price) 60
Bierce, Ambrose 114
Bishop, Zealia 20, 150
Blackwood, Algernon 114
Bloch, Robert 111, 112, 114, 114

C is for Cthulhu (Ciaramella) 227
"Call of Cthulhu, The" (Lovecraft) 68, 72, 94-95, 99, 111, 122, 123, 160, 177, 199, 204, 205, 212-13, 219
Campbell, Ramsey 114
Carroll, Noël 55
Case of Charles Dexter Ward, The (Lovecraft) 72, 94, 100, 104, 105, 113, 124. 229, 232
Castle Freak (1995) 148, 149n5, 153, 155n7

"Catholic Novelist in the South, The" (O'Connor) 67
"Celephaïs" (Lovecraft) 200
"Celestial Bodies" (Bataille) 197
Chambers, Robert 208
Chevalier double, Le (Gautier) 177
City of To-morrow and Its Planning, The (Le Corbusier) 82, 83
Clark, Lillian 76, 77, 85, 86
Cliffourd the Big Red God (Hite) 225, 226
College of Sociology (1937-1939), The (Bataille) 205n2
"Colour out of Space, The" (Lovecraft) 99, 101, 111, 113
Complete Guide to Asperger's Syndrome, The (Attwood) 120, 121, 124, 125, 126, 127, 128
"Comus" (Milton) 72, 73
"Confession of Unfaith, A" (Lovecraft) 37
Conspiracy against the Human Race, The (Ligotti) 222n7
"Cool Air" (Lovecraft) 110, 112
"Crawling Chaos, The" (Lovecraft-Jackson) 199
"Crime of the Century, The" (Lovecraft) 25
"Cthulhu's Polymorphous Perversity" (Hite) 226
Cuadernos del abismo (Broncano and Hernandez de la Fuente) 117
Curious Case of H. P. Lovecraft, The (Roland) 70, 71
"Curse of Yig, The" (Bishop) 110
Curtain: Poirot's Last Case (Christie) 209-10

"Dagon" (Lovecraft) 113, 122, 178, 179, 180, 187-88, 204

de Castro, Adolphe 20
Decline of the West (Spengler) 24
Derleth, August 72, 111, 112, 115, 147–48
Descent of Man, The (Darwin) 103, 133
"Diary of Alonzo Typer, The" (Lovecraft–Lumley) 109, 110
Documents (Bataille) 191, 194, 195, 202, 203, 204
"Doom That Came to Sarnath, The" (Lovecraft) 178, 182–83
Doyle, Arthur Conan 208, 209, 217
Dream Quest of Unknown Kadath, The (Lovecraft) 42, 73, 113
Dream World of H. P. Lovecraft, The (Tyson) 70
"Dreams in the Witch House, The" (Lovecraft) 72, 113, 125, 232
Dunsany, Lord 114
"Dunwich Horror, The" (Lovecraft) 20, 60, 72, 73, 123,124, 213. 228–29, 233
Dwyer, Bernard Austin 14, 14n3, 15, 16, 17, 33

"East India Brick Row, The" (Lovecraft) 86, 87, 88
Einstein, Albert 35, 40
Eighth Tower: On Ultraterrestrials and the Superspectrum, The (Keel) 67
"Elementary, My Dear Lovecraft" (Callaghan) 209n1
Encyclopedia Acephalica (Brotchie) 192, 194
Epicureanism at the Origins of Modernity (Wilson) 43
"Epistemology That Matters, An" (Foley) 216
Exorcist, The (Blatty) 69

"Facts concerning the Late Arthur Jermyn and His Family" (Lovecraft) 134–35, 142
"Factual Basis for 'The Green Meadow'?, A" (Vaughan) 13n2
"Festival, The" (Lovecraft) 178, 180, 181, 183, 185

Figures III (Genette) 185
Fort, Charles 67
Four Quarters (Eliot) 71
"From Beyond" (Lovecraft) 113, 192
Fungi from Yuggoth (Lovecraft) 57, 116

Galpin, Alfred 32, 199
Gamwell, Annie E. P. 76
Goodnight Azathoth (Hite) 227
Gothic in Children's Literature, The (Townshend) 233–34
Gothicka (Nelson) 226
"gran americano despreciado, El" (Mosig) 116
"Great American Throw-Away, The" (Mosig) 116
"Green Meadow, The" (Lovecraft–Jackson) 13n2
Greene, Sonia 20
Guide du mythe de Cthulhu (Allard) 176

H. P. Lovecraft: Against the World, Against Life (Houellebecq) 53, 117
H. P. Lovecraft Encyclopedia, An (Joshi and Schultz) 15n4
"H. P. Lovecraft: Myth Maker" (Mosig) 161n1. 223
H. P. Lovecraft: New England Decadent (St. Armand) 66
H. P. Lovecraft: The Decline of the West (Joshi) 24n16
"H. P. Lovecraft y su obra" (Llorens Borras) 113
Hatred of Poetry, The (Bataille) 197
"Haunter of the Dark, The" (Lovecraft) 72, 73
"Herbert West—Reanimator" (Lovecraft) 100, 105, 112, 126, 203
"Higher Criticism and the Necronomicon" (Price) 58
"Horror at Red Hook, The" (Lovecraft) 22, 95, 112, 122, 137–38
Horror in the Hills, The (Long) 14, 15, 15n5, 16, 16n7, 18
"Hound, The" (Lovecraft) 112, 126
House of the Seven Gables, The (Hawthorne) 228

Howard, Robert E. 73, 111, 132, 133n4
I Am Providence (Joshi) 15n4, 20n12, 24, 28, 35, 37, 43, 72, 93, 97, 99, 103, 132
Idea of the Holy, The (Otto) 66
Impossible, The (Bataille) 197
In the Dust of This Planet (Thacker) 161–62
"'The Innsmouth Look': H. P. Lovecraft's Ambivalent Modernism." (Bealer) 78
Inquiétante étrangeté, L' (Freud) 177
"Introducción" (Llorens Borras) 113
Jack the Ripper 217
John Brown, Abolitionist (Reynolds) 94
Joshi, S. T. 32, 34, 35, 36, 40, 41, 81, 97, 117, 131, 174

Keeping America Sane (Dowbiggin) 93
King in Yellow, The (Chambers) 208, 214–15, 219
Kleiner, Rheinhart 190, 195, 197
Knowing Fear (Colavito) 48

"Landscapes, Selves, and Others in Lovecraft" (Waugh) 78
Leiber, Fritz 33, 220
"'Life Is a Hideous Thing': Primate-Geniture in H. P. Lovecraft's 'Arthur Jermyn.'" (Lovett-Graff) 375
Literature After Darwin (Richter) 133–34
"Literary Composition" (Lovecraft) 48
"Literary Copernicus, A" (Leiber) 169n9
Littlest Lovecraft (Rex) 227
"Living Heritage, A" (Lovecraft) 79, 80, 81, 82n4, 83, 84
Long, Frank Belknap 14, 15, 20, 36, 66, 76, 78, 111, 114, 165, 190, 194–95, 196–97, 198, 231
"Lost in Lovecraft" (Hite) 13n1
Lovecraft: A Biography (de Camp) 117
"Lovecraft, Aliens, and Primitivism" (Colavito) 48

"Lovecraft and Classical Antiquity" (Joshi) 13n1
"Lovecraft Criticism: A Study" (Joshi) 222
Lovecraft: Disturbing the Universe (Burleson) 60
Lovecraft: El Grimorio Maldito (Lalia) 149
Lovecraft, H. P., and aesthetics 31, 66, 78, 80, 87, 150, 215; and Butler Hospital 93, 99, 105; and classicism 13–14, 19, 21–22, 31–33; and Darwinian Theory 94, 103, 132, 133, 141; and Lord Dunsany 34, 48, 113; on Freudianism 96–97
"Lovecraft: Reproduction and Its Discontents" (Lovett-Graff) 375, 136n7
Lovecraft's Syndrome: An Asperger's Appraisal of the Writer's Life (Myers) 119, 124
"Lovecraft's Things: Sinister Souvenirs from Other Worlds" (Weinstock) 44
Lurker at the Threshold, The (Derleth) 110
"Lurking Fear, The" (Lovecraft) 22, 136, 203
"Lycidas" (Milton) 72

Más allá de los eons (Molina Foix) 117
Milton on Himself: Milton's Utterances upon Himself and His Works (Diekhoff) 68, 69
Modern Science and Materialism (Elliot) 37–38
Moe, Maurice W. 199
Molina Foix, Juan Antonio 117
"Monster Culture (Seven Theses)" (Cohen) 234
"Moon-Bog, The" (Lovecraft) 112
Moore, C. L. 14n3
"More Things: Horror, Materialism and Speculative Weirdism" (Botting) 45
Morton, James F. 195
"Mound, The" (Lovecraft–Bishop) 17n8, 50, 53, 165n5, 203

"Murders in the Rue Morgue, The" (Poe) 211
"Music of Eric Zann, The" (Lovecraft) 111, 215
"Mystery of Marie Rogêt, The" (Poe) 211-12, 214
"Mythic Hero Archetype in 'The Dunwich Horror,' The" (Burleson) 60

"Nameless City, The" (Lovecraft) 113, 186-87
Narrativa completa (Molina Foix) 116-17
New England's Gothic Literature (Ringel) 64, 230n4, 231
New York Herald 204
New York Times 204
"Nietzscheism and Realism" (Lovecraft) 162n2
"Notes on Writing Weird Fiction" (Lovecraft) 40-41, 168n8
"Nyarlathotep" (Lovecraft) 199

Oedipus Rex (Sophocles) 209
On Monsters: An Unnatural History of Our Worst Fears (Asma) 51, 52, 55-56
"On the Grotesque in Science Fiction" (Csicsery-Ronay) 142
On the Origin of Species (Darwin) 133
Only Yesterday: An Informal History of the 1920's (Allen) 97
Out of the Shadows (Anderson) 214, 221
"Outsider, The" (Lovecraft) 95, 111, 112, 126, 145, 146, 177, 178-79, 185, 186
"Oven Bird, The" (Frost) 71

Paradise Lost (Milton) 72, 73
Paradise Regain'd (Milton) 65, 72, 73
ParaNorman (2012) 228-33
Passing of the Great Race, The (Grant) 101
Perucho, Juan 14
Philosophy of H. P. Lovecraft: The Route to Horror, The (Airaksinen) 122, 123, 125, 127

"Pickman's Model" (Lovecraft) 122, 123, 216
Poe, Edgar Allan 35n1, 38, 93, 96, 105, 106, 133, 146, 208, 218
"Poe-et's Nightmare, The" (Lovecraft) 34
"Polaris" (Lovecraft) 178, 184
Price, E. Hoffman 77, 163
"Prólogo" (Gosseyn) 112
Promise of Happiness, The (Ahmed) 164
Purity and Contamination in Late Victorian Detective Fiction (Pittard) 208

Quaker City, The (Lippard) 106
Queer Optimism (Snediker) 163-64

"Quest of Iranon, The" (Lovecraft) 116

"Race Mixture in the Roman Empire" (Frank) 22n14
Races of Europe, The (Ripley) 101
"Rats in the Walls, The" (Lovecraft) 44, 110, 112
Religion and Its Monsters (Beal) 49, 53
"Renaissance of Manhood, The" (Lovecraft) 24
Renshaw, Anne Tillery 96n1
"Retain Historic 'Old Brick Row'" (Lovecraft) 86
Rotation of the Galaxy, The (Eddington) 198

Schultz, David E. 43, 117, 174
"Seeing and Unseeing, Seen and Unseen" (Lehoux) 39
Sex and the Cthulhu Mythos (Derie) 133
"Shadow over Innsmouth, The" (Lovecraft) 22, 78, 94, 100, 104, 123, 138-40, 142-43, 201, 233
"Shadows over Lovecraft: Reactionary Fantasy and Immigrant Eugenics" (Lovett-Graff) 375, 136n7, 141-42n8
"The Shadow out of Time" (Lovecraft) 45, 98, 127, 156n8, 163, 166-68, 170-71, 174
"Shambler from the Stars, The" (Bloch) 17n8
"Shunned House, The" (Lovecraft) 113

"Silver Key, The" (Lovecraft) 113
Smith, Clark Ashton 14, 14n3, 15, 111, 114, 132, 190, 196, 197
"Solar Anus" (Bataille) 199
"Some Notes on Cthulhian Pseudobiblia" (Lauterbach) 212
"Statement of Randolph Carter, The" (Lovecraft) 110, 113
Strange Case of Dr. Jekyll and Mr. Hyde, The (Stevenson) 154, 217-18
"Sublime, Today?, The" (Most) 42
Sully, Helen V. 172-3
"Supernatural Horror in Literature" (Lovecraft) 47, 48, 74, 115, 165-66, 174, 220
Surrealism, Art and Modern Science (Parkinson) 191, 194, 197, 198
"System of Dr. Tarr and Professor Fether, The" (Poe) 93

"Temple, The" (Lovecraft) 178, 180, 181, 184-85
Thing from Another World, The (1951) 73
"Thing on the Doorstep, The" (Lovecraft) 94, 97, 98-99, 100, 105, 112, 124
A Thousand Plateaus (Deleuze and Guattari) 198, 203-4
Three Essays on the Theory of Sexuality (Freud) 97
"Through the Gates of the Silver Key" (Lovecraft-Price) 59, 72, 194
"To Nobodaddy" (Blake) 190

Toldridge, Elizabeth 76, 82n4, 83, 87
"Tomb, The" (Lovecraft) 113, 229, 233
Towards a New Architecture (Le Corbusier) 81
"Tree, The" (Lovecraft) 13
True Detective (2014) 208, 209, 211, 212, 215, 216, 218-20, 221, 222-23
"Unnamable, The" (Lovecraft) 230
Very Hungry Cthulhupillar, The (Mund) 227
"Very Old Folk, The" (Lovecraft) 14, 15, 16n6
Wandrei, Donald 13, 14n3, 15, 16, 19
"Weird Modernism" (Prida) 132
Weird Realism (Harman) 168-69
Weird Tale, The (Joshi) 166
Where the Deep Ones Are (Hite) 225, 226
Where's My Shoggoth? (Thomas) 227
"Whisper in the Dark, A" (Alcott) 105
"Whisperer in Darkness, The" (Lovecraft) 17n8, 40, 42, 72, 94, 95-96, 111, 112, 123, 125, 127, 165n5
Witchcraft Explained by Modern Spiritualism (Putnam) 231
"Wonders of the Invisible World, The" (Mather) 67
Wooley, Natalie H. 32
Wright, Farnsworth 160

www.ingramcontent.com/pod-product-compliance
Lightning Source LLC
Chambersburg PA
CBHW051041160426
43193CB00010B/1022